CHOOSING LIFE, CHOOSIN

Autonomy is a vital principle in medical law and ethics. It occupies a prominent place in all medico-legal and ethical debate. But there is a dangerous presumption that it should have the only vote, or at least the casting vote. This book is an assault on that presumption, and an audit of autonomy's extraordinary status.

The fightback against the hegemony of autonomy began long ago, but the original papers setting out the dissenters' contentions still have the feel of *samizdat* tracts. A lot of the modern academic literature does take a more moderate position. But that literature is not an accurate barometer of the *zeitgeist*. For that you need to hear speakers' tones at conferences, read the medical and legal broadsheets, trawl through the dictates of the GMC and the guidelines of the BMA and note the presumptions in the heads of (particularly young) doctors when they talk about their patients.

This book surveys the main issues in medical law, noting in relation to each issue the power wielded by autonomy, asking whether that power can be justified and suggesting how other principles can and should contribute to the law. Its structure is broadly chronological. It starts before birth (with questions relating to reproductive technology and the ownership of gametes) and ends after death (with the issues relating to the ownership of body parts). On the way it deals with the status of the early embryo and the fetus, the law of abortion, confidentiality, consent, medical litigation, medical research and end-of-life decision-making.

It concludes that autonomy's status cannot be intellectually or ethically justified, and that positive discrimination in favour of the other balancing principles is urgently needed in order to avoid some sinister results.

Choosing Life, Choosing Death

The Tyranny of Autonomy in Medical Ethics and Law

Charles Foster

·HART·
PUBLISHING
OXFORD AND PORTLAND, OREGON
2009

Published in North America (US and Canada) by
Hart Publishing
c/o International Specialized Book Services
920 NE 58th Avenue, Suite 300
Portland, OR 97213-3786
USA
Tel: +1 503 287 3093 or toll-free: (1) 800 944 6190
Fax: +1 503 280 8832
E-mail: orders@isbs.com
Website: http://www.isbs.com

© Charles Foster 2009

Hart Publishing Ltd, 16C Worcester Place, Oxford, OX1 2JW
Telephone: +44 (0)1865 517530 Fax: +44 (0)1865 510710
E-mail: mail@hartpub.co.uk
Website: http://www.hartpub.co.uk

British Library Cataloguing in Publication Data
Data Available

ISBN: 978-1-84113-929-6

Typeset by Hope Services, Abingdon
Printed and bound in Great Britain by
TJ International Ltd, Padstow, Cornwall

To my mother and father, who respected my own autonomy
when that respect required superhuman restraint.

And to Aharon Barak, whose belief in what the law can be and do
has been an abiding inspiration.

'[T]here is no morally correct solution which can be deduced from a single ethical principle like the sanctity of life or the right of self-determination. There must be an accommodation between principles, both of which seem rational and good, but which have come into conflict with each other.'

Airedale NHS Trust v Bland [1993] AC 789, 827 (Hoffmann LJ)

'[B]eing out of fashion is not the same as being philosophically disreputable.'

Joseph Boyle (2004) 'An Absolute Rule Approach'
in *A Companion to Bioethics* Kuhse H and Singer P (Oxford, Blackwells) 78

PREFACE

This is an assault on the presumption that autonomy ought to be the only voice heard in medical ethics and law. The fightback against the extraordinary hegemony of autonomy began long ago, but the original papers setting out the dissenters' contentions still have the feel of *samizdat* tracts. A lot of the modern academic literature, of course, does take a more moderate position. But that literature isn't a very accurate barometer of the *zeitgeist*. For that you need to hear speakers' tones at conferences, read the medical and legal broadsheets, trawl through the dictates of the GMC and the guidelines of the BMA, and note the presumptions in the heads of (particularly young) doctors when they talk about their patients.

The book is laced with ironies, but perhaps the greatest is that autonomy, which loves the rhetoric of free speech, is ruthless in its suppression of any other contenders for a voice in medical ethics debates. The reasons for this are partly historical. Autonomy grew up as a street fighter, and was blooded in some genuinely noble battles against medical paternalism. But like so many rulers with this sort of pedigree, it has quickly forgotten its democratic roots, and grown fat and brutal in power.

Of course there are many things wrong with this book, but three main criticisms should be answered pre-emptively.

The first is that I speak anthropomorphically about autonomy, as if it were a person with a character and an agenda. This anthropomorphism is mainly a literary device. It dramatises the debate. But there is a deeper truth in it. There is a remarkable homogeneity in autonomy's contentions, uttered through its high priests. The high priests, marinated in each others' papers and academic culture, do sound strangely similar. I ought to say, though, that I number some of these turbulent priests amongst my dearest friends. If the debate sounds as if it is getting personal, it's not.

The second is a related point. I could be accused of setting up straw men and then knocking them gleefully down. It might be said that I have caricatured 'autonomy' (perhaps by describing it in my anthropomorphic way), and that a properly nuanced view of autonomy would be able to respond more convincingly to me than the intellectually emasculated version that I have allowed to speak.

There are four responses to this.

First: it is perfectly true that I do not give a systematic account, with duly voluminous footnotes, of the origins and nature of the philosophical doctrine of autonomy. There are plenty of splendid books that do. I have read quite a lot of them. But this isn't that sort of book. I am well aware that there are lots of things to be said about autonomy which aren't said here, but none of them seems to me to be relevant to the argument I'm embroiled in. I have tried to simplify things that are too often thought of as so encrusted with venerable complexity as to be incapable of straightforward description. The wrong perception of complexity has often conferred an entirely unwarranted immunity to straightforward criticism. If I have oversimplified, I hope I haven't done so in a cowardly attempt to diminish the force of a difficult opposing contention.

My determination to simplify will go too far for some people. In particular the feminists will feel short-changed and under- and misrepresented. I took a deliberate decision in the abortion chapter, for instance, not to present the case as a fusillade against pro-abortion feminists (yes, I know that there are some anti-abortion feminists too). The relationship between feminism and autonomy is complex and close, but not hugely interesting from a medico-legal point of view. Feminism tends to conduct its business at high emotional temperatures. In both philosophy and chemistry, high temperatures often generate interesting novelties. And indeed feminism has produced some remarkable and valuable philosophic novelties, but (apart from its contribution to the idea of relational autonomy, which I do discuss) not in the territory covered by this book. Although feminism has drafted a powerful new language in which autonomy often articulates its claims, it has not fashioned entirely new claims. Or at least its claims are not sufficiently different from autonomy's generic claims to demand specific attention. I didn't want to open a can of worms for fear that their wriggling might distract from the main thesis.

Second: I only have a problem with the caricature—the icy self-determinist who talks about people's life plans as if they are demonstrable documents.

Third: the caricature is alive, well, tenured and to be heard on every conference platform, apparently intolerant of the saving nuances.

Fourth: when the nuances are invoked, they generally seem to me to call seriously into question many of the fundamentals of the autonomist creed: they are not subtle variations on the theme, but contradictions of it. Even if that is not right, a vast number of 'nuances' need to be invoked to retain autonomy's credibility as the sole arbiter of ethically acceptable action. 'Autonomy', when it is encrusted with all those 'nuances', doesn't look like autonomy at all. It looks just like a structure designed by all the desirable principles working together, and it is far more sensible to see it that way. You have to do tremendous violence to common and philosophical sense to see autonomy as the sole author of a decent textbook of medical ethics or law. So why do people bother? The only reason for bothering is a depressing lack of humility on the part of autonomy.

And fifth: this is primarily a book about the law, and even if the nuances are real, and even if they are genuinely held by the mainstream autonomists, they are not heard or considered by the judges—for reasons I consider in chapter 1.

Although medical ethics have been responsible for some of the most important and exciting intellectual experiences of my life, I have to admit to a deep suspicion of the discipline. I am embarrassed by the suspicion, because it is grounded in a sanctimonious and profoundly unattractive conviction that of the two disciplines—ethics and law—my own discipline of law is the senior partner. This is only because the law is forced to *decide* things, and decision seems to me to deserve a respect that mere discourse does not. Lying awake at night having decided that conjoined twins should be separated is a different and more laudable form of insomnia than the insomnia caused by worrying about how one's lecture has gone down. But *decision* is valuable not only because of the responsibility that is its concomitant, but also (and here is the really repellent sanctimony) because it produces better thinking. The judges themselves know this. If they comment in a judgment on a point that does not strictly fall to be decided, they acknowledge that the *obiter dictum* does not have the authority of the really necessary observations. This is not a piece of pointless tradition. Practical necessity transforms thought. It is the alchemy of necessity, rather than any magic mantle, that transmutes the meanderings of Mr X, (deserving only weary, patient, dinner-party politeness) into the coruscating judgment of Mr Justice X (worthy of a long, respectful piece in the *Law Quarterly Review*). And there is something intellectually and ethically antiseptic about the light of a courtroom: it deals very effectively with the viruses that persist happily in even (and possibly particularly) the most rigorously refereed journals.

That is not to say that the law is perfect. Very far from it. Much of this book is concerned with pointing out its radical deformities and its blemishes. Its practitioners, too (of which I am one), have an enormous amount to learn from the colossal creative energy and sheer cleverness of academics in the realm of medical ethics. It is a great pity that the close but estranged cousins, medical law and ethics, talk so little to each other. The estrangement is dangerous for both of them. There are real problems of language, but the hybrid vigour that would result from genuine cross-fertilisation could produce some really thrilling new syntheses.

I hope that I have stated the law correctly as of July 2008.

Charles Foster
Oxford
July 2008

ACKNOWLEDGEMENTS

My debts are many and huge. The heaviest obligations are to:

The Warden and Fellows of Green Templeton College, Oxford. This book was written in the vibrant calm given by a Visiting Fellowship there. There is no more congenial or stimulating place to work and to play.

Professor Tony Hope and Professor Michael Parker, of the Ethox Centre, The University of Oxford. Although they didn't know it, they have been suggesting this project to me for years. They both read the manuscript in draft and saved me from some dangerous extravagances.

All the staff and researchers at the Ethox Centre, for plying me with coffee, cake, good cheer and tremendous ideas.

Jonathan Herring of Exeter College, Oxford, whose penetrating insight into the strange workings of autonomy often showed the way.

The librarians of the Codrington Library, All Souls College, Oxford, for their patience and humour.

Professor Julian Savulescu, whose off-the-cuff comment in *The Royal Oak* was the final catalyst that propelled this book into existence.

Aharon Barak, formerly President of the Supreme Court of Israel, a mentor of great kindness, perception and wisdom.

Richard Hart and the team at Hart Publishing, for their efficiency, understanding and enthusiasm for this project.

As always, my wife Mary, who is too often a victim of the bad exercise of my autonomy.

Some of the outlines of the law that appear here have appeared before in the *New Law Journal, Solicitors Journal, Counsel* and *Elements of Medical Law*. I am grateful to the editors and publishers for permission to reproduce them here.

CONTENTS

Contents

TABLE OF CASES

United States

European Court of Human Rights

TABLE OF LEGISLATION

Part 1

Principles

1

Autonomy: Challenging the Consensus

MODERN DEBATES IN medical ethics are often very boring. Whatever the subject, there is usually little debate about the governing principle[1]: everyone assumes that it is 'autonomy' and only autonomy.[2] If the conference is about resource allocation there will no doubt be a nod to the principle of justice—but only a nod. Then it is back to listening in uncritical rapture to what the great god autonomy has to say. A daring or naïve delegate might ask: 'Which theory of autonomy are you using here?', but it won't do his career much good. Everyone who is anyone knows what autonomy means, and it means the straightforward libertarianism of John Stuart Mill,[3] Peter Singer[4] and Julian Savulescu.[5] It means that we all have a life-plan, we all have a right to have it respected, and if we're to talk about such disreputable, autonomy-truncating things as duties at all, we merely have duties not to interfere with others' life-plans. Anyone so contemptibly sub-rational or unreflective as not to have a life-plan is hardly human at all. If one can spare a little time in one's own life-plan to help the unreflective limp towards higher self-realisation, that is a Good Thing, and the god will be pleased.[6]

---

[1] Of course, as I acknowledge in the Preface, there is an active debate in the academic literature. But that debate does not reflect the dominant and dominating mindset in the medical profession. The medical mindset, mainly using the vehicle of the *Bolam* test, is imported into the courts too. This book spends a lot of its time discussing autonomy's fate there.

[2] This is 'the time of the triumph of autonomy in bioethics. . . . [T]he law and ethics of medicine are dominated by one paradigm—the autonomy of the patient.': Scheider CE (1998) *The Practice of Autonomy: Patients, Doctors and Medical Decisions* (New York, OUP) 3, 9. Wolpe PR (1998) 'The Triumph Of Autonomy In American Bioethics: A Sociological View' in Devries R, Subedi J (eds) *Bioethics and Society: Sociological Investigations of the Enterprise of Bioethics* (Englewood Cliff, NJ, Prentice Hall) 38–59. A typical example is in Jonas M (2007) 'The Baby MB Case: Medical Decision-Making in the Context of Uncertain Infant Suffering' 33 *Journal of Medical Ethics* 9, 541–4, in which autonomy is assumed to weigh much more heavily in any responsible ethical decision-making. See also A Tauber (2006) *Patient Autonomy and the Ethics of Responsibility* (Cambridge, Mass, MIT Press); Gillon R (2003) 'Ethics Needs Principles—Four Can Encompass the Rest—And Respect for Autonomy Should Be "First Among Equals"' 29 *Journal of Medical Ethics* 307–12.

[3] Mill JS (1929) *On Liberty* (London, Watts).

[4] Singer P (1993) *Practical Ethics* (Cambridge, CUP); Singer P (1995) *Rethinking Life and Death* (Oxford, OUP).

[5] See, eg, Savulescu J (2006) 'Conscientious objection in medicine' 332 *British Medical Journal* 294–7.

[6] Many have recruited philosophy as an ally in the feminist war, seeing it as a potent weapon against the paternalism that has often characterised medicine and other areas of life: see, eg, Jackson E (2001) *Regulating Reproduction* (Oxford, Hart Publishing) ch 1.

This is the orthodoxy, and it is policed with terrifying vigour. To depart from it is dangerous. It is like standing up at a meeting of the Royal Society and announcing that you are a New Earth Creationist who thinks that Darwin got his orders directly from Satan. And so the medical ethics journals are full of detailed descriptions of and reflections on the brocade on the Emperor's entirely absent clothes.

The orthodoxy is protected by innuendo too, and in particular by the absurd implication that anyone who does not join in the autonomist chorus is a benighted anti-Copernican who would have hanged Galileo, burnt *The Origin of Species*, and would withdraw all civil rights from homosexuals.

It is similar in the law, although not quite so bad.[7] It is not quite so bad for five reasons. The first is that law (at least in England) is made by practising lawyers. Judgments are cut and paste jobs from barristers' skeleton arguments. The second is that practising lawyers deal with real situations, and real situations do not read philosophy books. The third is that practising lawyers do not read philosophy books either. The fourth is that practising lawyers, although they love words, are not as respectful of them or the ideas that they convey as are pure thinkers. That gives them some immunity to the sheer incantatory power of the word 'autonomy'. And the fifth is that practising lawyers do not have the distaste for conservatism that academics do. In fact they tend to think that if a solution has been shown for quite a long time to work, that is a fairly good reason to continue to adopt it, unless a compelling case is made for an alternative. But since no-one gets a PhD by reiterating an old idea, novelty is the value that drives academia. This breeds a terrible chronological snobbery and fashion-consciousness. If something is old, it is deemed, without further evaluation, to be bad. If something is new, however ridiculous it really it, it tends to be smiled on. Many of the solutions to the ethical problems posed in this book are old. The lawyers' perspective is that this tends to show enduring value rather than doddering irrelevance.

Most of this book was written in the Codrington Library of All Souls College, Oxford. Above me towered august ranks of scholarly law journals. Many of the authors represented there had steeped themselves in Kant and Rousseau before commenting on what the law is and should be. Their papers are supposed to be one important route by which real scholarship metastasises into the body of the law. But it rarely happens that way. The busy-ness and plain philistinic indifference of practising lawyers means that the philosophers stay in the library and the papers are discussed only by fellow academics. Generally this is a crying shame, but since lawyers tend to have an unerring instinct for the wrong end of the

---

[7] Many English examples will be given. In international human rights jurisprudence autonomy often and increasingly seems to be regarded as the practical outworking of the notion of dignity. Thus in the UN Declaration of Human Rights of 1948, dignity is regarded as the philosophical background, rather than a right in itself. Its implementation is handed over to other agents including, notably, autonomy. Autonomy and dignity are often and increasingly identified with one another, despite having been ranged opposite one another in the courts on several occasions: see, eg, the *Conseil d'Etat* case, *Cne de Morsang-sur-Orge*, Dalloz Jur 1995; CE Ass, 27 *Octobre* 1995, in which the presumably autonomous decision of a dwarf to earn his living by being fired from a cannon was felt to be wholly at odds with the dwarf's dignity.

philosophical stick, and since in the realm of medical law there is a natural ten-dency to over-philosophise, it has probably prevented harm rather than stifling the hybrid vigour that usually comes from cross-fertilisation.

There are times, though, when practising lawyers (and therefore the law they make) are exposed to learning. This is at the higher appellate levels, and notably in the House of Lords. This is when the journals are dusted off and cited. The Law Lords feel a need to articulate principles, rather than just making a right judgment in the particular case, and that is when things start to go wrong. It is then that they start to try to be philosophers. They are all very clever, and most of them did a course in jurisprudence half a century earlier, but they have no real philosophical sense of smell, and they have very little time to consider the full philosophical fall-out of their dicta: the next case about marine insurance is waiting at the door. So they shoot from the hip, sometimes doing very great damage to the law. Given the ruling orthodoxy, it is inevitable that the highly edited samples of philosophical thinking to which they are exposed will paint Millian autonomy as the all-trumping principle. Probably their temperaments tend in that direction anyway: they are driven, self-made, highly motivated individuals who could have told you their own life-plans by the end of their first term at their ancient college. This is not to mock: it is just to explain. That, then, is how the orthodoxy gets the rub-ber stamp of the law.

It is not quite that simple, of course. While in theory the law is what a statute or a judgment of the House of Lords says, the reality is rather different. The law gov-erning Case X is what the judge who happens to be allocated to that case on the day of determination can be persuaded to do—provided that it is wrapped up in non-appealable language. It is difficult for law undergraduates and non-lawyers to understand how different this is from the law in the law reports. In this book we will come across several examples of judicial decision-making which no doubt made the editors of the law reports feel wholly redundant. Some reflect the ortho-doxy on autonomy; some do not.

There is another route by which philosophical ideas creep into the law. It is an increasingly important one and it, rather than judicial philosophising in the House of Lords, is mainly responsible for the dissemination of the autonomy orthodoxy in the law. It is a consequence of the peculiar respect that the English law has for the views of professionals. That respect is best exemplified by the famous and ubiquitous *Bolam* test[8]—whereby a doctor (for example) will not be found to be negligent if he has acted in a way which would be endorsed by a responsible body

---

[8] See *Bolam v Friern Hospital Management Committee* [1957] 1 WLR 583. There is an important gloss on *Bolam* in *Bolitho v City and Hackney Health Authority* [1998] AC 232, which essentially put in italics the word 'responsible', which had always formed part of the *Bolam* test but had often been over-looked by the lawyers. For assessments of the prognosis for *Bolam*, see Foster C (1998) 'Bolam: Consolidation and Clarification' *Health Care Risk Report* Vol 4 Issue 5 (April 1998) 5; Brazier M and Miola J (2000) 'Bye Bye Bolam: A Medical Litigation Revolution?' Spring 2000 8 *Medical Law Review* 85–114; Samanta S, Mello M, Foster C, Tingle J and Samanta J (2006) 'The role of clinical guidelines in medical negligence litigation: A Shift From the *Bolam* standard?' Autumn 2006 14 *Medical Law Review* 321–66.

of medical opinion in the relevant specialty. The spirit of *Bolam* has diffused into other areas of the medical law—notably confidentiality[9] and (controversially) consent.[10] The bridgehead used by autonomy is not the views of medical experts in litigated cases (doctors probably read even less philosophy than barristers do), but the codes of professional bodies such as the General Medical Council. Those codes are often drawn up by people who have done courses in medical ethics, and they express positions about autonomy culled from the standard textbooks. Those views are generally unnecessary: the codes would be perfectly workable without them. Do they reflect the view of the members of the profession? There is no reason to suppose that they do, other than the fact that the codes have emerged from consultation exercises. But once a view is expressed in a code produced by a notionally authoritative body such as the GMC, it is hard for a court to escape the conclusion that it is definitive of responsible medical thought and approach.

Once within the body of the law, autonomy shapes the law to make itself comfortable. There is an increasing tendency to view the whole of the law as simply a framework in which autonomy can be exercised.[11] There are many problems with this, but here are two. First: if the architecture of the whole law is determined by the need to enshrine autonomy in an appropriately reverential way then, if the reverence is misguided, the whole superstructure of the temple will be dangerously twisted—perhaps leading to weaknesses and weirdnesses a long way from the high altar of autonomy itself. A basic misapprehension about consent to treatment might affect the way in which Blackacre is conveyed to X. And second: gods, once enshrined, tend not to be examined as critically and questioningly as they should be. Once you brand something a god—and even more so once you spend a lot of money and effort building a shrine round it—it becomes increasingly difficult to acknowledge even that the divinity might be rather tarnished—let alone that the god is no god at all.

This book looks at the extent to which autonomy is already the ruling principle in English medical law, suggests other principles that should come into play, and indicates how those other principles might affect the law. But before looking at the possible competing principles, we need to note the various ways in which 'autonomy' is used in the vast and forbidding literature on the subject.

---

[9] See, eg, *R v Department of Health, ex p Source Informatics Ltd* [2000] Lloyd's Rep Med 76.

[10] See, eg, *F v West Berkshire Health Authority* [1989] 2 All ER 545.

[11] And indeed that the rule of law itself is consequently dependent on autonomy being properly enshrined: Thus Ronald Dworkin says, '[T]he 'rights' conception [of the rule of law] assumes that citizens have moral rights and duties with respect to one another, and political rights against the state as a whole. It insists that these moral and political rights be recognized in positive law, so that they may be enforced *upon the demand of individual citizens* through courts or other judicial institutions of the familiar type, so far as this is practicable. The rule of law on this conception is the ideal of rule by an accurate public conception of individual rights. It does not distinguish, as the rule-book conception does, between the rule of law and substantive justice; on the contrary it requires, as part of the ideal of law, that the rules in the rule book capture and enforce moral rights.': Ronald Dworkin (1985) 'Political Judges and the Rule of Law' in *A Matter of Principle* (Cambridge, MA, Harvard University Press) 11–12.

There are four senses in which the label 'autonomy' is used.[12,13] The first is the notion derived from Kant,[14] and depends on his metaphysical view of the world and of what humans are. He distinguished between the sensible (phenomenal) world and the intellectual (noumenal) world. Humans, as rational beings, are philosophical amphibians: we are in both worlds. But to be in a world is not necessarily to be a fully paid up citizen of it, subject to its laws. We are subject to the sensual promptings of the phenomenal world, but when we are urged to give in we can brandish our passports from the superior noumenal world and say, 'You have no jurisdiction over me.' There is an obligation not to give in to the blandishments of the sensual world: hence moral obligation. Proper autonomy, for Kant, is to act in accordance with the universal moral law. We are only acting freely when we freely opt to do the Right Thing. Then and only then are we our own master. Any other action demonstrates slavish obedience to the low desires of the sensual world. The Book of Common Prayer understood this very well: it describes 'perfect freedom' as the service of the true God.

The obvious problem is in determining what the Right Thing is. For Kant, and for most in the West until fairly recently, the Right Thing was Christian morality. For Kant, then, suicide and extra-marital sex, both of which contravene his understanding of the Universal law, cannot be decided upon in a truly autonomous way, and decisions to effect either can be vetoed without violating autonomy. Modern medical law disagrees with Kant about some of the content of the Universal law. It disagrees with him about sexual intercourse between consenting unmarried adults, for instance. But Kant would nod approvingly at (for example) the laws criminalising assisting suicide.

It has become unfashionable to speak about autonomy in straightforward Kantian terms, but most of the high priests of modern autonomy—despite their protestations—are thoroughgoing Kantians.[15] They only disagree with him about the content of the Universal law. They think that prescriptive Christian morality is ridiculous, and that the only law which, if followed, allows you to be properly free

---

[12] These headings are taken broadly from Spriggs M (2005) *Autonomy and Patients' Decisions* (Lanham, MD, Lexington Books). I see no justification for a detailed account here of the anatomy and embryology of the various theories of autonomy. The absence of such an account means that I will speak about autonomy in terms that are too general for some. There are real difficulties of nomenclature too. I recognise that, eg, although Ronald Dworkin contends vocally for a right of procreative autonomy, his view of procreative autonomy is very different from a theory that could equally be called 'procreative autonomy' but is based on a notion of what a person really is, and on what conditions are necessary for moral powers to be developed and exercised. I am not interested in those distinctions, because the law is not.

[13] There are good surveys in (inter alia): Frankfurt H (1988) *The Importance of What We Care About* (Cambridge, CUP); Christman J (ed) (1989) *The Inner Citadel: Essays on Individual Autonomy* (New York, OUP); Christman J and Anderson J (eds) (2005) *Autonomy and the Challenges of Liberalism* (Cambridge, CUP); Taylor JS (ed) (2005) *Personal Autonomy: New Essays on Personal Autonomy and its Role in Contemporary Moral Philosophy* (Cambridge, CUP).

[14] Kant I, *Groundwork of the metaphysics of morals*, Paton HJ (trans) (New York, Harper, 1964); Kant I, *Critique of Practical Reason*, Beck LW (trans) (New York, Garland, 1976). Of course he was foreshadowed by Rousseau.

[15] See Secker B (1999) 'The appearance of Kant's deontology in contemporary Kantianism: concepts of patient autonomy in bioethics' 24(1) *Journal of Medicine and Philosophy*, 43–66.

and properly human is the equally prescriptive law of middle class western liberalism. This book does not seek to say which of those contenders for the crown of 'universal law' should win.

At the heart of Kant's philosophy is a sinister presumption that your worth—indeed your very status as a human—depends on your ability to resist the blandishments of the sensual world or, depending on your reading of the Universal law, to have and to adhere to your life-plan. The only intrinsically human thing about you is your ability to make the right choices. Throw away the chance of the right choice and (despite the liberal wool with which the conclusion is cushioned in modern discourse), you are actually sub-human. It is there that both Kant and his modern liberal disciples part company with the Abrahamic faiths.[16]

The second way in which autonomy is described is as a psychological ideal.[17] An autonomous man is his own man, living a self-directed life, and that is to be applauded. Gerald Dworkin would say that he understands autonomy this way, and that he is interested not in autonomous acts per se, but in what it means to be an autonomous person.[18] To be autonomous is thus to have and to exercise an ability to reflect critically upon and to accept or reject consciously and critically one's preferences, desires and wishes. To do so is to become self-defining, coherent and meaningful. This all sounds like a pretty tall order. And surely there are distinct echoes here of that stern, rational, rather cold man who stalks around Kant's bleak world, dutifully choosing the Good. Is anyone capable of reaching Dworkin's high standard of autonomous living (which is actually the only thing you can describe with a straight metaphysical face as living at all)? Well, yes, says Dworkin. You don't have to be agonisingly self-examining. You show this sort of autonomy by your actions. What do you try to change in your life? What are your aspirations? To see if this sort of autonomy is present you have to look at a big slice of someone's life: a week won't do. And so it turns out that, despite all he says, his primary concern is with identifying autonomous acts after all. Dworkin turns out to be terribly shallow.

Third, autonomy is described as a reason for some constraint on action. X's 'autonomy' is invoked as a reason why Y should not do something to her. This is a common use of the notion of autonomy in the law. It is sometimes useful shorthand, but it does not in itself imply any real meaning of the word 'autonomy'. It begs many questions that the lawyers are often content to leave unanswered. All it comes to is that Y should not do something to X because: (a) X has a right to consent to things being done to her; and (b) the appropriate consent has not been

---

[16] There are various glosses on this, eg, Taylor C (1989) *Sources of the Self* (Cambridge, Mass, Harvard University Press): human beings are 'self-interpreting' animals, defined by our self-understanding. The ability to be a fully human agent depends on the 'languages' (in a very wide sense) used to articulate that self-understanding. This necessarily implies some cognitive qualification for membership of humanity.

[17] One of the most eloquent and sustained of such descriptions is in Young R (1986) *Personal Autonomy: Beyond Negative and Positive Liberty* (London, Croom Helm).

[18] Dworkin G (1988) *The Theory and Practice of Autonomy* (Cambridge, CUP).

given. This type of analysis (or non-analysis) does not locate the right to consent in any particular theory of rights.

And fourth, 'autonomy' is sometimes used in an evaluative way. Thus when we say that X is autonomous we are saying nothing at all about what it means to be autonomous, but simply that X or her decision deserves respect. Merle Spriggs notes[19] that in successive editions of their agenda-setting book *Principles of Biomedical Ethics*[20] Beauchamp and Childress lurch more and more towards this usage.[21] Note that this usage is only possible if the consensus about the primacy of autonomy is complete. If you behave autonomously, you and your decision are to be respected. And if you do not, then there is no other reason to respect you. We are back to the icy world of Immanuel Kant with his autonomous humans and his unrealised *untermenschen*. And since what amounts to autonomous living is, as we've seen, conditioned by one's beliefs about the Universal law, we are not far away from the conclusion: 'if you agree with us about the world, you are human, and if you don't, you're not'.

This intellectual fascism nestling at the core of the traditional notion of autonomy is one of the main reasons to question autonomy's qualification to have the casting vote in all ethical debates. The objection is not just a theoretical one: it has some brutally practical corollaries, some of which are explored in this book. If autonomy holds the keys of life and death, how safe are you when you are unconscious, insane, demented, a child or otherwise not in a position to discuss your life-plan with sufficiently impressive coherence? And what if you choose not to have the information necessary for you to make a fully informed decision about your medical treatment? Is there no right not to know? Can you not autonomously opt for your clinician to behave in an old-fashioned, paternalistic way? And so on.

But there are other objections to autonomy's hegemony. Isn't it absurdly simplistic, for instance, to think that one principle should rule?[22] Of course autonomy should have a prominent place in all thinking about medical law and ethics: it is a crucial principle, and the consequences of abandoning it are nightmarish. But are life, law and medicine really so straightforward that they can be adequately described using one concept only?[23] When one reads some of the headline-making

---

[19] See above n 12.

[20] Beauchamp TL and Childress JF (1979) (New York, OUP).

[21] This tendency is manifested particularly in their increasingly obsessive interest in the notion of competence.

[22] The autonomists are generally too canny to deny that there *are* other principles that can be used to discuss ethical dilemmas. The tactic is to patronise those other principles into irrelevance. If a competing principle seems to present a threat to autonomy's rule, a way is found to assert that the conflict is more apparent than real. For instance, '[The polarisation between autonomy and the sanctity of life] is flawed since it rejects the possibility of autonomy having sanctity and assumes that society will always be in conflict with the individual. It also ascribes an absolute value to life, which society ostensibly upholds. Such a valuation may be overstated.': Shaw PR and Thacker R (1993) 'Consent, Autonomy and the Infantilised Patient' 1 *Med Law Int* 33 at 47.

[23] One of the important early opening shots in the fight against the philosophical 'one size fits all' heresy was O'Neill O (1984) 'Paternalism and Patient Autonomy' 10(4) *Journal of Medical Ethics* 173–8. There are many clinical comments on the unreality of the 'one size' notion. See, eg, Winzeberg

autonomistic judgments there is often the feeling that the law is the way it is because the lawmakers want elegance and simplicity. There are great benefits in both, but mere intellectual aestheticism should not lead the way. Law should be the servant of reality, not its master. It doesn't exist for lawyers. Its real business is not with the university library, the lecture hall or the PhD thesis: it is in the heat and sweat and blood of the hospital. If the sweat stains the theory, then the theory, however pleasing, has to be thrown away. Law shouldn't be scared to take on the multi-facetedness of life. To do that properly it needs lots of weapons: just one won't do. Law should be as nuanced as it needs to be. A stultifying reductionism birthed, feeds and is fed by the notion that autonomy is all there is. That reductionism just isn't up to the job of producing appropriately nuanced law.

It is plain, too, that not all autonomous decisions deserve respect. All right-thinking people would condemn an autonomous decision to murder or rape. But does this tell us anything about autonomy's general claim to rule? John Keown would say that it did: that it calls fundamentally into question the ability of autonomy to give right answers unaided by other principles (such as his categorical imperative of choosing that which promotes 'human flourishing').[24] This goes rather too far for me: on the basis of the evidence of these beliefs of right-thinking people one might still conclude that autonomy can provide a good general rule, while acknowledging that there must be exceptions to it. But the need to carve out exceptions begins to silence some of the more extravagant arrogances of the autonomists. If you have a theory which boasts: 'I am all you need', the theory should becomes rather embarrassed whenever an exception is acknowledged. If you have more exceptions than you have examples of the theory working, it is hard to say that the boast is made out. If a blanket is mostly holes, do you have a blanket at all?

The embarrassment deepens when one points out that the usual ruse of the autonomists, faced with a tricky case of plainly unacceptable behaviour by apparently autonomous people, is to find a way of saying that they are not really autonomous at all. In *Re L (Patient: Non-consensual Treatment)*[25] a patient had a needle phobia. This made her refuse the caesarean section necessary to save her

---

GS, Hanson LC and Talky JA (2005) 'Beyond Autonomy: Diversifying End-of-Life Decision-Making Approaches to Serve Patients and Families' 53(6) *Journal of the American Geriatrics Society* 1046–50.

[24] Eg, Keown J and Gormally L, 'Human Dignity, Autonomy and Mentally Incapacitated Patients: A Critique of "Who Decides"' *Web Journal of Current Legal Issues*, 1999: <http://webjcli.ncl.ac.uk/1999/issue4/keown4.html>, accessed 24 December 2007: '[E]xercises of autonomy (ie of the capacity for self-determining choice) are not the fundamental source of worth and value in a person's life. Human beings possess an ineradicable value prior and subsequent to the possibility of exercising autonomy. Autonomy itself as a capacity is to be valued *precisely in so far as its exercise makes for the well-being and flourishing of the human beings who possess it.* But it is plain that many exercises of the capacity, that is, many self-determining choices, are destructive of human well-being—both in the life of the chooser and in the lives of others affected by his or her choices. The mere fact that someone has *chosen* to act or to be treated in a certain way establishes no title to moral respect for what has been chosen. The character of the choice must satisfy certain criteria in order to warrant our respect. The most basic criterion is that a choice should be consistent with respect for the fundamental dignity both of the chooser and of others.'

[25] [1997] 8 Med LR 217.

and the unborn child that she desperately wanted. The court's response was compassionate, wholly just and analytically wholly indefensible. It said that she lacked capacity—that she was not properly autonomous. But by all the usual canons of construction she clearly was. It was a decision that saved the woman, her child, and the fig-leaf of philosophical respectability worn by the autonomists. It was plainly right to decree that the caesarean section should be carried out, and on the law as it stood (dictated primarily by autonomy) it was the only way to achieve the right result. But it indicated that autonomy cannot by itself give the right result in hard cases: it needs to call in help. Other principles have the humility to acknowledge this, but humility is not a quality that comes naturally to autonomy. The case illustrates again a point we have already seen. It goes back to those Kantian fundamentals: autonomy is a device used to further whatever universal law is favoured by its advocates. Their universal law frowns on women killing themselves and the children that at one level they want to have. And thus, in their philosophy, one cannot autonomously choose that result, any more than Kant's properly autonomous man could choose to have extra-marital sex.

The universal law of the medical autonomists is not geographically universal. In fact it is only to be found in a relatively small, highly educated part of the west. There is a wider point: autonomy itself (as opposed to the universal liberal law at its heart) is a Western idea—mysterious to and frowned upon by those outside the West.[26] Westerners are perceived by many to value themselves at the expense of society—a view entirely concordant with autonomy, if not expressly demanded by it. To make autonomy rule is thus a sort of cultural imperialism. We will pick up this point again in dealing with the notion of 'relational autonomy', but it is worth saying here that in according unquestioned priority to autonomy we are making a statement about what human beings really are. The autonomist has no doubt: though a human being might choose to act selflessly, at bottom and by definition he is an atomistic unit. His primary and always overwhelming referent will be himself. If he decides to act altruistically, that is because it pleases him to do so. No, says the alternative view: man is primarily a relational animal. He was built for relationship; relationships are not merely things that happen to him or which into which he autonomously decides to opt. He was conceived as a result of relationship, grew inside a human and, after he is expelled from that human, only really

---

[26] A recent paper, by a Turkish academic, was emphatic: 'The concept of autonomy is a manifestation of Western culture, which emphasises individualism, personal happiness and self-actualisation. In this context, "personhood" is viewed from the perspective of autonomy and individual rights.' It concluded: 'It would be difficult to argue that there is no room for individual autonomy in Turkey, but the applicability of the principle of respect for autonomy probably depends on the interpretation of autonomy. It will be important to find a more flexible concept of autonomy that is compatible with the structure of the culture and with the various self-perceptions. The principle of respect for autonomy or the principle of beneficence may be more applicable, depending on the case. . . . Patients who are dependent on their family or social group because they perceive themselves as a strongly tied part of a community rather than as separate individuals may find it difficult or impossible to decide and act autonomously. There is no point in forcing autonomy on such patients.' Kara MA (2007) 'Applicability of the Principle of Respect for Autonomy: The Perspective of Turkey' 33 *Journal of Medical Ethics* 627, 627, 629–30.

continues to grow if he is in relationship with somebody or something. As a matter of definition, humans are social and sexual beings. The hermit is a social animal who has opted to be alone. Society is the default position, decreed by our biology. We are hard-wired for relationship. Much of the deep dissatisfaction of the west with itself is a result of its failure to construct its societies around this rather obvious premise.[27] Any theory about how to ensure the happiness and prosperity of intrinsically social animals which starts from the presumption that they are intrinsically islands unto themselves is likely to fail.

Even if one finds it impossible to join in this lyrically metaphysical view of humans, can it seriously be disputed that we are all enmeshed, for better or for worse, in an intricate matrix of causality which makes one man's autonomy another man's slavery? The capitalist's freedom of action depends crucially on the wage-slave's inability to change his job for something he would rather do. The fumes disgorged in the course of free-market enterprise cause the asthma of the village down the road and the desertification of Mali. The same is true wherever we look in health care law. Permit the autonomous designer death of X, and you endanger the autonomy rights of the vulnerable patients that the previous restrictive law was drafted to protect. Force doctors to kill on demand, and you take away the autonomous right to be treated by someone who is not a killer, as well as the doctor's right not to kill. Of course the fact that it is difficult to implement autonomy without autonomy itself being a casualty is not in itself a reason not to try, but the obvious impossibility of the project should perhaps cause us to question whether we really want autonomy to hold all the keys of all the compartments of our lives.[28]

Another reason for questioning the primacy of autonomy in medical law is its grotesquely exaggerated profile there—as opposed to in other areas of law. The criminal law and the law of tort that apply outside the consultation room are far more pragmatic and far less downright prissy about autonomy. They recognise that (for instance), non-consensual touching should sometimes go uncensured.[29] What is so special about the operating theatre? The autonomists' rejoinder would

[27] Eric J Cassell (2007) puts it like this: 'Thirty-five or forty years ago, it was acceptable to pretend that context, illness and other people, benevolent or otherwise, had no impact on autonomy. Or that there were such things as totally independent choices. Or that freedom of choice was just a manner of speaking. These ideas provided a way of underlining the importance of autonomy—especially in a sense larger than mere 'freedom of choice'. But they are also wrong. They arise from a view of the human condition as made up of atomistic individuals spinning in their own orbits among others doing the same, and they are just as wrong as the positivist model of science and atomistic facts on which they are probably based. Now the task is to develop an understanding of persons and their relationships that can form a solid intellectual and theoretical basis for contemporary and future ethics. . . . There are no . . . completely self-determining individuals who are not influenced in the strongest sense by others in their personal and social world.': 'Unanswered Questions: Bioethics and Human Relationships' *Hastings Center Report* Vol 37, No 5, September–October 2007, 20–23, 21, 22.

[28] For a robust counter-attack by autonomy against these allegations, see May T (2005) 'The Concept of Autonomy in Bioethics: an Unwarranted Fall From Grace' in Taylor JS (ed) *Personal Autonomy: New Essays on Personal Autonomy and its Role in Contemporary Moral Philosophy* (Cambridge, CUP), 299–309.

[29] See Herring J (2006) *Medical Law and Ethics* (Oxford, OUP) 125.

presumably be that, when you are in hospital you are closer to life's and death's fundamentals, and so it is unsurprising that naked principles are more obviously visible. There may be something in that, but the scale of the disparity is surprising; it suggests that autonomy in medical law has been allowed to range (at least relatively) unchecked.

The autonomy debate is a complex one. It is sometimes easy to lose sight of things precisely because they are big and basic. Stripped of all the (vital) caveats, autonomy is the notion that one should be able to choose what it is done to you and by you. But what happens if being able to choose what happens to you is not your primary concern? If that is so, then all the wind is taken out of the autonomist's sails. Onora O'Neill's powerful contention (none the less powerful for appealing to common sense as well as to the learned literature) is that our ability to make healthcare choices for ourselves is well down our list of healthcare priorities.[30] At the top is trust in our treating clinicians. If this is true, autonomy is immediately demoted from top philosophical dog, and values such as beneficence and non-maleficence (traditionally more associated with benevolent medical paternalism), get promoted.

There are other, practical, quibbles with autonomy too. Practical problems shouldn't be dismissed quickly with a professorial sneer: if the law isn't practical it has failed utterly.

The most obvious practical quibble (we meet many others later) is that it is impossible to know when a truly autonomous decision has been made, or what conditions must pertain for it to be made. When, if ever, will a patient be in a sufficiently receptive state of mind for perfectly autonomous decision-making? And what about the relevance of the information provided? The degree of autonomous action is traditionally and understandably said to be a function (inter alia) of the information on which the decision to act is based. If Doctor A lies to Patient B about Patient B's prognosis, Patient B's autonomy rights are said to have been violated since, had Doctor A not lied, Patient B might have acted in a different way. He has been cheated out of his autonomous right to be master of his destiny. He could not alter the prognostic facts, but he could alter his response to them.

One of the problems with this is that an infinite amount of information is potentially relevant to a perfectly autonomous decision. Patient X might have a particular phobia about a vanishingly rare complication associated with a proposed drug. *Bolam* may never require the clinician to mention the complication. The complication may be recorded in a legendarily obscure journal in a foreign language. Patient X, had they heard of this complication, might have wanted to meet up with the person who had experienced the complication. Had they met up it might have changed the course of Patient X's life dramatically. And so on, and so on. If perfect knowledge is a pre-requisite of truly autonomous thought and action, Patient X did not have it. No human being will ever have perfect knowledge about even the simplest decision they face. All that the autonomist can hope for,

---

[30] O'Neill O (2002) *Autonomy and Trust in Bioethics* (Cambridge, CUP).

then, is to be his own master insofar as the inevitably incomplete view of the facts allowed him by the world permits him to be. 'That's a lot better than nothing', the autonomist asserts, and of course that is right. But then nobody is suggesting that autonomy is irrelevant and should be abolished. The only point here is that the autonomist's claim for his own all-trumping principle seems rather grandiose, given that principle's very limited capacity to deliver according to its own rules.

There has been a quiet, tentative questioning of the supremacy of traditional autonomy.[31] It is a mark of the strength of the mainstream position that the critics have not sought to dethrone autonomy itself, or to get it to share power, but merely to mitigate some of the more extravagant excesses of its totalitarianism. One of the main ideas that has resulted is 'relational autonomy'.[32] Relational autonomy recognises that no man is an island, but that we all exist in a network of relationships. Indeed most of us *define* ourselves in terms of those relationships. To the question 'What are you?' we reply: 'I am a Muslim. I am the mother of my sons and the wife of my husband'. Accordingly, say the relational autonomists, the most appropriate question for most people is not 'what is best for me?' (the cornerstone question presumed by traditional autonomy), but 'given the nexus of relationships in which I exist, the duties I owe and the duties that are owed to me, what should be done?'

Traditional autonomists say that those who articulate relational autonomy have simply misunderstood what traditional autonomy is all about. They recognise, they say, that most people will value their relationships and take them into account in coming to their own autonomous conclusions about how to act. They point out that some of the contentions of the relational autonomists seem to stem from a

---

[31] Eg, Tauber AI (2003) 'Sick autonomy' 46 *Perspectives in Biology and Medicine* 484–95; Stirrat GM, Gill R (2005) 'Autonomy in Medical Ethics After O'Neill' 31 *Journal of Medical Ethics* 127–30; Holm S (1995) 'Not Just Autonomy: The Principles of American Biomedical Ethics' 12 *Journal Of Medical Ethics* 332; Ross LF (2002) 'Patient Autonomy: Imperfect, Insufficient, But Still Quite Necessary' 13(1) *Journal of Clinical Ethics* 57–62.

[32] See Agich GJ (2003) *Dependence And Autonomy in Old Age: An Ethical Framework For Long Term Care* (Cambridge, CUP) and Donchin A (2001) 'Understanding Autonomy Relationally: Toward a Reconfiguration of Bioethical Principles' 26(4) *Journal of Medicine and Philosophy* 365–86 for clear statements of this notion. Herring J (2007) *Relational Autonomy*, unpublished manuscript, identifies six notions at the heart of relational autonomy: (a) relational life is inevitable; (b) relational life is good; (c) decisions must be understood in a social context; (d) emotions are part of autonomy—whereas individualised autonomy tends to emphasise the rational side; (e) other values such as trust, responsibility, care and attention to the needs of others are important; they are essential to the maintenance of relationships, which are themselves essential to autonomy; and (f) Autonomy is a fluid concept—not a state that one either has or do not have, but a state that one acquires, and which can ebb and flow with the state of our relationships. Feminist philosophers, for obvious reasons, have been prominent in the evolution of relational autonomy: see, eg, Mackenzie C and Stoljar N (2000) *Relational Autonomy: Feminist Perspectives on Autonomy, Agency and the Social Self* (New York, OUP); Friedman M (2004) *The Autonomy Myth* (New York, New Press); Friedman M (1997) 'Autonomy and Personal Relationships: Rethinking the Feminist Critique' in Myers DT (ed), *Feminists Rethink the Self* (Boulder, Co, Westview); Friedman M (1989) 'Autonomy in Social Context' in Sterba J and Peden C (eds) *Freedom, Equality and Social Change* (Lewiston, NY, Edwin Mellen Press) 158–69. Marilyn Friedman observes that popular US ideology is fixated on the myth that citizens are and should be autonomous. She notes that we are all inevitably dependent at some stage, and contends that carers provide most of the glue that holds societies together, so permitting the notion of autonomy to persist.

parody of the traditionally autonomous man—the austere, selfish, distant, scarily dispassionate thinker. I think they are right. Parody is not argument. Relational autonomy amounts to advice about how to exercise one's autonomy, rather than to a fundamental critique of the extraordinary status of autonomy. The elements of such a critique have been set out in this chapter.

This book calls autonomy to justify its status, subject by subject. But first, having suggested that autonomy should not be the only voice at the table in medical ethics or medico-legal discussions, we need to look at some of the other contenders for a place there.

2

Other Contenders for a Voice

T HIS CHAPTER SUGGESTS some of the principles other than autonomy that should contribute to medical ethics and medico-legal debates. It
is a short and rather trite chapter. The three main principles cited here
are cited in all undergraduate textbooks on medical ethics as relevant to medical
decision-making. They derive from Beauchamp and Childress.[1] The basic premise
of this book is that, despite that universal citation, they are all more or less ignored,
and at great cost.

The claims of these principles are modest. All that they want is to be allowed to
comment where it is appropriate, and to comment without being shouted down
by autonomy. None of them claims to rule. They are introduced here mainly so
that they are recognised in the rest of the book when they stand up to contribute.

Non-maleficence: *Primum Non Nocere*:
Above All, Do No harm

Having said that none of the principles claims supremacy, here is the first one
appearing to do just that: 'Above all, do no harm.'[2] The basic injunction, ('do no
harm') and indeed the claim of priority, ('above all'), sound rather uncontroversial. Even if we cannot expect our doctors to cure us, we expect them not to make
us worse, or to kill us, torture us, cheat us, sexually abuse us, or spitefully get us
detained under the Mental Health Act when there is no indication for detention.
Often when doctors appear in the criminal courts or at the Fitness to Practise

---

[1] *Principles of Biomedical Ethics*, see ch 1 n 20. They have been helpfully revisited in: Gillon R (2003)
'Four Scenarios' 29 *Journal of Medical Ethics* 267–8; Beauchamp TL (2003) 'Methods and Principles in
Biomedical Ethics' 29 *Journal of Medical Ethics* 269–74; Macklin R (2003) 'Applying the Four
Principles' 29 *Journal of Medical Ethics* 275–80; Campbell AV (2003) 'The Virtues (and Vices) of the
Four Principles' 29 *Journal of Medical Ethics* 292–6; and Gillon R (2003) 'Ethics Needs Principles—
Four Can Encompass the Rest—And Respect for Autonomy Should be "First Among Equals"' 29
Journal of Medical Ethics 307–12, and the other papers in that number of *Journal of Medical Ethics*.
[2] See McLean SM (ed) (2006) *First Do No Harm: Law, Ethics and Healthcare* (Aldershot, Ashgate);
Burgio G, Lantos (eds) (1994) Primum non nocere *Today—A Symposium on Paediatric Ethics*
(Amsterdam, Elsevier) Excerpta Medica International Congress Series; Raz J (1987) 'Autonomy,
Toleration and the Harm Principle' in Gavison R (ed) *Issues in Contemporary Legal Philosophy* (Oxford,
OUP).

Committee of the General Medical Council they are there because they fall foul of this rule, and nobody questions that they should be there.

There are two reasons why the principle cannot regulate medical conduct on its own. The first is that it imposes no positive obligations at all. It will not complain if a doctor does no more than stay in bed—as long as he is not in bed with a vulnerable patient. The second is that 'harm' is very much in the eye of the beholder. One man's harm might be another man's wish. Other principles (notably autonomy and justice) are needed to help in the definition of 'harm' adopted for the purpose of satisfying the maxim.

Beneficence

The pledge to 'do no harm' is generally interpreted as meaning that a doctor will not do harm unless it is outweighed by the good consequences of the act that causes harm. Hence beneficence: the obligation to do good overall. But again, a number of questions are begged—notably, again, about the definition of 'harm'.[3] 'Harm' in whose eyes? The patient's? The doctor's? The GMC's? Society's? Those of other patients whose treatment might have been funded by the money spent on the treatment? The hospital accountants'? Similar questions might be asked about the definition and the appropriate definer of the countervailing good. Some of the answers may be provided by the final principle, justice.

Justice

Justice takes a long, societal view of medico-legal problems. It is rather better than non-maleficence and beneficence, and much better than autonomy, at remembering that there is more than one patient in a hospital, and that in a world of finite resources one patient's treatment is another patient's denial of treatment. For a principle it is rather unprincipled. It has one basic canon which it applies rigidly: like cases should be treated alike. But where this maxim doesn't produce an answer, it gets pragmatic, and starts drawing parasitically and inconsistently on other ethical ideas—notably various shades of utilitarianism. We will see that this pragmatic philosophical catholicity has contributed significantly to the highly variegated ethical tapestry that we call medical law.

---

[3] See Wear S (1993) *Informed Consent: Patient Autonomy and Physician Beneficence Within Clinical Medicine* (Kluwer).

Professional Integrity

To these cornerstone principles it is at least convenient and possibly important to add the amorphous quality: professional integrity. To some extent its use is tautological: a doctor who acts with professional integrity will presumably be guided by (at least his perception of) beneficence and non-maleficence, will strive for justice insofar as justice's demands are within his remit, and will in any event obey the professional codes which are supposed to take account of those demands. The notion of professional integrity is most useful when the word 'integrity' is taken literally. The notion applauds doctors who are whole people; whose personal standards are internally consistent and consistent with those of the profession; whose professional ethics don't stop operating when they drive out of the hospital. Only whole doctors can minister to whole patients, and holism is far better medical practice than narrow technical reductionism. We return to this issue in dealing with the vexed question of conscientious objection.

Rights and Duties

Autonomy loathes the idea of duties. It applauds loudly the rights-based jurisprudence that has swept through the English common law over the last decade. But it fails to notice one very obvious thing. It is something we noted in discussing non-maleficence. In order for autonomy to become relevant at all in medicine—indeed in order for medicine to occur at all—doctors have to get out of bed, go to the hospital and treat patients. They do this because they have a duty to do so, and throughout the time that they are treating patients they are acting under duties. It is impossible to describe those obligations other than in terms of duties. It is of course true that the doctors autonomously chose to become doctors and autonomously choose to continue being doctors, but the whole framework in which medicine operates rests on doctors' duties even more fundamentally than it does on any autonomy rights that the patients might have. Autonomy therefore tolerates duties in the same way that swagger-stick-brandishing colonials tolerated the natives. Ideally you don't want them in the house, and you certainly wouldn't dream of inviting them to dinner, but in fact they do all the work.

That is not to say that doctors do not have autonomy rights of their own. They do. There is something of a civil war raging between doctors' autonomy rights and patients' autonomy rights. The fact of that war turns out to be yet another reason why we should be reluctant to hand over all ethical governance in medicine to autonomy. We need to look at that war. It is the subject of the next chapter.

3

Whose Autonomy?

A 23 YEAR OLD woman attends her general medical practitioner (GP). She is 12 weeks pregnant, is unhappy being pregnant, and wants an abortion. Her GP has no particular religious objection to abortion, but having seen the procedure being carried out when he was a medical student, finds it distasteful and wants to have nothing to do with it. He declines to refer the woman for an abortion, saying that if she wants one she will have to make other arrangements. He does not give her the name of another doctor who might be prepared to refer her, or the address of any abortion clinic. Suppose for the sake of this example that it is impossible for her to find another provider, and that the doctor's refusal deprives her of the chance of getting the abortion she wants.

The woman's 'right' to an abortion appears to clash head on with the doctor's 'right' not to be involved in a procedure he finds offensive. (It may also clash with any 'right' to life that her unborn child might have: that matter is dealt with later in this book). Both of these 'rights' are properly located in the doctrine of autonomy. Autonomy created the problem: can autonomy get us out of it?

In recent years there has been mounting academic criticism, on both sides of the Atlantic, of the use of medical conscientious objection.[1] This is probably a consequence of the increased invocation of conscientious objection clauses. That increased use has led to practical problems for healthcare providers and patients. It is increasingly difficult, for instance, to recruit medical practitioners to do abortions. It is rather ironic that as increasing numbers of health care professionals demonstrate that conscientious objection is important to them, the pressure mounts to restrict the right to objection.

The case against conscientious objection is put stridently by Julian Savulescu:

> Conscience . . . can be an excuse for vice or invoked to avoid doing one's duty. When the duty is a true duty, conscientious objection is wrong and immoral. When there is a grave

---

[1] See, eg, Cook RJ (2006) 'The Growing Abuse of Conscientious Objection' 8 *Virtual Mentor* 337–40; Greenberger MD and Vogelstein R (2005) 'Pharmacist Refusals: A threat to Women's Health' 308(5728) *Science,* 10 June 2005, 1557–8; Swartz MS (2006) '"Conscience Clauses" or "Unconscionable Clauses": Personal Beliefs Versus Professional Responsibilities' 6(2) *Yale Journal of Health Policy, Law and Ethics* 269–350; Wall LL and Brown D (2006) 'Refusals by Pharmacists to Dispense Emergency Contraception: A Critique' 107(5) *Obstetrics and Gynaecology* 1148–51; Wicclair MR (2006) 'Pharmacies, Pharmacists and Conscientious Objection' 16(3) *Kennedy Institute of Ethics Journal* 225–50: Appel JM (2005) 'Judicial Diagnosis: 'Conscience' vs Care: How Refusal Clauses Are Reshaping the Rights Revolution' 88(8) *Medicine and Health Rhode Island* 279–81: Dickens BM (2006) Ethical Misconduct by Abuse of Conscientious Objection Laws 25(3) *Medicine and Law* 513–22.

duty, it should be illegal. A doctor's conscience has little place in the delivery of modern medical care. What should be provided to patients is defined by the law and consideration of the just distribution of finite medical resources, which requires a reasonable conception of the patient's good and the patient's informed desires. If people are not prepared to offer legally permitted, efficient and beneficial care to a patient because it conflicts with their values, they should not be doctors. Doctors should not offer partial medical services or partially discharge their obligations to care for their patients.[2]

Charo agrees. The problem, she says, is that the 45-plus states in the United States that have abortion conscientious objection clauses on their statute books give medical professionals the exclusive right to offer (inter alia) abortion services.

> By granting a monopoly, they turn the profession into a kind of public utility, obligated to provide service to all who seek it. Claiming an unfettered right to personal autonomy while holding monopolistic control over a public good constitutes an abuse of the public trust—all the worse if it is not in fact a personal act of conscience but, rather, an attempt at cultural conquest.[3]

Although Savulescu and Charo sometimes sound here as if they are concerned with the state of the conscientious objector's mind per se, they elsewhere make it clear that they are not, and that their only real concern is with the delivery of the health services they deem necessary. Here is Savulescu:

> When a doctor's values can be accommodated without compromising the quality and efficiency of public medicine they should, of course, be accommodated. If many doctors are prepared to perform a procedure and known to be so, there is an argument for allowing a few to object out. A few obstetricians refusing to perform abortions may be tolerable if many others are prepared to perform these, just as a few self-interested infectious disease doctors refusing to treat patients in a flu epidemic, on the grounds of self-interest, might be tolerable if there were enough altruistic physicians willing to risk their health. But when conscientious objection compromises the quality, efficiency or equitable delivery of a service, it should not be tolerated. The primary goal of a health service is to protect the health of its recipients.[4,5]

Savulescu and Charo have a low view of medicine. For them, doctors are just technical functionaries, standing with entirely unengaged consciences on a clinical production line, churning out medical services. Charo is quite open about it, and she frankly blames autonomy for it.

> [T]he emerging norm of patient autonomy . . . has contributed to the erosion of the professional statute of medicine. Insofar as they are reduced to mere purveyors of medical

---

[2] (2006) 'Conscientious Objection in Medicine' 332 *British Medical Journal* 294–7, 294.
[3] Charo RA (2005) 'The Celestial Fire of Conscience—Refusing to Deliver Medical Care' 352 *New England Journal of Medicine* 2471–3, at 2473.
[4] See n 2 above, 295.
[5] Similarly, Charo states: 'Accepting a collective obligation does not mean that all members of the profession are forced to violate their own consciences. It does, however, necessitate ensuring that a genuine system for counselling and referring patients is in place, so that every patient can act according to his or her own conscience just as readily as the professional can.' See n 3 above, at 2473.

technology, doctors no longer have extraordinary privileges, and so their notions of extraordinary duty—house calls, midnight duties, and charity care—deteriorate as well.[6]

The point is well made. If you make doctors mere technicians (by requiring them to suspend their own consciences as soon as they put on their white coats), you gain the advantage of having somebody who will give every patient what he or she wants, but you lose a lot too. Charo identified tangible things—extra hours unmandated by contract, and so on—but surely the intangible things are equally or more important: sympathy, warmth and downright humanity. Medicine talks increasingly about the crucial importance of holistic care. You can't get holistic care from someone who is not allowed to be whole. What most autonomous patients in most clinical situations really want is sympathetic, holistic care. If autonomy culls from the medical ranks the clinicians who can give it, autonomy, once again, proves tragically self-defeating.[7] If the price of a truly holistic medical workforce is some logistical difficulty for some women in obtaining an abortion when and where they want it, many would think that that is a price worth paying.

And then there is the law. Savulescu appeals to it. 'What should be provided to patients is defined by the law', he says.[8] Well, yes, but what law exactly is he talking about? There is no absolute legal right to an abortion. The Abortion Act 1967 merely decriminalises abortion in some carefully specified circumstances. What the 1967 Act does do, however, is provide expressly for conscientious objection. The ambit of that provision is outlined below. There is similar protection for conscientious objection in the European Convention on Human Rights.[9]

It is tactically unwise of Savulescu to invoke the law on behalf of the right of patient autonomy to trump doctors' autonomy rights. The law in this area, at least in theory, is stoutly supportive of doctors. The ethical roots of that support seem to be autonomy itself, professional integrity in the literal sense, and some sort of virtue ethic.

But there is a wide and widening gulf between law and practice. It is notoriously hard for doctors who say that they will not perform abortions to obtain training

---

[6] See n 3 above, at 2472.

[7] See Pellegrino ED (1994) 'Patient and Physician Autonomy: Conflicting Rights and Obligations in the Physician-Patient Relationship' 10 *Journal of Contemporary Health Law Policy* 47–68: '[B]eneficence and autonomy must be mutually re-enforcing if the patient's good is to be served, if the physician's ability to serve that good is not to be compromised, and if the physician's moral claim to autonomy and the integrity of the whole enterprise of medical ethics are to be respected.' Elsewhere he comments: 'The emergence of autonomy as a sociopolitical, legal, and moral concept has profoundly influenced medical ethics. It has shifted the center of decision-making from the physician to the patient and reoriented the whole physician-patient relationship toward a relationship more open, more honest, and more respectful of the dignity of the person of the patient. But autonomy is insufficient to guarantee the nuances and the full meanings of respect for persons in medical transactions. As a foundation for medical relationships, the concept of integrity is richer, more fundamental, and more closely tied to what it is to be a whole human person. So . . . we should deepen our grasp of the notion that autonomy depends upon preserving the integrity of persons and that both integrity of persons and autonomy depend on the physician.': Pellegrino ED (1990) 'The Relationship of Autonomy and Integrity in Medical Ethics' 24(4) *Bulletin of the Pan American Health Organization* 361–71.

[8] See n 2 above.

[9] Art 9 of the Convention.

posts in gynaecology, and the legal right not to participate in abortion is coming under direct and systematic attack. The pro-abortion lobby has announced the latest phase in its offensive. One of the leading abortion providers, Marie Stopes International, wants to force GPs' surgeries to display lists indicating which doctors in the practice will refer women for abortion, and the pressure group 'Doctors for a Woman's Choice on Abortion' is encouraging patients to report to the GMC doctors who refuse to play any part in abortion.[10]

What does the law say?

There is widespread confusion about the extent of the conscientious objection clause in the Abortion Act 1967. Section 4(1) reads:

> Subject to subsection (2) of this section, no person shall be under any duty, whether by contract or by any statutory or other legal requirement, to participate in any treatment authorized by this Act to which he has a conscientious objection:[11]

Subsection (2) relates to treatment 'necessary to save the life or to prevent grave permanent injury to the physical or mental health of a pregnant woman.'

What is covered by 'participate in any treatment'? The point was considered by the House of Lords in *R v Salford AHA, ex p Janaway*.[12] Mrs Janaway was a secretary at a health centre. She was a Roman Catholic and believed that abortion was wrong. She was asked by a doctor to type a letter relating to referral of a patient to a consultant with a view to abortion. She refused, and further refused to type any other letters concerned with abortion. Apart from section 4(1) this refusal would have been a breach of her contract of employment. She relied on s 4(1), but was nonetheless dismissed. Did section 4(1) apply to typing letters which were a part of the referral process? No, said the House of Lords. 'Participate', said Lord Keith, should have 'its ordinary and natural meaning' and

> referred to actually taking part in treatment administered in a hospital or other approved place . . . for the purpose of terminating a pregnancy.

This citation has been repeatedly quoted as authority for the proposition that anything that occurs outside the operating theatre falls outside the ambit of section 4(1). But it not clear that this is the case. First, and obviously, *Ex p Janaway* was not to do with a doctor. Is there really no distinction between a secretary

---

[10] See 'Abortion lobby in campaign to expose pro-life doctors' *Sunday Times* (London, 17 July 2005) <http://www.timesonline.co.uk/article/0,,2087-1697523,00.html> (Accessed 24 December 2007).

[11] The Human Fertilisation and Embryology Act 1990 also preserves an express right to refuse to participate in any treatment authorised under that Act. Section 38 provides: '(1) No person who has a conscientious objection to participating in any activity governed by this Act shall be under any duty, however arising, to do so. (2) In any legal proceedings the burden of proof of conscientious objection shall rest on the person claiming to rely on it.' There is no statutory protection for individual conscientious objectors in many other contentious areas—eg post-coital contraception and gender reassignment. For a consideration of the position of conscientiously objecting NHS GPs in practices holding contracts for the provision of contraceptive services and maternity medical services, see the National Health Service (General Medical Services Contracts) Regulations 2004, SI 2004/291, and the discussion in Foster C (2008) 'Conscience in the consultation' *Triple Helix*, Summer, 10–11.

[12] [1988] 3 All ER 1079.

typing a letter and a doctor referring? To assert that there is not downgrades the professional act of referral into a merely administrative business. Is not the initiation of the professional process which leads to the 'treatment' necessarily part of the 'treatment'? For all other purposes the doctor at the point of referral owes to the patient the duty of a doctor, not that of a secretary. This point was never argued in *Ex p Janaway*.

Second, in *Ex p Janaway* itself there was discussion of the Abortion Regulations 1968, which deal with the 'green form' to be signed by the two registered medical practitioners pursuant to section 1 of the Act. While noting that

> The Regulations do not appear to contemplate that the signing of the certificate would form part of the treatment for the termination of pregnancy,

Lord Keith went on to say:

> It does not appear whether or not there are any circumstances under which a doctor might be under a legal duty to sign a green form, so as to place in difficulties one who had a conscientious objection to doing so . . . So I do not think it appropriate to express any opinion on the matter.

While of course the signing of a green form is much nearer the actual act of termination than the act of referral is, the general question of whether the medical steps preliminary to the act of termination are covered by section 4 must be regarded as still open to argument.

Third, *Ex p Janaway* was decided long before the European Convention on Human Rights was grafted into English law. Article 9 of the Convention provides that

> Everyone has the right to freedom of thought, conscience and religion; this right includes . . . freedom . . . to manifest his religion or belief in worship, teaching, practice and observance.

The Human Rights Act 1998 requires judges to interpret UK legislation, if it is at all possible to do so, in accordance with the Convention rights. If a UK law is incompatible with those rights, a 'declaration of incompatibility' can be granted—effectively an authoritative direction to the government to make the legislation concordant with the Convention. It can be argued strongly that Article 9 should require the conscientious objection clause to encompass a refusal to refer. The arguments are technical and outside the scope of this book.[13]

The British Medical Association has given detailed guidance. It appears to assume that *Ex p Janaway* applies to referral. It asserts:

> Doctors with a conscientious objection to abortion should make their views known to the patient and enable the patient to see another doctor without delay if that is the patient's wish.[14]

---

[13] For detailed discussion, see Hammer L (1999) 'Abortion objection in the UK within the framework of the European Convention on Human Rights and Fundamental Freedoms' [1999] EHRLR, Issue 6, 564.

[14] British Medical Association. *The Law and Ethics of Abortion*, March 1997, revised December 1999.

The GMC, in the previous edition of 'Good Medical Practice' stated:

> If you feel that your beliefs might affect the advice or treatment you provide, you must explain this to patients and tell them of their right to see another doctor.[15]

The new version of Good Medical Practice[16] appears to go further. It says:

> If carrying out a particular procedure or giving advice about it conflicts with your religious or moral beliefs, and this conflict might affect the treatment or advice you provide, you must explain this to the patient and tell them they have a right to see another doctor. You must be satisfied that the patient has sufficient information to enable them to exercise that right. If it is not practical for a patient to arrange to see another doctor, you must ensure that arrangements are made for another suitably qualified colleague to take over your role.[17]

It further provides that:

> You must not express to your patients your personal beliefs, including political, religious or moral beliefs, in ways that exploit their vulnerability or that are likely to cause them distress.[18]

The change in the wording is an important indication of the way that the ethical wind is blowing. It is not a consequence of a new appraisal of the meaning of section 4 of the 1967 Act, or of *Ex p Janaway*. The new wording may impose a more onerous duty on a conscientiously objecting doctor. It is, like so many edicts issuing from the GMC's offices, a simple joining in with the chant of the zeitgeist. GPs are seen, insofar as compatible with section 4, as merely administrative animals—post-offices dispatching women on the road to wherever they decide they want to go. Any sort of directive counselling—any expression by the doctor of any view at all—would be met by immediate and draconian sanction. The doctor's autonomy rights—while supposedly protected by section 4—are truncated almost to nothing. Put another way, if the doctor ventured to say where he thought beneficence, non-maleficence or even justice led, he would be strung up.

The wording could be attacked under Article 9; the outcome would not be certain. But the rather craven attitude of the English courts towards the medical profession's statements about itself, and the massive girth of the margin of appreciation in medical cases, would make the Article 9 struggle a difficult one for a conscientiously objecting doctor.

There may be some comfort in the GMC's guidance 'Personal Beliefs and Medical Practice'[19] It purports to be a commentary on 'Good Medical Practice'. It acknowledges expressly that 'personal beliefs and values, and cultural and religious practices are central to the lives of doctors and patients'[20] and recognises that

---

[15] General Medical Council, 2001.
[16] General Medical Council, 2007.
[17] *Good Medical Practice*, para 8.
[18] *Good Medical Practice*, para 33.
[19] General Medical Council, March 2008.
[20] Para 4.

doctors as well as patients have rights.[21,22] While this is a step in the right direction, there are the steps of a vast marching army in the other.

Should it be different? Should the rule of patient autonomy in the abortion debate be so absolute that it should be able to determine the whole nature of the doctor-patient relationship? The public good is not ultimately served by having doctors sculpted entirely by patients. In order to stop the chisels from doing irrevocable damage, you need to recruit beneficence, non-maleficence and justice. They are needed to give doctors the full-blooded, three-dimensional personality required of a properly effective clinician.

This is as good a place as any to note, too, how patronising and how fearful autonomy is. In the context of the GP abortion consultation it says: 'The woman shall not be exposed, unless she expressly invites it, to any views which might affect her fixed determination to have an abortion.'

Why is this? It is deeply ironic: autonomy itself, in all other arenas of medical practice, insists that all relevant information is given—to the extent, as we shall see, of ramming unwanted information down the throat of a patient who would be quite happy with some good, old-fashioned, doctor-knows-best medical paternalism. In many ways abortion seems to exist on a little island, untouched by the normal rules of consent. Women in the UK undergo abortions without any of the counselling about risks and benefits appropriate to a procedure of that magnitude. Perhaps what we are seeing here is yet another example of the neo-Kantian devotion to the liberal consensus. Abortion is perceived as one of the immovable givens of that consensus. A woman who can choose it guiltlessly is acting in accordance with the universal law, and is therefore perfectly free. A woman who feels inhibited about choosing it is, if not actually legally incapacitated, hardly free. The Kantian autonomists want to help everyone to perfect freedom—which equates to perfect concordance with the universal law. And that means that one should not

---

[21] Para 7: '[The guidance] attempts to balance doctors' and patients' rights—including the right to freedom of thought, conscience and religion, and the entitlement to care and treatment to meet clinical needs—and advises on what to do when those rights conflict.'

[22] The guidance refers specifically to abortion, in terms which are ambiguous: 'Patients may ask you to perform, advise on or refer them for a treatment or procedure which is not prohibited by law or statutory code of practice in the country where you work, but to which you have a conscientious objection. In such cases you must tell patients of their right to see another doctor with whom they can discuss their situation and ensure that they have sufficient information to exercise that right. In deciding whether the patient has sufficient information, you must explore with the patient what information they might already have, or need.' (para 21); and 'Where a patient who is awaiting or has undergone a termination of pregnancy needs medical care, you have no legal or ethical right to refuse to provide it on grounds of a conscientious objection to the procedure. The same principle applies to the care of patients before or following any other procedure from which you have withdrawn because of your beliefs.' (para 26). These paragraphs raise some obvious questions. Will doctors be obliged (on pain of disciplinary sanction) to sign abortion authorisation forms? Will they have to carry out pre-abortion examinations and assessments? Will they be obliged to refer patients seeking abortion to others doctors who will authorise it? The answers so far given by the GMC to each of these questions is a reassuring 'no': see the answers given by the GMC to questions posed by CMF, discussed by Foster C (2008) 'Conscience in the consultation' *Triple Helix*, Summer, 10–11.

trouble the woman with a full discussion, at what will inevitably be a particularly turbulent time.

A tort lawyer would listen with furrowed brow to this debate about conscientious objection. In the world of tort, a doctor can stalk out of the consulting room at any time, propelled by conscience, boredom or the lure of the golf course. The law steadfastly refuses to impose on doctors (other than by contract) any obligation to perform any particular medical treatment.[23] Also, a doctor can choose with whom he enters into a doctor-patient relationship: his conscience may trouble him if he sees a bleeding patient, and walks by on the other side of the road, but the law will not.

Since Patient X cannot demand of Doctor Y that procedure Z be performed by Y, can X legitimately complain that his autonomy rights are affected? Since these rules are designed (inter alia) to protect the autonomy rights of Y, that is a complaint that autonomy will be slightly embarrassed to support. Autonomy, too, is careful about being represented as the philosophy of the spoilt brat.

Autonomy in the medico-legal arena is (rightly) much more concerned with preventing unwanted violations than in guaranteeing a right to positive benefits. For that reason it has little to say about the vexed business of resource allocation: it is happy to acknowledge that that is the province of other principles. Likewise, it is slow to accept the brief from the patient with body image disorder who begs the surgeon, in autonomy's own language, to remove the objectively normal but subjectively horrific limbs. This makes autonomy's stridency in the abortion debate all the more curious. Autonomy is slow to say that someone has a right to removal of an abdominal tumour, but rushes to assert that a woman has a right to removal of a foetus—despite the arguably competing rights of the foetus, and despite the conscientious objection of clinicians. This is a discordant anomaly. It is explored more fully in chapter 5.

---

[23] See ch 9.

Part 2

Before Life

4

Reproductive Autonomy

Should One Be Required to Reproduce?

O F COURSE NOT. This is what autonomy says, and it is right. Reproduction is a serious business. Subject to the important issue of abortion, autonomy should speak with an uncontradicted voice when it comes to the question of whether or not one should be required to embark on the business of parenthood.[1] If somebody does not want to be a parent, they should not be forced to be. Things change ethically and legally once an embryo has been created, but if you don't want to let your gametes to fuse with someone's else's, no one should make you.

This, broadly, is what the English law says too, insofar as it says anything at all. The Human Fertilisation and Embryology Act 1990 has detailed provisions dealing with the use that can be made of sperm and eggs provided in the course of treatment governed by the Act. Those provisions are fairly clear and often heartbreakingly inflexible. Thus when Diane Blood sought to use the sperm of her dead husband to conceive a child, the HFEA said no: the husband had not given the requisite written consent for its use.[2] This is autonomy ruling with a brutally firm hand. The judgment of the court was not philosophically fecund. Rules were rules, it said. The rules were made for perfectly comprehensible reasons. Parliament, in endorsing the rules, was perfectly entitled to be scared of the spectres that it saw: a man being confronted by a son, of whom he had no knowledge, claiming an emotional relationship, or a mother seeking some sort of financial support from a father who never knew he was a father.

Of course the mother in such situations has autonomy rights too. They are best articulated in term of Articles 8 and 12 of the European Convention on Human Rights (ECHR). Article 8 provides:

---

[1] See McLeod C (2002) 'Self-Trust and Reproductive Autonomy (Basic Bioethics)' (Cambridge, Mass, MIT Press). Cf Bennett R and Harris J (2002) 'Are There Lives Not worth Living? When Is It Morally Wrong to Reproduce?' in Dickenson D (ed) *Ethical Issues in Maternal-Fetal Medicine* (Cambridge, CUP) 321–34; McHale J (2002) 'Is There a Duty Not to Reproduce?' *Ibid* 101–12.

[2] *R v Human Fertilisation and Embryology Authority, ex p Blood* [1997] 2 WLR 806; see also *U v W (A-G Intervening)* [1997] 2 FLR 282. For general discussion of the ethics of post-mortem gamete use, see Spriggs M (2004) 'Woman Wants Dead Fiancé's Baby: Who Owns a Dead Man's Sperm?' 30 *Journal of Medical Ethics* 384–5; Cannold L (2004) 'Who Owns a Dead Man's Sperm?' 30 *Journal of Medical Ethics* 386. Parker M (2004) ''Til Death Us Do Part: The Ethics of Post-Mortem Gamete Donation' 30 *Journal of Medical Ethics* 387–8.

(1) Everyone has the right to respect for his private and family life, his home and his correspondence.

(2) There shall be no interference by a public authority with the exercise of this right except such as is in accordance with the law and is necessary in a democratic society in the interests of national security, public safety or the economic well-being of the country, for the prevention of disorder or crime, for the protection of health or morals, or for the protection of the rights and freedoms of others.

This is the most elastic of all the Convention articles. It stretches to places that the original draftsman never dreamed of. It has long been assumed that autonomy is one of the principles that inspired Article 8 and continues to give it life. The European Court of Human Rights has now confirmed this:

Although no previous case has established as such any right to self-determination as being contained in Article 8 of the Convention, the Court considers that the notion of personal autonomy is an important principle underlying the interpretation of the guarantees.[3,4]

Article 12 provides:

Men and women of marriageable age have the right to marry and to found a family, according to the national laws governing the exercise of this right.

Of these, Article 12, unburdened by any caveats such as in Article 8(2), looks the more promising. But neither stands any chance in the face of the overwhelming force of the father's autonomy argument, as Natallie Evans found recently when she went to Strasbourg, claiming that since her only chance of motherhood was to use the embryos created by consent before her ovary-ablating chemotherapy, she should be allowed to use them. Her ex-boyfriend, who had fathered the embryos, had changed his mind about their use. He was entitled to do so, said the court. This was a case about embryos, not merely gametes. We return to it when considering the rights of the embryo, but it indicates that the father's autonomy rights are so strong that they cannot prevail even against a coalition of maternal and embryonic forces.[5]

Is this right? Although one might bemoan the bureaucratic inflexibility in *Blood* and the callousness of the boyfriend in *Evans*, it is difficult to see that the principle propelling the law is wrong, that the fathers' autonomy rights were given disproportionate weight, or that recruitment of principles other than autonomy would or should yield a radically different result.

Outside the ambit of the 1990 Act, however, the legal position is much less clear. What happens, for example, if a woman removes semen from a condom used by

---

[3] *Pretty v United Kingdom* (2002) 35 EHRR 1.

[4] See Marshall J (2008) 'A right to personal autonomy at the European Court of Human Rights' 3 *European Human Rights Law Review* 337–56, which surveys, through a feminist lens, the way that the Strasbourg Court has interpreted Art 8, referring particularly to the sexual identity of transsexuals and the right of access to information about origins and identifying two notions of personal autonomy—self-determination/self-creation and self-realisation/self-discovery.

[5] See *Evans v United Kingdom* (6339/05) (2006) 1 FCR 585.

her boyfriend and, knowing that he would object, inseminates herself with it? The simple answer is that we don't know. The difficulty arises from the English law's uncertainty about the ownership of body parts and body substances. The uncertainties relevant here have largely survived the Human Tissue Act 2004. The 2004 Act governs dealing with elements that consist of or include human cells. Semen certainly qualifies.[6] But what if the culpability relates to the use made of the gametes—not covered by the Act? If one considers first the criminal law possibilities, has the girlfriend committed any criminal offence at all? Even if the law would regard the semen as capable of constituting property (and there is a big and inconclusive debate about that),[7] can she sensibly be said to have stolen it? Has the boyfriend not abandoned it, in a way analogous to throwing a empty bottle into a dustbin? If so, it is not 'property belonging to another', within the meaning of the Theft Act 1968, and cannot be stolen. Probably the better position is that no offence has been committed.

The position in civil law is equally uncertain. Presumably, in order for the girlfriend to have 'converted' the sperm to her own use (acted with it in a way inconsistent with the rights of the owner), one would have to assert not only that there was property in the sperm (facing the same difficulties as in the criminal law definition of property, discussed above), but also that the boyfriend had a continuing proprietary right (facing the same difficulties as in the criminal law definition of abandonment, discussed above). The law should be more pragmatic in its definition of property and abandonment. It should assert that there is property when to fail to do so would lead to an obviously unjust result, and conclude that there is no abandonment where the abandoner would decree that the abandoned material should not be used in the way that it has been. A proprietary right, in other words, should persist for as long as: (a) nobody else has acquired better title; and (b) the original title holder wishes to assert his right, for purposes in accordance with the general policy of the law.

Answers to these criminal and civil questions will be needed sooner or later. An answer to the criminal question is needed for the same policy reasons which lie behind the 1990 Act: this mishandling of gametes is obviously undesirable and needs to be discouraged. An answer to the civil question is needed because, under the existing family law, a man propelled unknowingly and unwillingly into fatherhood in the self-insemination circumstances described above might well be saddled with financial liability for the child. Most people would think that this is wrong. The main reason that it is wrong is that here, just as under the 1990 Act, the autonomy rights of the boyfriend should rule. The family legislation could be altered, but a re-draft would create some big problems of its own. It would be neater if the civil law entitled a man to bring an action for conversion of his semen—part of the damages for which would be any financial liability he shouldered under the Child Support legislation. He would no doubt want to annex to

---

[6] S 53.

[7] Summarised in Foster, C (2003) 'Dandruff, Data Protection and Dead Bodies' *Counsel*, April 2003, 12. See too Jansen RPS (1985) 'Sperm and Ova As Property' 11 *Journal of Medical Ethics* 123–6. See also *Yearworth v N Bristol NHS Trust*, (CA) unreported, 4 February 2009.

this claim a plea for damages for breach of his right under Article 8 of the European Convention on Human Rights—a plea which would merely translate into Strasbourgeoise the straightforward, undiluted and undilutable plea of autonomy.

When it comes to gametes, then, it seems that the law, wherever the law is clear, adopts a straightforward autonomy analysis. Your gametes are your own, and you can do with them whatever you like. Whenever the law is unclear, it should tend in the same direction, and for the same reasons.

Should You Be Entitled to Have a Child?[8,9]

Natallie Evans and Diane Blood thought so.[10] They thought that Articles 8 and 12 helped them. But their Article 8 rights could not prevail against those of the partners', and Article 12, despite its apparently absolute nature, has to give way to a really stark self-determination plea such as the partners could make. In such a straightforward competition the outcome will always be certain, and for good reasons.

But what if both partners want a child? The issue has come before the courts in three main contexts: applications in ordinary, everyday family law proceedings by a couple who want to adopt; and applications by prisoners or other people in comparable situations, saying that their right to reproduce has been unlawfully truncated by the detaining authorities; and applications for judicial review of decisions of the Human Fertilisation and Embryology Authority,[11] refusing couples permission to undergo some assisted reproduction procedure. Consideration of the third of these contexts is ethically and legally complicated by the issue of the status of the embryo. That issue is dealt with in detail in the next chapter. Accordingly only the first two situations are considered here. They are both a long way from medical law, but sometimes you get a better view from a distance.

Applications to Adopt

Adoption is 'the complete severance of the legal relationship between parents and child and the establishment of a new one between the child and the adoptive

---

[8] The extent to which one is generally entitled to demand the provision of healthcare is considered in detail in ch 9 'Litigation, rights and duties'.

[9] A superb defence of reproductive autonomy generally is in Jackson E (2001) *Regulating Reproduction: Law, Technology and Autonomy* (Oxford: Hart Publishing).

[10] See above. For a general discussion of the law and ethics, see Chan S and Quigley M (2007) 'Frozen Embryos, Genetic Information and Reproductive Rights' 21: 8 *Bioethics* 439–48.

[11] The regulatory body created by the Human Fertilisation and Embryology Act 1990, which is responsible for licensing procedures involving the use of most reproductive technology.

parent.'[12] It is now established that the ECHR does not itself grant any right to adopt. In *Frette v France*[13] a single homosexual man, seeking to adopt, sought to say that it did. The Strasbourg court said that it did not. But it does not follow from this that Article 8 has nothing to say on the matter. It has a great deal to say. An adoption order is

> undoubtedly an interference by a public authority, in the shape of the court that makes it, with the exercise of the right to respect for family life, whether by the child . . . or by anyone else with whom [the child] enjoys 'family life'. Indeed it is the most drastic interference with the right which is permitted by the law.[14]

An adoption order will accordingly be compliant with Article 8 only if the interference with the basic Article 8(1) right that it necessarily involves falls within Article 8(2): it must be in accordance with the law and necessary in a democratic society to protect the rights and freedoms of others. The 'others' most clearly in focus here will generally be the children whom it is sought to adopt. Plainly the rights of many people are potentially engaged, conflicting, and standing in mutual alliance with one another in most adoption disputes. Certainly other children of the family from whom it is sought to sever a legal relationship have Article 8 rights; likewise, presumably, other children in the family of the would-be adopters.[15]

But there is limited intellectual satisfaction (at least in England) in dissecting out the possible strands of Article 8 entitlement. All the arguments, however elegant, get crudely subsumed, just like almost everything else in English child care law, into the principle that the overriding concern is the welfare of the child.[16] The governing statute is now the Adoption and Children Act 2002.[17] The Act declares that the 'paramount consideration of the court or adoption agency must be the child's welfare, throughout his life.'[18] The court or agency must have regard to a statutory checklist, which directs it to consider the child's wishes and feelings, needs, age, sex, background and any harm that the child has suffered or is likely to suffer.[19] Yes, other relationships are relevant,[20] but wholly subordinate to the welfare of the child.

All the lurid media interest in (for example), adoption by gay couples, looked at first blush like promising material for an exploration of reproductive rights. On one level the law is so simple and so emphatic that all those headlines turn out to be legal damp squibs. They tell us nothing except that children are more important than anyone else in the decision-making process, which is surely uncontroversially right.

---

[12] Report of the Houghton Committee (Cmnd 5107, 1972) at para 14.

[13] [2003] 2 FLR 9; the court relied inter alia on *X v Belgium and Netherlands* (1975) D & R 75.

[14] *Re B (Adoption by One Natural Parent to Exclusion of Other)* [2001] 1 FLR 589, [37] (Hale LJ).

[15] The issue is discussed in Lowe N (2001) 'English Adoption Law: Past, Present and Future' in Katz S, Eekelaar J and Maclean M (eds) *Cross Currents—Family Law and Policy in the US and England* (New York, OUP) 307, 337–8.

[16] The general principle in childcare law is enshrined in the Children Act 1989 s 1.

[17] It repealed the Adoption Act 1976, and came fully into force on 30 December 2005.

[18] S 1(1), (2).

[19] S 1(4).

[20] S 1(4)(c).

They pose no really interesting ethical conundrums. They do not let us say (for instance) that gays have more or fewer autonomy rights than heterosexuals. The gay couple has no right to adopt. Nobody has any right to adopt. The only criterion to be applied is the welfare of the child. If, on the evidence, the child's welfare is best served by adoption by the gay couple, then the adoption will be endorsed by the court.

But it is worth looking further at what happens in adoptions. The welfare determination required by the Act is a holistic one. It is analogous to the determination demanded by the law of best interests in the context of medical decision-making. The detailed stipulations in the statutory checklist under the 2002 Act are supposed to help the agency or the court to grope towards 'best interests'.

The Act requires an agency 'to give due consideration to the child's religious persuasion, racial origin and cultural and linguistic background.'[21] In deciding whether an adoption order is the best thing for the child, the court and an agency must have regard to 'the child's ascertainable wishes and feelings regarding the [adoption] decision (considered in the light of the child's understanding',[22] but the child's consent is not required.

In terms of rights and principles, what is going on here? There is a clear nod to autonomy in the requirement to take the child's wishes on board, but a plain acknowledgment (in the absence of any requirement for the child's consent), that many children will be insufficiently appraised or appraisable of the relevant issues for their autonomy to have the final word. In practice, the law of adoption works very like medical consent so far as the child's consent is concerned. If the prospective adoptee is *Gillick* competent, the court is likely to endorse the child's decision to approve the adoption, and in doing so is likely to rely heavily on the child's decision. This is analogous to a decision by a *Gillick* competent child to undergo recommended treatment: that decision makes the doctors entirely legally secure: such a child can validly consent to treatment. But it is not the same for a decision by a *Gillick* competent child not to consent to recommended treatment. Here the child's decision can be trumped. Similarly with adoption: If the child is *Gillick* competent and does not want to be adopted, but the court thinks that adoption is a good thing, the adoption will nonetheless go ahead, with a flurry of well-meaningly paternalistic comments in the judgment.

If the child's autonomy is so conveniently adopted if it says the 'right' thing, and so conveniently dismissed if it does not, what other principles are acting? The list of other factors gives a clue: religious persuasion, racial origin and cultural and linguistic background. One shouldn't philosophise too much here. Many considerations made under the label of these criteria are simple, practical ones. Is it generally going to be in the child's best interests to go with parents who speak a different language from the child's native language? All other things being equal, plainly not—for reasons too obvious to need spelling out. A black child with white

---

[21] S 1(5).
[22] S 1(4)(a).

parents will plainly not be the biological child of those parents. That could lead to embarrassing questions in the playground which, all other things being equal, are best avoided.[23] But it is not too fanciful to see at least the outline of other, more fundamental considerations here. Surely there is a concern not just to make the child happy and comfortable, but to make the child secure in a more metaphysical sense: to make it happy in its own actual and cultural skin. There is a sort of substituted judgment happening here, and it is a substituted judgment that rests on some possibly controversial premises. The court is saying: 'We will make for you the judgment that you would make were you in possession of all the material facts and had the perspective and wisdom that we have. Were you to make that decision you would decide that it is best to grow up with parents the same colour as you are, and in the same culture and religion that you were born into. These considerations would still pertain even if you were very, very young, and incapable of having absorbed any cultural or religious norms yourself. That is because, deep down, we are determinists, and recognise that we are prisoners of our genes. We are happiest and most liberated when we acknowledge our imprisonment.'

The court, of course, is trying to do good, to avoid harm, and to be just. One might say that we have here a clear example of those principles outdoing autonomy, and it is hard to argue that they should not. All sorts of legal monstrosities would be conjured up by any of the alternatives—most of them accurately described as some sort of sinister social engineering.

Applications by Prisoners

Mr Mellor, aged 29, was serving a life sentence for murder. While in prison he had met and married his wife. The tariff element of his sentence was due to expire when he would be 35 and his wife would be 31. The earliest he could expect to be granted temporary release was two years before this. He wanted to start a family. He said that if he had to wait until his release before trying for a family his wife might be too old. He applied to the prison for access to artificial insemination facilities. It could not be seriously said that the security considerations that justify the banning of conjugal visits applied here.[24] The prison refused. He sought judicial review, saying that the refusal infringed his rights under Articles 8 and 12 of the ECHR. His application failed. Part of the punishment of imprisonment is the surrender of rights. The right to found a family was one of them.[25] Lord Phillips MR said that:

---

[23] *An NHS Trust v A and B* [2003] 1 FLR 1091.

[24] Bans on conjugal visits have been held by the European Commission on Human Rights not to violate Art 8: see *X v UK* App 6564/74 2 D & R 105 (1975) and *X and Y v Switzerland* App 8166/78, 13 D & R 241 (1978).

[25] See *ELH and PBH v United Kingdom* (1997) 91 ADR 61.

It does not follow from this that it will always be justifiable to prevent a prisoner from inseminating his wife artificially, or indeed naturally. The interference with fundamental human rights which is permitted by Article 8(2) involves an exercise in proportionality. Exceptional circumstances may require the normal consequences of imprisonment to yield, because the effect of its interference with a particular human right is disproportionate.[26]

Thus, if (for example because of the prisoner's wife's age, and the length of his sentence) the refusal to allow artificial insemination might not merely delay but actually prevent the founding of a family, the position might be different. But no such circumstances pertained here.

It was also legitimate, said Lord Phillips, to consider the implications of children being brought up in a single-parent family.[27]

The autonomy interests of both the prisoner and his wife, represented by Articles 8 and 12, together (although it was not put like this, and could not in any conceivable state of the law be put like this), with any right of a putative child to exist, thus gave way to wider societal interests, as envisaged by Article 8(2). The absolute nature of Article 12 gave surprisingly little trouble to the court. It was side-stepped by the curious introduction of proportionality. One cannot reputably say that an absolute right is subject to any considerations of proportionality. Rightly or wrongly, here is autonomy beaten again by (at least perceived) beneficence, non-maleficence and justice.

Precisely the same point could be made by any case (and there are thousands) in which an engaged Article 8(1) right gives way to the broader demands of Article 8(2). Indeed one might say that almost all of the jurisprudence of the entire ECHR can be described in a similar way. Autonomy asserts a right. Wider considerations generally out-argue it.

The purpose of dealing with adoption and the prison case in such detail is to make the point that once we step outside medical law we do not expect autonomy to have the last word. Quite the opposite. And when it does not have the last word we do not get constitutionally worried. Civil liberties do not cease; the world does not end. This brief excursion to prison perhaps begins to suggest that if we abandon some of the uncritical reverence with which we listen to autonomy in the hospital, the world might not end for medical law either.

'Reproductive autonomy' is often spoken of as if it is a discipline all of its own, unaffected by principles from other areas, and even by autonomy considerations from other areas—notably the general law of consent.[28] This compartmentalisa-

---

[26] *R (Mellor) v Secretary of State for the Home Department* [2002] QB 13 [45].

[27] *Ibid* [67].

[28] See, eg, Clarke A (2001) 'Genetic Screening and Counselling' in Kuhse H and Singer P (eds) *A Companion to Bioethics* (Oxford, Blackwell) 215–28, 216: 'The importance of client autonomy in decisions about reproduction and about genetic testing is enshrined in the canons of modern bioethics, and is confirmed in numerous policy documents from Britain, Europe and North America. The importance of genetic counsellors adopting a "non-directive" stance is frequently emphasised and, even if non-directiveness is unattainable in practice, the ethos of genetic counselling is certainly non-prescriptive.' Clarke notes that 'This respect for client autonomy is challenged in two areas. In the

tion and deference are unjustified and inappropriate. The voices of the other principles are nowhere more insistent than in the law of abortion. It is there that we go next.

context of testing within families, there have been suggestions that genetic testing should be obligatory under certain circumstances if the results would be important for other family members. In the context of genetic screening programmes, there is a danger that individuals will be offered testing in a routinised manner by health professionals who clearly expect them to comply; the clients may participate without having adequately considered the possible consequences.'

5

Abortion

MEDICAL LAW IS at its most dismally incoherent when it comes to the status of the embryo and the foetus. A foetus can exist for the purposes of the law of succession (robustly defending, through its counsel, its right to inherit a field), while simultaneously, in a court just down the corridor in the same building, be unblushingly described by a judge as non-existent in the eyes of the law when its very life is at stake. The Strasbourg judges have shamefully refused to adjudicate on the status of the embryo, even when that issue was right at the heart of the issue they were being paid to decide.[1]

We need not review in any detail here the ethical arguments relating to the state of the foetus. They have been well summarised elsewhere, and we return later to deal with them in broad outline.[2] Generalisations are even more dangerous and unsatisfactory in this arena than they are elsewhere, but insofar as there is any consensus, perhaps there is general lip service given to the idea expressed by the Polkinghorne Committee, which contends for

> a special status for the living human foetus at every stage of its development which we wish to characterise as a profound respect based on its potential to develop into a fully formed human being.[3]

Some find it difficult to see how the 'respect' so sanctimoniously spoken of is compatible with the provisions permitting experimentation on the embryo up until the age of 14 days after conception, and indeed with the law of abortion itself.

The reason why it is unnecessary to deal in detail with the ethical arguments is because the law up until now has shown itself wholly unwilling to grapple with or

---

[1] *Vo v France*, below.

[2] One of the best summaries is in Herring J (2006) *Medical Law and Ethics* (Oxford, OUP) 247–57 and 330–2. See also: Brock D (2006) 'Is a Consensus Possible on Stem Cell Research? Moral and Political Obstacles' *Journal of Medical Ethics* 32–42; Deckers J (2007) 'Are Those Who Subscribe to the View That Early Embryos Are Persons Irrational and Inconsistent? A Reply to Brock' 33 *Journal of Medical Ethics* 102–6; Brock DW (2006) 'Is a Consensus Possible on Stem Cell Research? Moral and Political Obstacles' 32 *Journal of Medical Ethics* 36–42; Parker C (2007) 'Ethics for Embryos' 33 *Journal of Medical Ethics* 614–16: Gibson S (2007) 'Uses of Respect and Uses of the Human Embryo' 21: 7 *Bioethics* 370–8; Lizza JP (2007) 'Potentiality and Human Embryos' 21: 7 *Bioethics* 379–85; Steinbock B (1992) *Life Before Birth: The Moral and Legal Status of Embryos and Foetuses* (New York and Oxford, OUP); Cameron C and Williamson R (2005) 'In the World of Dolly, When Does a Human Embryo Acquire Respect?' 31 *Journal of Medical Ethics* 215–20; Stanton C and Harris J (2005) 'The Moral Status of the Embryo Post-Dolly' 31 *Journal of Medical Ethics* 221–5.

[3] Polkinghorne J (1989) *Review of the Guidance on the Research Use of Fetuses and Fetal Material* (London, HMSO).

incapable of grappling with anything approaching nuance in the realm of embryonic or foetal life. The nearest we come to biological or ethical sophistication is in
the ban on the storage of or experimentation on embryos after the emergence of
the primitive streak at 14 days.[4] In the present rudimentary state of the law there
is simply no point in troubling the judges with arguments based on the correlation
of emerging biological characteristics with personhood, or any of the other theses
so carefully synthesised in the philosophical laboratories of the world. They would
be met with pen-tapping irritation.

In *Re T (Adult: Refusal of Medical Treatment)*[5] Lord Donaldson MR, when holding that an adult patient suffering from no mental incapacity has an absolute right
to choose one rather than another of the treatments being offered, said that:

> The only possible qualification is a case where the choice may lead to the death of a viable
> foetus. That is not this case and, if and when it arises, the courts will be faced with a novel
> problem of considerable legal and ethical complexity.

There was, therefore, in the mind of one of England's most experienced and
respected judges, the thought (it was no more than that), that in a contest between
maternal autonomy and some foetal rights, it was at least conceivable that the
foetus might win.

Where a pregnant and apparently competent woman was refusing, for religious
reasons, to have the caesarean section which was the only way of saving her life and
that of her unborn child, Sir Stephen Brown P, referring to Lord Donaldson MR's
caveat in *Re T*, and to the US case of *Re C*,[6] granted a declaration allowing the section to go ahead without her consent. The reasoning is extremely brief, as was the
hearing, but nonetheless the decision seems to have been based at least in part on
the notion that foetal interests could outweigh those of the mother.

In *St George's NHS Trust v S*[7] (which concerned the wrongful deployment of the
Mental Health Act 1983 to force the treatment on an apparently competent pregnant woman that the clinicians thought was necessary to allow her child to be born
safely), Judge LJ noted that:

> Whatever else it may be, a 36 week foetus is not nothing; if viable, it is not lifeless, and it
> is certainly human.[8]

These words seem self-evidently true. But from now on, policy and sophistry com-
bine to confuse and frustrate what should be the self-evident corollaries.

In *A-G's Reference (No 3 of 1994)*[9] a pregnant woman had been stabbed. She
went prematurely into labour and gave birth to a child who survived for 121 days
before dying as a result of the stabbing. The Court of Appeal decided that the
foetus should be treated as an integral part of the mother—no different in

---

[4] See below for further discussion.
[5] [1993] Fam 95, 102.
[6] (1990) 573 A 2d 1235.
[7] [1998] 3 All ER 673.
[8] At 687.
[9] [1998] AC 245.

principle to her foot or her arm. The House of Lords disagreed. Lord Mustill said this:

> There was, of course, an intimate bond between the foetus and the mother, created by the total dependence of the foetus on the protective physical environment furnished by the mother, and on the supply by the mother through the physical linkage between them of the nutriments, oxygen and other substances essential to foetal life and development. The emotional bond between the mother and her unborn child was also of a very special kind. But the relationship was one of bond, not identity. The mother and the foetus were two distinct organisms living symbiotically, not a single organism with two aspects. The mother's leg was part of the mother; the foetus was not. . . . I would, therefore, reject the reasoning which assumes that since (in the eyes of English law), the foetus does not have all the attributes which make it a 'person' it must be an adjunct of the mother. Eschewing all religious and political debate, I would say that the foetus is neither. It is a unique organism. To apply to such an organism the principles of a law evolved in relation to autonomous beings is bound to mislead.[10]

He did not explain why such an application was 'bound to mislead'. An explanation would have been helpful.

Lord Hope agreed with Lord Mustill that a foetus was not merely a maternal body part:

> [The Human Fertilisation and Embryology Act 1990] serves to remind us that an embryo is in reality a separate organism from the mother from the moment of its conception. This individuality is retained by it throughout its development until it achieves an independent existence on being born. So the foetus cannot be regarded as an integral part of its mother in the sense indicated by the Court of Appeal, notwithstanding its dependence upon the mother for its survival until birth.[11]

So far so good. But now we go into a forensic Wonderland. For Lord Mustill's 'unique organism' is not only uniquely unprotected by the law but, despite having had its characteristics described in detail, does not exist. Lord Mustill went on to say:

> [I]t is established beyond doubt for the criminal law, as for the civil law (*Burton v Islington Health Authority* [1993] QB 204), that the child en ventre sa mère does not have a distinct human personality, whose extinguishment gives rise to any penalties or liabilities at common law.[12]

Accordingly the defendant 'committed no relevant violence to the foetus, which was not a person.'[13]

This was indeed of a piece with other decisions made in the context of compulsory treatment. In *Re F (in Utero)*,[14] Balcombe LJ had observed that there was no jurisdiction to make an unborn child a ward of court because it 'has, ex hypothesi,

---

[10] At 255–6.
[11] At 267.
[12] At 261.
[13] At 262.
[14] [1988] Fam 122, at 143.

no existence independent of its mother'. In *Paton v Trustees of the British Pregnancy Advisory Services*[15] Sir George Baker said that:

> There can be no doubt that in England and Wales the foetus has no right of action, no right at all, until birth.

And in *Re MB (An Adult: Medical Treatment)*[16] Butler Sloss LJ asserted that:

> The foetus up to the moment of birth does not have any separate interests capable of being taken into account when a court has to consider an application for a declaration in respect of a Caesarean section operation. The court does not have the jurisdiction to declare that such medical intervention is lawful to protect the interests of the unborn child even at the point of birth.

The English courts are in good colonial company in making these assertions. One typical example, relied upon by the Court of Appeal in the St George's NHS Trust case, is *Winnipeg Child and Family Services (Northwest Area) v G*,[17] a decision of the Supreme Court of Canada.

The mother there was addicted to glue sniffing, and five months pregnant. Two of her previous children had been born with permanent disability as a result of her glue sniffing. It was ordered that she should be detained for treatment, with the objective of protecting her unborn child from the effects of the glue-sniffing. This, said the Supreme Court, was unlawful. McLachlin J gave the judgment of the majority:

> To permit an unborn child to sue its pregnant mother-to-be would introduce a radically new conception into the law; the unborn child and its mother as separate juristic persons in a mutually separable and antagonistic relation. Such a legal conception, moreover, is belied by the reality of the physical situation; for practical purposes, the unborn child and its mother-to-be are bonded in a union separable only by birth . . . Judicial intervention . . . ignores the basic components of women's fundamental human rights—the right to bodily integrity, and the right to equality, privacy and dignity . . . The fetus' complete physical existence is dependent on the body of the woman. As a result, any intervention to further the fetus' interest will necessarily implicate, and possibly conflict with the mother's interests. Similarly, each choice made by the woman in relation to her body will affect the fetus and potentially attract tort liability.[18] . . . [T]he common law does not clothe the courts with power to order the detention of a pregnant woman for the purpose of preventing harm to her unborn child. Nor, given the magnitude of the changes and their potential ramifications, would it be appropriate for the courts to extend their power to make such an order.[19]

This reasoning is dismal. As noted already, in some areas of the law some judges regularly acknowledge the legal existence of unborn children, and the legal moon

[15] [1979] QB 276, at 279.
[16] [1997] 2 FCR 541, 561.
[17] (1997) 3 BHRC 611.
[18] See Royal Commission Report on New Reproductive Technologies *Proceed with Care* (1993) Vol 2, 957–8.
[19] (1997) 3 BHRC 611, 620, 622, 628.

has not turned to blood because they have. And as we shall see, the European Convention on Human Rights does not rule out the possibility of a foetus, at least at some stage of gestation, having Convention rights. If it has Convention rights, presumably it exists. But even if this is not so, is it really so frightening to 'introduce a radically new conception into the law'? In the past, common law judges thought that that was what they were paid for. The 'radically new conception' in this case would be an acknowledgment by the law of what every child studying biology will tell you—that a mother and her unborn child are importantly distinct. The assertion that 'for practical purposes, the unborn child and its mother-to-be are bonded in a union separable only by birth', is advanced, without further or any reasoning, as the core of the decision. It is not explained why the person who is the chronologically senior partner in the relationship should have the casting vote in every single decision, even if the vote is to kill the junior partner to avoid some discomfort or inconvenience on the part of the senior.[20]

But it gets worse. Why should worries about fixing the mother with tortious liability in relation to her unborn child deter the court from recognising that the foetus has a right that should be protected by the law? Would there be anything wrong in principle in fixing a mother with liability for negligent or deliberate harm to her unborn child? Anyone else can be sued by the child, after it is born, for causing it harm.[21] Why should the person with the greatest ability to harm the child enjoy, uniquely, an absolute immunity from suit in relation to any harm?[22]

The answer, of course, is that we are here in one of the little pockets of law, adjacent to the territory of consent, where autonomy enjoys supreme, and supremely irrational, rule. If the mother wants to exercise her autonomous right to sniff glue, the foetus's right to life or bodily integrity has to give way.

Many hoped that the European Convention on Human Rights would iron out many of the absurdities in the law relating to the foetus; that it would act like a sort of forensic mortar, bridging the gaps between the disparate areas of relevant law, and welding it into a coherent whole. So far, though, the Convention has disappointed.

There is considerable confusion about whether Article 2 (and, by extension, Articles 3 and 8) can protect the foetus. The possibility that Article 2 might apply to the foetus was not ruled out by the Commission in *H v Norway*,[23] but the facts of that case give few grounds for foetal comfort. A 14 week foetus was aborted on the grounds, legal in Norway, that 'pregnancy, birth or care for the child may place

[20] See: Steinbock S (1998) 'Mother-Fetus Conflict' in Kuhse H and Singer P (eds) *A Companion to Bioethics* (Oxford, Blackwell) 135–46; Murray T (1987) 'Moral Obligations to the Not-Yet-Born: The Fetus as Patient' 14 *Clinics in Perinatology* 329–43; Murray T (1991) 'Pre-Natal Drug Exposure: Ethical Issues' *Future of Children* 105–12; American College of Gynaecologists and Obstetricians Committee Opinion No 55 (1987) *Patient Choice: Maternal-Fetal Conflict*; Bewley S (2002) 'Restricting The Freedom of Pregnant Women' in Dickenson D (ed) *Ethical Issues in Maternal-Fetal Medicine* (Cambridge, CUP) 131–46.
[21] See the Congenital Disabilities (Civil Liability) Act 1976.
[22] For detailed discussion of the issues, see Scott R (2000) 'Maternal duties toward the unborn? Soundings from the law of tort' 8 *Medical Law Review* 1–68.
[23] (1992) 73 DR 155.

the woman in a difficult situation of life'—a provision analogous to section 1(1)(a) of the English Act of 1967. Those provisions were held to be Article 2 compliant. In other words, any application of Article 2 to the foetus (it not being admitted that there is any such application) must be restricted by consideration of the mother's competing claims. The Commission relied expressly on this feto-maternal competition in its decision in *Paton v United Kingdom*.[24] It said that to assert an absolute right to foetal life under Article 2 might endanger the mother's life: it might have the effect of preferring the life of the unborn child to that of the mother. That, the Commission said, could not be right, and accordingly if the foetus had any Article 2 right, it must be qualified by reference to maternal interests.

As an abstract proposition this seems logical enough. If one has to choose between two lives, it is reasonable to opt for the mother's. It seems correct that the absolute nature of Article 2 should not have the ironic effect of depriving the mother of the protection which Article 2 is designed to give. But if one acknowledges that the notion of a competition between the interests of the mother and the interests of the foetus is a valid analytical tool, one must be prepared to weigh those competing interests. If in one pan of the scales one has the life of the foetus, and in the other one has, not the death or serious injury of the mother but her social convenience, where should the balance lie? Can Article 2 really be said to be honoured at all if convenience wins over life?

In reality, most battles between the foetus and the mother are best described as battles between the foetus's Article 2 and Article 3 rights and the mother's Article 8 rights. In other areas of human life that contest should be and is an entirely one-sided one: Article 2 and Article 3 should win every time. But the legal referees seem to have a blind spot when it comes to this particular dispute.

The easy way off the horns of this dilemma is simply to say that Article 2 should not apply to foetal life at all. But that itself would be an odd result. It would entail saying (for example) that a 40 week foetus which had simply not been expelled from the uterus, but would be perfectly capable of medically unsupported life if it were expelled, should have no right to life (or, presumably, other basic rights), whereas a foetus which, by medical accident or design had been born prematurely and required intensive maintenance should have (as it uncontroversially does) all the basic rights. That elevates the arbitrary moment of birth to a significance which science suggests that it should not have.

It was widely hoped that the judgment of the European Court of Human Rights in *Vo v France* would indicate, once and for all, the extent of the protection given by the Convention to the foetus. But those hopes were dashed.[25] It was billed as the cornerstone judgment on the application of Article 2 of the ECHR to the human embryo and foetus. And indeed it is an important judgment. It is the ultimate masterpiece of Strasbourgeois equivocation: the clearest possible indication that Strasbourg will refuse to grasp the nettle in difficult cases: an illustration of the

[24] (1981) 3 EHRR 408.
[25] [2004] 2 FCR 526.

fact that, in the jurisprudence of the Strasbourg court, philosophically tricky problems can just be flushed down the forensic toilet which lawyers call the 'margin of appreciation'.

The facts were simple and tragic. In 1991 two women, both called Mrs Vo, went at the same time to the Lyons General Hospital. The Mrs Vo who was to become the applicant in these proceedings was six months pregnant. She wanted the baby very much. The other Mrs Vo was due to have a coil removed. There was a mix up. The applicant was called in to have her non-existent coil removed. The doctor did not examine her before trying to remove it. He pierced the amniotic sac. This meant that the pregnancy could not continue, and a termination was duly carried out.

The applicant was distraught. She pursued the doctor through the French courts. She had some successes, but finally the Court of Cassation concluded that the doctor was not guilty of unintentional homicide. The applicant went to Strasbourg, saying that if the offence of unintentional homicide did not apply to the death of an unborn child, the State had failed to discharge its obligations under Article 2.

The Government said, first, that Article 2 did not apply to the unborn child, and, second, that there was an adequate domestic remedy apart from a criminal sanction—namely an action for damages. The first of those submissions is the interesting and fundamental one.

The relevant part of Article 2 of course provides that 'Everyone's right to life shall be protected by law.' The central point was: Does 'everyone' ('toute personne' in French) include an unborn child? The existing case-law of the Strasbourg court made it possible for both sides to claim the jurisprudential high ground. In *X v UK*,[26] *H v Norway*[27] and *Boso v Italy*,[28,29] the court, considering abortion, admitted the possibility that the foetus might have an Article 2 right, but would not say that it did. In *Vo* the court rather overstated the effect of the previous cases by saying:

> in the circumstances examined to date by the Convention institutions—that is, in the various laws on abortion—the unborn child is not regarded as a 'person' directly protected by Article 2 . . . and that if the unborn do have a 'right' to 'life' it is implicitly limited by the mother's rights and interests. The Convention institutions have not, however, ruled out the possibility that in certain circumstances safeguards may be extended to the unborn child.[30]

The applicant said that, as a matter of scientific fact, life began at conception. An unborn child at any stage of gestation could not be regarded as either a cluster of cells or an object. It was quintessentially human (all the more so if it would have

[26] (1980) DR 19.
[27] (1992) DR 73.
[28] (2002) No 50490/99.
[29] See too *Bruggemann and Scheuten v Germany* (1981) 3 EHRR 244, in which the Commission noted that the issue of abortion is not simply a matter of the private life and rights of the mother—although without deciding that an unborn child has rights under the ECHR.
[30] Para 80

been capable of life outside the uterus). It had, in the past, been regarded as legally convenient for some purposes to invest humans with legal personality as soon as they were expelled from the uterus, but that view was an unbiological archaism. The only modern way of interpreting 'toute personne' in Article 2 was to regard it as meaning human beings rather than individuals who possessed the artificial attribute of legal personality. Pressing the argument perhaps rather counter-productively far, she asserted that this interpretation of Article 2 should outlaw all forms of abortion, with the exception of therapeutic abortion. This may have been a serious tactical blunder. The strength of this case, from the applicant's point of view, was that this was an involuntary abortion: none of the delicate business of balancing the mother's wishes against the foetus's interests arose here.

The Government seized eagerly on this assertion. The Government agreed with the applicant's logic: if Article 2 applied to the foetus, of course it followed that abortion was contrary to Article 2. But abortion had been expressly endorsed by the court. One could therefore infer from all the abortion decisions that Article 2 could not have the effect contended for by the applicant. Neither metaphysics nor medicine had given a definitive answer to the question of when human life began: how then could the court, which had to reflect the different philosophical traditions of the various Convention signatories, do any better? It went on to say that if the Convention had intended to apply to the foetus, it would have said so. The other rights protected by the Convention, anyway, applied to post-natal people. It would be strange if one could be a person for the purposes of Article 2, but not for the other Articles. Consistency therefore demanded that the foetus did not fall within the ambit of Article 2.

This was a judgment of the Grand Chamber. There were 17 judges. 14 of them held that there had been no violation of Article 2, and there were three blistering dissents.

The court reviewed in detail the various international declarations there have been which deal with the rights of the unborn child. There are many of these, including the Orviedo Convention on Human Rights and Biomedicine, (with its additional protocols on biomedical research and on the prohibition of cloning), the report of the Working Party on the Protection of the Human Embryo and Fetus, and the opinion of the EC European Group on Ethics in Science and New Technologies. None of these deals squarely with the issue of the time from which human embryos ought to be treated as legally equivalent to post-natal humans. Their failure appeared to the court to be a ground for not grappling with the issue in the case of *Vo*. One might have thought that the lead of the court was needed precisely because no definitive lead could be found elsewhere. If a question comes to court for determination precisely because the question is difficult, it is curious for the court to refuse to answer it on the grounds that it is too difficult. The court observed that:

> at European level . . . there is no consensus on the nature and status of the embryo and/or fetus . . . although they are beginning to receive some protection in the light of scientific progress and the potential consequences of research into genetic engineering, medically

assisted reproduction or embryo experimentation. At best, it may be regarded as common ground between States that the embryo/fetus belongs to the human race. The potentiality of that being and its capacity to become a person—enjoying protection under the civil law . . . require protection in the name of human dignity, without making it a 'person' with the 'right to life' for the purposes of Article 2 . . . Having regard to the foregoing, the Court is convinced that it is neither desirable, nor even possible as matters stand, to answer in the abstract the question whether the unborn child is a person for the purposes of Article 2.[31]

How should that undesirability or impossibility be framed in the legal language of Strasbourg? By using the ultimate refuge of the indecisive—the 'margin of appreciation.'

[T]he issue of when the right to life begins comes within the margin of appreciation which the Court generally considers that States should enjoy in this sphere, notwithstanding an evolutive interpretation of the Convention. . . . The reasons for that conclusion are, firstly, that the issue of such protection has not been resolved within the majority of the Contracting States themselves . . . and, secondly, that there is no European consensus on the scientific and legal definition of the beginning of life.[32]

It went on to say that even assuming Article 2 was applicable, on the facts, France had not failed to comply with the obligations that Article 2 would impose.

There are grave difficulties with this judgment. The main one is the refusal of the court to answer the question that it was being asked. Two of the judges were disgusted by that abdication of responsibility. They pointed out that judges are there to judge:

Does the present inability of ethics to reach a consensus on what is a person and who is entitled to the right to life prevent the law from defining these terms? I think not. It is the task of lawyers, and in particular judges, especially human-rights judges, to identify those notions . . . that correspond to the words or expressions in the relevant legal instruments . . . Why should the Court not deal with the terms 'everyone' and 'the right to life' (which the European Convention does not define) in the same way it has done from its inception with the terms 'civil rights and obligations', 'criminal charges' and 'tribunals', even if we are here concerned with philosophical, not technical, concepts.[33]

The second, and perhaps most worrying, difficulty is the way in which, having decided to dodge the issue, the court dodged it. It invoked the idea of the margin of appreciation. That idea has a legitimate place in the construction of several Articles, but how can it relate at all to the most fundamental and absolute Article of all, Article 2? With Article 2, to dilute is to abolish. Judge Ress agreed:

There can be no margin of appreciation on the issue of the applicability of Article 2. A margin of appreciation may, in my opinion, exist to determine the measures that should be taken to discharge the positive obligation that arises because Article 2 is applicable, but it is not possible to restrict the applicability of Article 2 by reference to a margin of

---

[31] Paras 84–5
[32] Para 82
[33] Separate opinion of Judge Costa, joined by Judge Traja, para 7

appreciation. The question of the interpretation or applicability of Article 2 (an absolute right) cannot depend on a margin of appreciation. If Article 2 is applicable, any margin of appreciation will be confined to the effect thereof.[34]

It is tempting to say that, having read *Vo*, we are none the wiser. But we are. It tells us two things. First, we know that the Convention cannot be relied upon in areas of biomedical controversy. That makes it all the more important to get our domestic legislation right.[35] And second, it is yet another black mark in autonomy's record. The architects of the Convention were thoroughgoing autonomists. Despite its many caveats (exemplified well by that in Article 8(2), at which we have already looked) its basic picture of the world is of nuclear individuals, each with a hard coating which prevents them from real contact with others. Each individual is a discrete bundle of rights, enforceable against anyone else in the world.[36] *Vo* was a testing *viva* for the Convention and for the whole philosophy of autonomy. Autonomy had the wit to know that it could not answer the questions being put to it, and so it simply didn't try. That is perhaps slightly better than trying and getting a wrong answer, but the result is the same: it means outright failure.

It is easier to knock down than to build up. If autonomy cannot do alone the job of coherent law-making in the realm of foetal life, what help does it need? As before, beneficence, non-maleficence and justice have something to say. The answers they give are familiar, and shared by many whose company all right-thinking people will eschew.[37] But one cannot necessarily judge an idea by the company it keeps.

The agreed invocation of beneficence and maleficence presupposes some agreement about what amounts to 'harm'. The traditional autonomist pro-abortionist would say that there is only one type of harm worth considering: harm to the woman's right to self-determination.[38] If the foetus has any moral or legal weight at all, and if one ever begins the exercise of weighing it against the woman's right to self-determination, the woman's right is so disproportionately heavy that it massively outweighs the foetus. The moral or legal weight of the foetus may increase as its biological age and size increase, but still there is never any real com-

---

[34] Dissenting opinion of Judge Ress, para 8

[35] A postscript: the court itself noted that the Orviedo Convention on Human Rights and Biomedicine and its various protocols do not attempt a definition of the terms 'everyone' or 'human being'. The Strasbourg court can be asked, however, under Art 29 of the Oviedo Convention, to give advisory opinions on the interpretation of that Convention. That might well be the way in which Strasbourg will have to be forced to do its job in relation to construction of these crucial terms.

[36] This picture is viewed and discussed again in ch 9.

[37] I am thinking, of course, of the shrill, violent and violently anti-intellectual religious fundamentalists, particularly of the US.

[38] Thus, eg, in a passionate conflation of several ideas on a feminist website: 'It isn't really a question of whether a woman can have an abortion. It's a question of whether women are people: we claim the personal and sexual autonomy that men take for granted.' <http://the-goddess.org/wam/blog.html> accessed 8 September 2008. The reasoning appears to be: (a) a person is defined by their ability to self-determine (or at least that self-determination is a necessary condition of being a human being); (b) accordingly, denial of the right to self-determination represented by the freedom to have an abortion denies a woman her humanity; (c) this denial is harm so obvious and immense that no competing interests make denial legitimate.

petition.[39] Two main philosophical routes are used to arrive at this position. The first is to contend that a foetus has no 'personhood', and accordingly is not a member of the moral community. If you adopt this view, then you have no real intellectual problem. You can go blithely on to assert that any rights the foetus may have therefore cannot trump those of the woman, who is a fully paid-up member of that community.[40,41]

The autonomists who so confidently assert that there is no 'personhood' are resting something of colossal moral importance on an idea (personhood) that is manufactured in a philosopher's study—not demonstrated on the ward or the laboratory. The idea really isn't robust enough to bear the weight. What too often pass for arguments from the premise of absent personhood are generally not arguments at all: they are mere unevidenced assertions.

If you are happy with this, though, there is no denying that the 'personhood' argument is philosophically neat. But philosophical neatness comes at a price. It comes at the price of ignoring biological facts and human intuition. I will say little about intuition. It is too amorphous, too variable and too hard to quantify to be dialectically useful, but one cannot ignore completely the conviction of many pregnant women that their unborn child has joined the human community. Some choose to die for their unborn child (no doubt driven by Darwin rather than coherent metaphysics). When they do so they are convinced that they are dying for 'another'. The conviction deserves at least a footnote in the debate.

On one view, the biological facts (given their uncertain relationship to the elusive notion of personhood) might be thought to help neither side. But surely the fact that at some stage a foetus could survive outside its mother begins to argue powerfully against those who would sanction abortion on 'non-personhood' grounds all the way to term. The arguments are familiar, but none the less potent for that. A 23 week old foetus stands a reasonable chance of survival in a modern unit. Does it not have 'personhood' at 23 weeks? If it does not, it should not be murder to stab to death a 23 week gestation baby in the Special Care Baby Unit. If it does, why is it not wrong to kill it when it is dependent on its mother's internal

---

[39] Of course this is something of a parody. There are nuances within the pro-abortionist view. Good surveys of the issues are in McMahan J (2002) *The Ethics of Killing: Problems at the Margins of Life* (Oxford, OUP) 267–421 and Harris J and Holm S (2003) 'Abortion' in La Follette H (ed) *The Oxford Handbook of Practical Ethics* (Oxford, OUP) 112–35.

[40] See, eg, Warren MA (2002) 'On the moral and legal status of abortion' in La Follette (ed) *Ethics in Practice* (Malden and Oxford, Blackwell): 'A foetus, especially in the early stages of its development, satisfies none of the criteria of personhood. Consequently, it makes no sense to grant it moral rights strong enough to override the woman's moral rights to liberty, bodily integrity, and sometimes life itself... Nor... is a foetus's *potential* personhood a threat to the moral permissibility of abortion, since merely potential persons do not have a moral right to become actual—or none that is strong enough to override the fundamental moral rights of actual persons.' (p 73). (Original emphasis)

[41] I have outlined in the Preface my reasons for declining to deal in any detail with feminist writing on abortion. The literature is immense. Perhaps the high-water mark of the feminist-as-autonomist school is Saharro S (2003) 'Feminist Ethics, Autonomy and The Politics of Multi-Culturalism' 4(2) *Feminist Theory* 199–215, which concludes that the imperative of protecting female autonomy is so overwhelming that it legitimates even the selective abortion of female foetuses—a practice generally antithetical to feminism.

life-support system rather than the artificial one in the hospital? Is it the fact of dependence that disqualifies it from 'personhood'? If so, the elderly and incapacitated need to be beware. Why should the fact of a person's location determine so crucially whether it has all the protection of the law against being killed, or no protection at all? Is it really sensible to say that some sort of powerful legal magic occurs when a baby is pushed through its mother's vagina, whereby a person existed that was not there seconds before or inches higher? Isn't that superstitious mediaevalism of a far greater order than that that of which secular pro-abortionists accuse their religious opponents? And so on.

The other route is used by those who concede that the foetus does have moral rights, but nonetheless contend that abortion is permissible. If this is your view, there are two real justifications open to you. You could rest on the notion of self-defence, asserting that the foetus is like an armed and dangerous invader to your home, and, and it is therefore morally and legally legitimate to use fatal violence against it. Or you could say that no real injustice arises, because it is no worse for the foetus to cease to exist through abortion, than it is not to have existed at all. And since the person morally responsible for the cessation is the person morally responsible for the creation (the mother), it is ethically quits.

Jeff McMahan imagines the mother justifying herself to the foetus like this:

> I know my voluntary act created the condition of forced choice. But if I had not done that act, you would never have existed at all. So how can that act be cited as a reason why I should be harmed rather than you?[42]

He then imagines the foetus responding:

> Your killing me would inflict a terrible harm on me. I recognise, of course, that if you do not kill me, my presence will cause you to suffer a terrible harm. But that predicament is entirely the result of your voluntary action. That I would never have existed if you had not done that act is irrelevant. You certainly did not do the act with any intention of benefiting me. The fact is that I do exist and have an interest in continuing to exist that is at least as strong as yours. You have no right to kill me to save yourself from the consequences of your own action.[43]

McMahan comments: 'I am uncertain which of the two has the better argument.'[44] I do not share his uncertainty, and do not think that many others would either.

Suppose that a mother and her 21 year old son are taken captive. The kidnappers say to the mother. 'We are going to kill your son or graze your knee. You decide which.' By the logic of the argument articulated by the mother through McMahan, the mother would be entitled to say that the son should be killed in order to spare her the graze. There is no reason to distinguish between a foetus *in utero* and a child *ex utero*. Yet all would think the decision of the kidnapped mother obscene. To talk about the trauma of having an unwanted child as analogous to a

---

[42] See n 34 above, 420.
[43] See n 34 above, 421. Such a response would not be possible from a foetus conceived as a result of rape.
[44] See n 34 above, 421.

grazed knee is of course absurd and insulting. But it highlights the point that what should really be in issue here is the relative magnitude of the harms done by performing an abortion and by not performing an abortion. The obscenity of the mother's reaction is a good indication, too, of the moral limits, recognised by most decent people, of autonomy's rule. Autonomy smiles on her decision.[45] Everyone else is nauseated. Autonomy needs other principles to moderate its excesses.

What, then, of the relevant harms? If the mother has a child that she does not want, that is certainly distressing and life-disrupting—although she may well come subsequently to be glad that she had the child. In some circumstances it could be said that her rights under Article 8 of the ECHR have been violated. Certainly her harm can be expressed in terms of truncated autonomy. Others too (for example a reluctant father) may be upset and financially compromised. If the mother has an abortion, any right to life the foetus may have (whether describable as an Article 2 right or otherwise), has been violated. It has been denied autonomy in the most final and emphatic way possible.

Perhaps others, too, are affected—for instance the biological father, or the grandparents. Without embarking on the technically tricky and controversial business of arguing the point, there is mounting evidence that abortion may hurt the woman too. Rates of prematurity in subsequent pregnancies seem to be significantly raised, and many contend powerfully that there is evidence of a significantly enhanced risk of significant psychiatric sequelae—enhanced, that is, above the risk of such sequelae were the pregnancy taken to term. If one takes the rights of the foetus and other third parties out of the equation for a moment, then most would agree that a woman should be allowed to shoulder such risks if she is properly counselled about them. But anecdotal evidence in the UK suggests strongly that abortion exists on an anomalous island in the sea of medical consent. Abortions routinely take place without any of the systematic safeguards against inadequate consent-taking appropriate to a procedure of abortion's magnitude. The Abortion Act 1967 contains a requirement to obtain the signatures of two registered medical practitioners.[46] The main reason for this was to protect not the woman or the foetus, but the doctors: it was designed to protect them against being prosecuted under the Offences Against the Person Act 1861. But it also had perceived (and, for a time, real) collateral benefits: Parliament was solemnly assured that it would ensure that the criteria of the Act were properly met and that the woman had been given the minimally acceptable information necessary to a proper balancing of risks and benefits. As is generally accepted, the requirement is now a joke. Forms are sometimes signed without the relevant practitioners even seeing the woman, let alone giving her balanced advice.[47] Abortions, then, are

---

[45] Although perhaps a little ruefully, realising that the son's autonomy is about to be extinguished for good.

[46] S 1(1).

[47] See, eg, the evidence of Dr Vincent Argent, former medical director of British Pregnancy Advisory Service (one of the UK's biggest abortion providers), to the UK Government's Science and Technology Committee in the course of its enquiry into abortion: October 2007.

often performed in circumstances which, if they pertained to any other surgical procedure, would land the practitioner concerned in front of the GMC, or facing a High Court claim in negligence or assault for performing surgery without adequate consent. This is just the sort of thing that autonomy hates, as we shall see when we come to deal more generally with the law of medical consent. It is curious and anomalous that autonomy gives such unconditionally ringing endorsement to abortion.

How do the relative harms look now, through the eyes of those principles? Surely autonomy, on consideration, having conducted a more diligent audit of the damage on each side, should come down against abortion in many more circumstances than it generally does. Beneficence and non-maleficence, similarly, will tend to let nature take its course. And as for justice? Well, justice has always been uneasy about abortion. It instinctively dislikes bullying, tries to stand for the weak against the strong, and prefers Article 2 to Article 8. It also dislikes being elbowed out of court by notions that say it should have no jurisdiction over something; and that of course is precisely the effect of the statement that a foetus is for some reason (no personhood or otherwise) beyond the protection of the court. And, finally, it dislikes inconsistency, and is embarrassed by many things in the English law. It is embarrassed, for instance, that a baby that survives 48 hours after being born can sue for damage that occurs through an innocently negligent, well-meaning intervention any time during its gestational life,[48] but has no way at all to protest against being killed. It is similarly embarrassed that although a foetus can be killed at any time up to term in some circumstances,[49] if one steps outside the law of abortion a human life is so conclusively presumed to be a good thing that: (a) a very disabled child cannot go to court and claim damages because its existence is more miserable than its non-existence;[50] and (b) the parents of an unwanted child cannot claim damages to represent the cost of its upkeep, since its existence is conclusively presumed to be a blessing that outweighs the detriment of the associated financial liabilities.[51]

[48] Congenital Disabilities (Civil Liability) Act 1976: for discussion, see above.
[49] Abortion Act 1967 s 1(1)(b), (c), (d).
[50] *McKay v Essex Area Health Authority* [1982] QB 1166.
[51] *McFarlane v Tayside Health Board* [2000] AC 59; *Rees v Darlington Memorial Hospital NHS Trust* [2004] 1 AC 309. The costs associated with bringing up a disabled child which are over and above those associated with bringing up a non-disabled child are recoverable: see *Parkinson v St James's and Seacroft University Hospital NHS Trust* [2001] 3 WLR 376, but this does not disturb the principle that a child—and even a disabled child—is legally and unarguably a blessing.

6

Questions Raised by Reproductive Technology

MOST ETHICAL DILEMMAS at the very start and the very end of life are creatures of medical technology and other advance. The law in relation to reproductive technology tends to be a couple of steps behind the technology it purports to regulate. That may or may not be a good thing.

The primary legislation governing the artificial management of human reproduction is the Human Fertilisation and Embryology Act 1990.[1] We need not bother with its details. The Act delegates a lot of decision-making to the Human Fertilisation and Embryology Authority (HFEA). Some say that there is too much delegation, and that the HFEA is making decisions which go so fundamentally to what we perceive human beings and society to be that they should be the province of Parliament alone.

Some of the litigation under the Act has concerned questions which sound philosophically interesting—like what an 'embryo' is. But it has all turned on narrow questions of statutory construction, and is of no interest to any but the most black-letter of black-letter lawyers.

The general thrust of the 1990 Act was to facilitate the use of new technology. Since 1990 scientific advance has run fast. It has run ahead of anything that the draftsmen of the 1990 Act could have envisaged. The Act has therefore creaked at the seams, and the judges have had to be more than usually purposive in their interpretation.

Broadly, the 1990 Act is liberal so far as very early, pre-implantation embryos are concerned. There are, of course, many such 'spare' embryos created as the by-products of IVF procedures. Embryos at this stage are not regarded by the law as quintessentially human. They can, for instance, be used for experimentation in a way that even the most legally incompetent person could not be. But they are not, legally, mere blobs of protoplasm. The philosophy of the law is to treat them with respect. Indeed there is a whole Act of Parliament and a very expensive quango devoted to regulating the way that they are dealt with.

At this stage they are composed of multi-potent stem cells—cells which have the potential to become any type of cell. Later in development, differentiation occurs:

---

[1] The ethical issues are well summarised in Shenfield F (2002) 'Ethical Issues in Embryo Interventions and Cloning' in Dickenson D (ed) *Ethical Issues in Maternal-Fetal Medicine* (Cambridge, CUP) 149–60.

stem cells transmute into specialised cells. At this stage the die begins to be cast at the cellular level. Potential becomes realised. And it is broadly at this stage that the 1990 Act starts to be much more jealously protective of embryos.[2]

The proponents of the Act say that this is philosophically coherent: that it has the effect of protecting human beings even in the very early stages of their march towards the individuality which the law is so keen to guard. The Act's opponents say that there is obviously individuality well before the stage of differentiation. It is inherent in the genes that each cell possesses. The fact that it is not yet expressed in differentiated cells is neither here nor there: if one purports to protect human potential, one has to protect even a zygote.

It is unnecessary for present purposes to argue about what the law has decided about the status of the very early embryo. The outline given above will do. But one blatant discordance has to be pointed out: if the Act really does honour human potential, lots of its sister legislation does not. One can hardly claim philosophical consistency for the law if 10-cell embryos are safe in the hands of the 1990 Act but normal 23 week foetuses can be aborted under the Abortion Act 1967.

Clinics providing assisted reproduction services necessarily have to make decisions about whether someone should be entitled to reproduce. We have come across this issue before—notably in the context of a serving prisoner's entitlement to have his wife artificially inseminated with his semen. But other cases point up rather better the actuating principles. What if the only possible result of a pregnancy is a child who will be so compromised as to lead an utterly miserable life, unmitigated by any pleasure or satisfaction? Should the autonomous parental impulse be allowed to prevail? And if so, over what, exactly, would it be prevailing?

What rights and whose rights are considered by the clinic and the courts when determining what should be done? The first thing to note is that, due to the erratic provision of assisted reproduction under the NHS, many will have to pay for private treatment. The National Institute for Clinical Excellence (NICE) has noted that this is unsatisfactory, and suggested some criteria that should be employed by the NHS in order to decide whether or not free NHS treatment should be given. The Department of Health has decided that it cannot pay for the treatment recommended by NICE. The legal interest of this is primarily that it shows the relative weakness of any parental rights. However strong they are, they are not strong enough to force the state to reach into its pocket—presumably because they are beaten by the competing Article 2 and Article 8 rights of other patients who would be denied treatment if public funding went on fertility treatment. The putative parents' rights are certainly considered by the clinics, although judges rarely get to analyse them. They are no doubt rights under Article 12 of the ECHR—those curiously non-absolute absolute rights—and under Article 8 (whose caveats,

---

[2] Thus the 1990 Act provides that an embryo cannot be stored for more than 14 days after the mixing of the gametes: see s 4(3). By this time the primitive streak will have appeared. The HFEA has no power to authorise the storage of or any intervention in relation to an embryo after this 14-day watershed.

under Article 8(2), seem so eager to migrate and attach themselves without obvious legislative warrant to other Articles).

And then there are the rights of the putative child. Section 13(5) of the Human Fertilisation and Embryology Act 1990 provides:

> A woman shall not be provided with treatment services unless account has been taken of the welfare of any child who may be born as a result of the treatment (including the need of that child for a father), and of any other child who may be affected by the birth.

We are again in the strange, legally amorphous world of the family lawyers here, and it is a bad mistake in that jurisdiction to be too legally rigorous. But surely this language of welfare is a coded language of rights. The child under consideration has a right not to be treated badly. But here is the conundrum: who is the child under consideration? It does not exist, and may never exist. Indeed the whole point of section 13(5) is to invite consideration as to whether it should exist or not. We have noted already that in other areas of the law public policy forbids a child from saying 'It were better that my mother had not borne me'[3] and a parent from unwishing a child.[4] But here, section 13(5) has no similar embarrassment in saying: 'If the child's life is going to be unsatisfactory, as judged by our not very transparent criteria, it is better that the child should not be born. Not only so, but this conclusion is so obviously correct that it outweighs the passionate desire of the parents to bring that child into the world.'

We have yet another barn door inconsistency and, more pertinently to our debate, we have yet another example of parental autonomy being trounced. Yet nobody, surely, could dissent from a word of section 13(5)? The rhetorical point is, again: if autonomy is wholly dethroned on the edges of the medical law, will it really be so awful if it has to share power in other areas?

What happens if we add other interests into the equation? How does autonomy react then?

Zain Hashmi suffered from beta thalassaemia. His best chance of survival, and his only real chance of remotely normal life, was to obtain stem cells from the umbilical cord of a suitably tissue-matched sibling. The chances of creating such a sibling by natural conception were low, but technology could help. It was proposed that embryos should be created in vitro, a sample taken from each embryo at about the eight-cell stage to check compatibility with Zain, and a matched embryo implanted into the mother. The mother would then take the pregnancy to term and, when the child was born, its cells would be used in the attempt to help Zain. There was no reason at all to suppose that the child born in this way would not be loved, valued and cared for, although the primary purpose of its birth was to help its brother. Indeed it would be natural to think that the sibling would probably be loved particularly intensely, having saved its brother. The HFEA endorsed

---

[3] *McKay v Essex Area Health Authority* [1982] QB 1166.
[4] *McFarlane v Tayside Health Board* [2000] AC 59.

this procedure. Its endorsement was judicially reviewed by the pro-life campaigner Josephine Quintavalle. The details of the case do not matter: it turned on some nuances of statutory construction which are irrelevant to this book.[5] It might even be said that it establishes no principles at all. But that would be to invest the judges with a superhuman and entirely undesirable ability to forget the context of the case.

The conclusion was that the IVF, the pre-implantation testing and the implantation of the embryos could go ahead. The conclusion was reached by a bit of fancy judicial footwork, and reached not because the argument on statutory construction was compelling—it most certainly was not—but because the judges thought that the conclusion was, in broad ethical terms, the right thing to do. The judges saw the case the way the parents and the readers of the newspapers saw it—as a straightforward competition between an otherwise doomed three-year-old on the one hand, and some eight-cell embryos and some academic principles on the other. It was a case that divided the pro-life community bitterly. Many were not prepared to sacrifice a three-year-old on the altar of their convictions about the status of the very early embryo and the evil of creating life for the purpose of serving another.[6]

What, in terms of our principles, was happening in the Hashmi case?[7]

It *can* be expounded purely in terms of autonomy. Zain's autonomy rights were dependent on his continued existence, and that meant that the procedure should go ahead. The 'spare' embryos, all of which had been invaded by the biopsy, could scarcely complain, or at least not complain loudly. If they had any autonomy rights at all, those rights were of a much more rudimentary kind and of far smaller magnitude than Zain's.[8] The selected embryo was enormously advantaged by the invasion. If it had not been invaded it would never have been selected; if it had not been selected it would never have been born, and if it had not been born it would never have had any fully fledged autonomy rights at all. The parents, who surely have some say in the decision-making, were keen for the procedure to go ahead. If it did not they were likely to be deprived of Zain (thereby interfering with their Article 8 rights), and likely to be deprived of a another child (since they said they would not have another child naturally)—so arguably interfering with their Article 12 rights.

---

[5] See *R (Quintavalle) v Human Fertilisation and Embryology Authority (Secretary of State for Health intervening)* ('the Hashmi case') [2005] 2 AC 561. The case is discussed in detail in Foster C (2007) *Elements of Medical Law* (London, Claerhout Law Publishers) 7–8.

[6] Ronald Dworkin (1993) has said that most pro-lifers do not really believe that killing a foetus is morally equivalent to killing a born person: see *Life's Dominion* (London, Harper Collins). The significant support within the pro-life movement for the decision in the Hashmi case suggests that he might have been right.

[7] See the discussions in: Spriggs M (2005) 'Is Conceiving a Child to Benefit Another Against the Interests of the New Child?' 31 *Journal of Medical Ethics* 341–2; Delatycki M (2005) 'Response to Spriggs: Is Conceiving a Child to Benefit Another Against the Interest of the New Child?' 31 *Journal of Medical Ethics* 343; Sheldon S and Wilkinson S (2004) 'Should Selecting Saviour Siblings Be Banned?' 30 *Journal of Medical Ethics* 533–7; Devolder K (2005) 'Pre-implantation HLA Typing: Having Children to Save Our Loved Ones' 31 *Journal of Medical Ethics* 582–6.

[8] The issue of the rights of the embryo and foetus are dealt with in detail above.

This hangs together, just about, but it is strained, artificial and unsatisfactory. It is far better to say that beneficence and non-maleficence are both acting here. Surely the judges thought much more in those terms than in terms of stark autonomy. It was the voices of these principles that would have kept them awake at night while they were hearing the case. By declining to endorse the procedure they would have felt that they would actively be doing harm to Zain, to his family, and indeed to the savior sibling; by ordering it they would have felt that they were doing good to them all. Autonomy would doubtless counter: 'by "doing good", or "avoiding harm" here, you really mean "facilitating autonomy rights" '. But is that really right? The only way that autonomy can sustain the argument is by saying that the only real purpose of life is to exercise autonomy rights. We looked at this vaultingly grandiose claim in chapter 1, noted some of its frightening corollaries, and concluded that a principle that leads so directly to such dangerous consequences cannot be the sole helmsman of medical ethics or law.

Pre-implantation genetic testing (PGT) was mentioned in passing in the context of the Hashmi case, but the very fact of its endorsement by the HFEA under the 1990 is worth a closer look. Does autonomy give a satisfactory account of that endorsement?

We have already noted: (a) that English medical law is reluctant to concede any legal personhood to the embryo or foetus; and (b) that existence—even a compromised existence—is deemed so emphatically to be a blessing that a child cannot bring a claim saying that its life is so miserable that it would have been better had it never been born,[9] and a parent cannot bring a claim for damages for the upkeep of a child born as a result of clinical negligence.[10]

When PGT is performed it is performed with the express intention of avoiding the birth of a person with a specified disability, and with the express intention of ensuring the birth of a person without that disability. While it is important to identify both of those two intentions (and indeed the Hashmi case can be said to have turned on it), it does not do to lose sight of the wood for the trees. The analytical bottom line is that PGT is about avoiding an undesirable characteristic—or rather, to be frank, about avoiding an undesirable person.

McKay, McFarlane, et al forbid this kind of talk. And autonomy surely blushes to hear it, because if you do not have existence, it is nonsense to talk about the exercise of autonomy. The highest that the autonomist can put the case for PGT is to say:

(a) PGT allows a person to exist and be autonomous who would not otherwise have existed;
(b) the other non-selected embryos have no complaint, since if the technique were not available the parents would have chosen not to have children at all

---

[9] *McKay v Essex Area Health Authority* [1982] QB 1166, see above.
[10] *McFarlane v Tayside Health Board* [2000] AC 59; *Rees v Darlington Memorial Hospital NHS Trust* [2004] 1 AC 309; cf *Parkinson v St James's and Seacroft University Hospital NHS Trust* [2001] 3 WLR 376.

rather than to run the risk of having disabled children. Accordingly they never stood any chance of life or autonomy;

(c) the person selected will be better able to enjoy his autonomously lived life because he will not have the condition selected against; and

(d) the parents' reproductive autonomy rights are importantly in play. If they
    (i)   want children; and
    (ii) do not want a child disabled in a specific way,

then that should be the end of the matter. They should be able to have the child with and without the characteristics they specify, and those characteristics include disease or disability.

The assertion at (a) is true. The assertion at (b) may or may not be true: it will depend on the facts of each case. If this factor is decisive, all other things being ethically equal, it may ground an argument against genetic testing of the parents or indeed of clinical genetics in general. The assertion at (c) is offensive to the law and to all properly adjusted sensibilities. The assertion at (d)(ii) is identically offensive (although it is the justification for many abortions in the UK), and the assertion at d(i) adds nothing to the assertion at (b). Thus if (b) on the facts is true, autonomy can make a case for PGT without having to enlist other principles. If (b) is not true, or cannot be shown to be true, autonomy seems unable to break the stalemate generated by the conflict of the interests of the embryos affected by the condition and the unaffected embryos.

If autonomy cannot break the impasse, what can? Beneficence, non-maleficence and justice, of course. Each has a holistic view of the issues that autonomy fatally lacks. Indeed, whether or not autonomy can provide a solution, the other principles give, both individually and together, a far more satisfactory perspective. The HFEA recognises this. In the performance of its licensing functions it is primarily concerned with doing good, avoiding harm and doing justice. Eyebrows would be raised high were anyone around the HFEA table to say: 'It's autonomy and only autonomy for this problem.' It is not possible to say usefully (or at least uncontentiously), what answers the principles should decree, but it is possible to say that without them the answer to most practical problems in the world of reproductive technology is likely to be wrong and/or incomprehensible.

One short further example makes the point about autonomy's inadequacy. The 'enhancement' of human beings by the positive selection of 'desirable' characteristics (rather than the elimination of disease genes or the non-selection of diseased embryos) is increasingly feasible.[11] In the UK all the primary legislation necessary

---

[11] There has been a rash of recent literature on the ethics of enhancement. See, eg, Harris J (2007) *Enhancing Evolution: The Ethical Case for Making Better People* (Princeton and Oxford, Princeton University Press); Harris J (2006) 'Cognitive Regeneration or Enhancement' 1(3) *Regenerative Medicine* 361–6; Gordijin B (2006) *Medical Utopias: Ethical Reflections About Emerging Medical Technologies* (Leuven, Peeters); British Medical Association (2007) *Boosting Your Brainpower: Ethical Aspects of Cognitive Enhancements—A Discussion Paper* (London, British Medical Association, 2007) at <http://www.bma.org.uk/ap.nsf/Content/CognitiveEnhancement2007?OpenDocument&Highlight=2, Ethical,Aspects,Cognitive,Enhancements> accessed 8 September 2008; Savulescu J and Harris J (2004) 'The Creation Lottery: Final Lessons from Natural Reproduction: Why those who accept natural

for its endorsement is already on the statute book. Genetic modification of embryos is unlawful, except for the purposes of research,[12] but in principle (although the HFEA has said that it would not permit it), a licence could be granted for the selection (by PGT) of embryos with the genes for blue eyes, and their implantation into the mother.

Assuming that in the absence of a licence for blue eyes, the parents would have had a child anyway, autonomy has two possible arguments[13]; first: there is straightforward reproductive autonomy, which asserts that a child is a commodity no different in principle from anything one buys in a shop. If you can choose a pair of blue shoes, why not a pair of blue eyes? Most people would reject this out of hand, for reasons too obvious to articulate. And second: it could be argued that the desired characteristic would make the child's life better than it would otherwise have been. This is only an argument for autonomy if it can be said with a straight face that the characteristic would increase the child's ability to live an autonomous life. For many characteristics this will not be true. It is hard to say that a blue eyed person is more free than a brown-eyed person—although in a particular community that despised brown-eyed people it might be. It is easier to argue that, for example, greater intelligence (if that could be selected for) gives greater freedom, but the empirical basis for that is somewhere between the slender and the wholly non-existent. If it were true, though, it would provide the glimmerings of an argument.

Note, here, that the intelligent child X, selected by the PGT, is itself not more free than it would have been had there not been the PGT. If the PGT had not been done the probability is (and an overwhelming probability if natural conception would have been the alternative) that X would never have existed at all. The same applies if a significantly intelligence-enhancing drug could be provided to the mother in pregnancy, since a significant increase in intelligence would be likely to be identity-changing: it would not simply be like adding more RAM to a computer. With less fundamental changes that might not be the case, although who is to say how fundamental a part of me is the colour of my eyes?

Although the autonomy argument is not necessarily completely hopeless, it is very strained and artificial. In groping towards a solution to the ethical and legal problems thrown up by enhancement, it is far better, surely, to ask the broader questions posed by the other three principles.

---

reproduction should accept cloning and other Frankenstein reproductive technologies.' 13:1 *Cambridge Quarterly of Healthcare Ethics* 90–96; Bostrom N (2005) 'The Fable of the Dragon Tyrant' 31 *Journal of Medical Ethics* 273–7; Harris J (1992) *Wonderwoman and Superman: The Ethics of Human Biotechnology* (Oxford, OUP).

[12] Human Fertilisation and Embryology Act 1990 Sch 2, para 1(4).

[13] If this is not the case we are in the same position as set out in assertion (b) in the foregoing paragraphs. Some authors have argued that human reproductive cloning and genetic engineering should be outlawed because they undermine the autonomy of any child resulting from them. For a discussion of these views, see Mameli M (2007) 'Reproductive Cloning, Genetic Engineering and the Autonomy of the Child: The Moral Agent and the Open Future' 33 *Journal of Medical Ethics* 87–93.

Julian Savulescu, in company with several others,[14] says not only that the couple have a right to choose the child who is likely to have the best life: they have a duty to do so. He has coined the term 'procreative beneficence' to describe this obligation.

[C]ouples (or single reproducers) should select the child, of the possible children they could have, who is expected to have the best life, or at least as good a life as the others, based on the relevant, available information.[15]

The 'best life', here, is the freest life; the most autonomous life. All sorts of hackles rightly rise at the whole notion of 'procreative beneficence',[16] but for present purposes it is enough to make three observations:

(a) However one expresses one's distaste, it is an offensive idea, and autonomy dictated it. The notion makes autonomy look bad.
(b) As pointed out above, since such selection necessarily denies any autonomy at all to the children who are not born, this is a situation of autonomy's house divided against itself. Because autonomy has not acknowledged the force of the non-identity problem, the notion makes autonomy look stupid.
(c) The law will countenance embryo selection to avoid a significant detriment, but draws the line at attempts to enhance. The distinction might be difficult to sustain in practice, but is clear enough in principle. Thus we have yet another situation of the law, despite its autonomistic language, choosing to side with beneficence rather than autonomy.

[14] Notably John Harris, Raanan Gillon, Derek Parfit and Allen Buchanan.
[15] Savulescu J (2001) 'Procreative Beneficence: Why We Should Select the Best Children' 15 *Bioethics* 413–26.
[16] For a detailed critique, see *Procreative Beneficence and the Prospective Parent*, Herissone-Kelly P (2006) 32 *Journal of Medical Ethics* 166–9.

Part 3

Between Birth and Death

7

Confidentiality

EVERYONE AGREES THAT patients' medical secrets should be entitled to some degree of protection. There are several reasons given for this. As we will see, autonomy is certainly one of them. Autonomy represents the patient's perspective. Your information is your own. It is an out-pouching of you. To treat it in an unauthorised way is a sort of intellectual assault or theft. But autonomy is not the only justification for confidentiality, and it is often elbowed from the prime place. Pragmatic considerations are also important. Confidences should generally be kept because if they are not, patients generally will feel inhibited about giving to doctors generally the information needed for proper diagnosis and treatment.[1] And that is good for neither patients nor doctors.[2]

In its guidelines on confidentiality the General Medical Council notes:

> Patients have a right to expect that information about them will be held in confidence by their doctors. Confidentiality is central to trust between doctors and patients. Without assurances about confidentiality, patients may be reluctant to give doctors the information they need in order to provide good care.[3]

In very broad outline the elements of an actionable breach of confidence are:

(a) Was the information given to the clinician 'in circumstances of confidentiality'? There are two subsidiary questions here:

   (i) Did the disclosure occur in the context of a relationship in which confidentiality is expected? Almost all disclosures to doctors qualify. So do disclosures to lawyers, religious confessors etc. Even where the relationship is not one which necessarily implies confidence, a requirement of confidentiality may exist if the information disclosed is obviously of a highly personal nature, or if the confidee is expressly or impliedly asked not to pass the information on.

   (ii) Was the disclosed information of a confidential kind? If the information is already in the public domain, any confidentiality it might originally

---

[1] There is good empirical evidence that this may be the case. See, eg, Thrall JS, McCloskey L, Ettner SL *et al* (2000) 'Confidentiality and Adolescents' Use of Providers for Health Information and for Pelvic Examinations' 154 *Archives of Paediatrics and Adolescent Medicine* 885–92; Carlisle J, Shickle D, Cork M, and McDonagh A (2006) 'Concerns Over Confidentiality May Deter Adolescents from Consulting Their Doctors. A Qualitative Exploration' 32 *Journal of Medical Ethics* 133–7.
[2] For an accessible account of confidentiality from a ethicist's perspective, see Gillon R (1998) 'Confidentiality' in Kuhse H and Singer P (eds) *A Companion to Bioethics* (Oxford, Blackwell) 425–31, and Higgs R (1998) 'Truth-Telling' *Ibid* 432–40.
[3] General Medical Council (April 2004) *Confidentiality: Protecting and Providing Information* 3.

have had will have evaporated. Some information, although disclosed in the context of an otherwise confidential consultation, will not be protected by the law of confidentiality because it is clearly not the stuff of real secrets. This is probably best looked at as a matter of the intention of the parties. Vacuous tittle-tattle between doctor and patient may well not be 'confidential', even if it contains material personal to the patient, because it was clearly not the intention of the patient, at the time the matter was mentioned, that the information should be kept secret. This is a vague class: do not rely on it. Assume that anything said inside the consultation room is confidential.

(b) Has the clinician disclosed the information without the consent of the patient? This is a matter of evidence. The unauthorised disclosure need not be deliberate: it can be inadvertent—for example, being overheard in a lift, or leaving patient notes on the bus.

(c) Does the public interest in disclosure outweigh the public interest in non-disclosure? This is the classic balancing act, exemplified by *W v Egdell*.[4]

Although the courts have never expressly put it this way, the real test for the liability of a professional for wrongful disclosure of information must be the *Bolam* one: Is there a responsible body of professional opinion which, in weighing the public interest in disclosure against the public interest in non-disclosure, would decide that the interest in disclosure won? What the courts have done, however, is to use the conscience of the professional as the benchmark of liability.[5]

This is really a lightly-veiled *Bolam* analysis: *Bolam*-responsible doctors have decent professional consciences. In looking at the way that reasonably directed professional consciences work/what responsible bodies of professional opinion would say, the courts have regard to the principles laid down in the various professional guidelines—notably those of the GMC.

What Principles Are Embodied in the Law of Confidentiality?

Autonomy is a central principle in the law of confidentiality. There is no difficulty, for instance, in expressing most of the substantive principles of the English law of confidentiality in terms of Article 8(1) of the European Convention on Human Rights, which is straightforwardly autonomistic. The Strasbourg Court said, in *Z v Finland*[6]:

> The protection of personal data, not least medical data, is of fundamental importance to a person's enjoyment of his or her right to respect for private and family life as guaranteed by Article 8 of the Convention.

[4] [1990] 1 Ch 359.
[5] In *R v Department of Health, ex p Source Informatics* [2000] Lloyd's Rep Med 76: see discussion below.
[6] (1998) 25 EHRR 371, [95].

The English courts' respect for the codes of professional bodies means that the General Medical Council's guidelines on confidentiality are readily regarded as definitive of the ambit of a doctor's duty. We return to this issue below. The GMC states that:

> If you are asked to provide information about patients you must:
> Inform patients about the disclosure, or check that they have already received information about it;
> Anonymise data where unidentifiable data will serve the purpose;
> Be satisfied that patients know about disclosures necessary to provide their care, or for local clinical audit of that care, so that they can object to these disclosures but have not done so;
> Seek patients' express consent to disclosure of information, where identifiable data is needed for any purpose other than the provision of care or for clinical audit—save in [exceptional specified circumstances].
> Keep disclosures to the minimum necessary.[7]

The assumptions lying behind this text are those of classical 'life-plan' autonomy.[8] The text assumes that patients will or may have a view about how their information should be used, and will want to exercise power over that use. The assumptions are those at the heart of Article 8(1).

Some might quibble at this, and want to adopt a narrower view of autonomy. It might be argued, for instance, that if X's medical secret is wrongfully divulged, but (a) X never gets to find out about the breach of confidence, and (b) the wrongful disclosure has no effect on the way that others view X or act towards her, that no autonomy issues arise—that X's ability to live her life in the way she chooses has not been affected at all. This would be to read autonomy in a very narrow way, and the judges have not read it that way. But the observation is a challenging and creative one. It perhaps forces us to define autonomy more carefully. What the judges have generally meant by autonomy seems to be something along the lines of: 'A right to dominion over things pertaining to oneself.' Such a definition can be accommodated within the 'life-plan' idea. To do it one would have to say that it is part of one's plan for one's life that one's intimate secrets are not bandied about in the hospital canteen. That plan is frustrated if they are. Obviously the fact of the breach cannot be in any way conditional upon anyone's knowledge of the breach. To say otherwise is to make a category mistake similar to the legal mistake of confusing a breach of duty with the loss that resulted from the breach of duty.

But this accommodation is not comfortable. It rubs nastily. The fact that it does so is yet another example that autonomy is not a satisfactory one-stop analytic solution to all problems in medical ethics. It is far more natural to recognise a

---

[7] See n 3 above, 3.

[8] Some see in the Strasbourg jurisprudence an idea that human dignity, rather than autonomy, is ultimately what the ECHR is protecting in the arena of confidentiality: see, eg, Krajewska A (2007) 'Genetic Information in the Medical Context and the Scope of Personal Autonomy in the European Legal Space—A Comparative Perspective' Seminar at the Ethox Centre, University of Oxford, November 2007.

separate right to dignity—perhaps related closely to autonomy—but not dependent on it. Dignity has a more objective perspective than autonomy—which is by
definition wholly subjective. If X knows wrongfully about Y's secrets, but Y does
not know that X knows, it makes much more sense to talk about dignity being
outraged than autonomy being upset. Article 8 of the ECHR certainly can express
itself in terms of dignity. We will see several examples of this in the context of end-
of-life decision-making, and indeed in the key confidentiality case of *Campbell v
MGN*[9] autonomy and dignity were spoken of in the same breath as being rights
relevant to the issue of confidentiality, both of which came under the umbrella of
Article 8.[10] But there is no doubt that, whether they are being philosophically
literate or not in doing so, most judges regard confidentiality as essentially an old-
fashioned, autonomistic, self-determination issue. This is not just because of judicial sloppiness: it is also a consequence of the judicial intoxication with the notion
of autonomy. If the judges sober up, dignity can expect to be deployed more often.
It has a lot to contribute.

We have already noted in other contexts how easily Article 8(1) gives way to
the wider societal considerations of 8(2), and the law reports are littered with
examples of the autonomy rights in Article 8(1) submitting. Thus in *MS v
Sweden*[11] there was no breach of Article 8 when a Social Insurance Office was sent
information about an applicant's medical history, including the fact that she had
had an abortion. It was held to be in the interests of society generally, and therefore justifiable under Article 8(2), for assertions made in the course of a claim for
state compensation to be checked.

The GMC guidelines, after stating the principles cited above, spend most of the
rest of the booklet dealing with the many exceptions, statutory and otherwise, to
the default rule of non-disclosure. One of the exceptions is indeed embedded in
the fourth of the quoted principles. Non-consensual disclosure is permitted in
principle for clinical audit—a classic illustration of how individual rights are
sometimes presumed to give way to those of a cohort.[12] The law of confidentiality
is composed of two elements: (a) the default rule, and (b) its exceptions. It would
be pointless to cite all the exceptions here. The most important class of exceptions
(into which all the others arguably fall), is the public interest. Other specific excep-

---

[9] [2004] 2 AC 457.
[10] (Lord Hoffmann), see below.
[11] (1998) 45 BMLR 1.
[12] Paras 13–15 of the Guidelines (pp 8–9) deal in detail with clinical audit. They assert: '13. Clinical
audit is essential to the provision of good care. All doctors in clinical practice have a duty to participate
in clinical audit. Where an audit is to be undertaken by the team which provided care, or those working to support them, such as clinical audit staff, you may disclose identifiable information, provided
you are satisfied that patients have been informed that their data may be disclosed for clinical audit,
and their right to object to the disclosure; and have not objected. 14. If a patient does object you should
explain why information is needed and how this may benefit their care. If it is not possible to provide
safe care without disclosing information for audit, you should explain this to the patient and the
options open to them. 15. Where clinical audit is to be undertaken by another organisation, information should be anonymised wherever that is practicable. In any case where it is not practicable to
anonymise data, or anonymised data will not fulfil the requirements of the audit, express consent must
be obtained before identifiable data is disclosed.'

tions include the notification of births and deaths,[13] the notification of abortions,[14] the notification of specified diseases,[15] the notification of information relating to terrorism,[16] the notification of information may lead to the identification of someone alleged to be guilty of a road traffic offence,[17] and the whole corpus of law relating to disclosure in the course of criminal and civil investigations and proceedings. There is even a subsection of an Act of Parliament designed to enable exceptions to the principle to be carved out expeditiously,[18] and the GMC specifically urges its members to invite the Secretary of State to use his powers under this section to overcome tedious and burdensome obligations of non-disclosure.[19] While there are some anomalies here which one might gleefully highlight (such as the fact that there is an obligation to disclose information relating to the identity of someone cycling without lights, but no obligation to disclose information relating to the identity of a bank robber), the general thrust of the law is clear enough.

These principles are easy enough to identify in the data protection legislation too. The Data Protection Act 1998 states that 'personal data' and 'sensitive personal data'[20] can only be 'processed' (dealt with in any way) if the processing is in accordance with the 'data protection principles'. These are fairly anodyne. Almost any principle could lay claim to them if it wanted.[21] Then there are the Freedom

---

[13] National Health Service Act 1977 s 124(4); National Health Service (Notification of Births and Deaths) Regulations 1982 SI 1982/286.

[14] Abortion Regulations 1991 SI 1991/499.

[15] Public Health (Control of Disease) Act 1984; Public Health (Infectious Diseases) Regulations 1998 SI 1988/1546.

[16] Prevention of Terrorism (Temporary Provisions) Act 1989—renewed annually since 1989.

[17] Road Traffic Act 1988 s 170(b).

[18] Health and Social Care Act 2001 s 60(1), which provides: 'The Secretary of State may by regulations make such provision for and in connection with requiring or regulating the processing of prescribed patient information for medical purposes as he considers necessary or expedient—(a) in the interests of improving patient care, or (b) in the public interest.' To date, regulations have been made under this subsection allowing, inter alia, disclosures to cancer registries, disclosures considered necessary to control communicable diseases, and the collection of data for various data bases including the NHS-wide Clearing Service, the Health Episode Statistics, the National Health Authority Information System and the Patient Episode Database for Wales. The Patient Information Advisory Group advises on how the s 60(1) powers should be deployed, and is supposed to act as a watchdog in relation to the use made subsequently of data by the bodies endorsed by s 60(1) regulations.

[19] Eg, in the guidelines on confidentiality (see n 3 above, 8): 'If you believe that it is not practicable to seek patients' consent, (eg, where a patient cannot be traced, or is unconscious) or to act on patients' decisions (eg, because computer systems do not allow for individual choice about disclosure), you must always seek further, impartial advice before disclosing data. In England and Wales you should seek a regulation under s 60 of the Health and Social Care Act 2001.' This statement is wholly bizarre. Of course it would be ridiculous to 'seek a regulation' in the case of an untraceable or unconscious patient. This is an example of the very poor drafting of GMC guidelines, which should lead the courts to view them with less reverence than they often do.

[20] See ss 1(1), 2(e).

[21] In a medical law context six of these principles are particularly important:

(a) The first principle: personal data may only be processed fairly and lawfully.
(b) The third principle: personal data shall be adequate, relevant and not excessive.
(c) The fourth principle: personal data shall be accurate and kept up to date.
(d) The fifth principle: personal data shall not be kept for any longer than necessary for the purpose for which they were processed.   (cont.)

of Information Act 2000, the Access to Medical Reports Act 1988, and the almost redundant Access to Health Records Act 1990. Nothing in any of this legislation grates uncomfortably against anything that the common law of confidentiality, refreshed by the ECHR, has to say.

Article 8(2), then, reminds autonomy that individuals aren't the only factors in the equation, and accordingly that autonomy cannot dictate the law alone. While it is a reasonably interesting taxonomic exercise to try to devise categories into which the various Article 8(2) justifications for overriding autonomy fall, it is rather pointless. The courts are resolutely (and, for the academic lawyer, infuriatingly), pragmatic.

The lack of one obvious principle governing the exercise of Article 8(2) might look like an opportunity for autonomy. Philosophy hates a vacuum. A thorough-going autonomist, trying to maintain his philosophical monopoly, will say that Article 8(2) is actually about autonomy too; that 8(2) is actually about maintaining the sort of civilised democratic society in which autonomy can flourish. But this is not legal analysis; it is philosophical megalomania. It is a symptom of the pathological tendency, noted in chapter 1, to see the whole of law as simply a structure in which autonomy can live comfortably, or a cathedral in which it can be worshipped. The absence of a single identifiable principle does not mean that principle does not actuate Article 8(2). Nor is the asserted dichotomy between pragmatism and principle a fair one. One should not criticise Article 8(2) for taking everything necessary into account in order to reach a fair result. What one can say is that it requires far less intellectual strain to attribute Article 8(2)'s ability to trump Article 8(1) to beneficence, non-maleficence or justice rather than to autonomy. Indeed surely most societal claims are likely to be the children or step-children of justice.

The specifically English law of confidentiality has often been expressed in language other than that of fundamental rights. Sometimes it has been described in terms of breach of trust; sometimes as a tort. But it is impossible to think of a situation in a medical context where the language of analysis would have the slightest effect on the final result. For all practical and most impractical purposes the English courts have been operating the European Convention on Human Rights for at least the last couple of centuries. Since the late 1980s it has been fashionable to talk in terms of the central forensic exercise in any confidentiality problem as the balancing of the balancing of a public interest in non-disclosure against a public interest in disclosure.[22] This was a change from the previous language, which talked about the balancing of private rights in non-disclosure against public rights in disclosure. The change made the law books easier to read: lawyers

(e) The seventh principle: adequate technical and organisational measures shall be taken to prevent unauthorised or unlawful processing of such data, and against loss, destruction or damage.

(f) The eighth principle: personal data may not be transferred outside the European Economic Area unless the recipient country or territory has adequate levels of protection for the rights and freedoms of data subjects.

[22] See *X v Y and others* [1988] 2 All ER 648, and *W v Egdell* [1990] 1 Ch 359.

were denied the luxury of essays about the precise nature of the right to confidence. But since nothing at all turned on those essays apart from the lawyers' ability to pay their mortgages, nobody was denied a remedy that the previous analysis would have given them, or vice versa.

The Article 8 language is now ubiquitous in the English law of confidentiality. It is convenient enough. Thus in *Campbell v MGN*[23] Lord Nicholls said:

> The time has come to recognise that the values enshrined in Articles 8 and 10 [of the ECHR: Article 10 relates to freedom of expression] are now part of the cause of action for breach of confidence. . . . Further, it should now be recognised that for this purpose these values are of general application.[24]

What are those values? In *Campbell* Lord Hoffmann said that:

> What human rights law has done is to identify private information as something worth protecting as an aspect of human autonomy and dignity. . . . Instead of the cause of action being based upon the duty of good faith . . . it focuses upon the protection of human autonomy and dignity—the right to control the dissemination of information about one's private life and the right to the esteem and respect of other people. . . . As for human autonomy and dignity, I should have thought that the extent to which information about one's state of health, including drug dependency, should be communicated to other people was plainly something which an individual was entitled to decide for herself.[25]

Few judges are as eager as Lord Hoffmann often is to descend to philosophical fundamentals, but this is a reasonably representative sample of modern judicial thinking on the question of 'Why confidentiality?' Baroness Hale, for instance, appeared happy to adopt the expression 'the protection of the individual's informational autonomy' in indicating what the law of confidentiality is designed to achieve.[26]

But there is no time in most confidentiality cases to dwell long on the nature of the protected right. Autonomy is not in the limelight for long. This is because one has to race on to consider what all these cases are really all about, namely, how the autonomy right—if it is best described that way—is balanced against all the other competing considerations. Sometimes the other considerations are mentioned in the very same judicial breath as autonomy is invoked:

> Respecting the confidentiality of health data is a vital principle in the legal systems of all the Contracting parties to the Convention. It is crucial not only to respect the sense of privacy of a patient, but also to preserve his or her confidence in the medical profession and in the health service in general. Without such protection, those in need of medical assistance may be deterred from revealing such information of a personal and intimate nature as may be necessary in order to receive appropriate treatment and, even, from seeking such assistance, thereby endangering their own health and, in the case of transmissible diseases, that of the community.[27]

[23] [2004] 2 AC 457.
[24] *Ibid* [17].
[25] At [50], [51] and [53]. Lord Hoffmann was dissenting, but this part of his judgment was apparently uncontroversial.
[26] [2004] 2 AC 457, [134].
[27] *Z v Finland* 25 EHRR 371, [95].

We have heard all this before, but note the significance, now that we are in forensic territory, of the fact that all this material is loaded into one paragraph. Instead of getting the detailed and lengthy attention that it would like, autonomy is almost sidelined. The law moves straight from individual to societal considerations: from the health of the data subject to the health of the community: from Article 8(1) to Article 8(2).

Although the ECHR analysis endorsed by *Campbell* is the preferable one, there are other ways of looking at the question of medical confidentiality.

Still hanging gamely in is the idea that the conscience of the discloser is a crucial determinant of whether a breach of confidence is actionable. In *R v Department of Health, ex p Source Informatics Ltd*,[28] a case about pharmacists, Simon Brown LJ said, having reviewed a number of cases:

> To my mind the one clear and consistent theme emerging from all these authorities is this: the confidant is placed under a duty of good faith to the confider and the touchstone by which to judge the scope of his duty and whether or not it has been fulfilled or breached is his own conscience, no more and no less. One asks, therefore, on the facts of this case: would a reasonable pharmacist's conscience be troubled by the proposed use to be made of patients' prescriptions? Would he think that by entering [the data collection agency's] scheme he was breaking his customers' confidence, making unconscientious use of the information they provide?[29]

Can this be reconciled with the approach in *Campbell et al*? Indeed it can. Perhaps the best way is to regard these words as a summary of the demands, in a medical context, of Article 8(2). There is a prima facie breach, but so what? The conscience of the reasonable professional is taken to have weighed up all the criteria necessary in deciding where the balance between disclosure and non-disclosure should lie. If all relevant societal considerations have been assessed, and the disclosing professional can sleep at night, then the disclosure is not actionable. Why? Because Article 8(2) is satisfied. The *Ex p Source Informatics* test conflates the Article 8(1) and 8(2) exercises, but nothing is lost in the conflation except redundant verbiage.

There are two obvious practical consequences. We have noted the first of them already. It is that in determining the complexion of the reasonable professional's conscience, the court will have regard to the rules of the professional's governing body. We have already noted that in the case of the GMC, the relevant rules are replete with considerations of beneficence, non-maleficence and justice. It could hardly be otherwise.

The second is in practical terms the same point: reasonable professionals, regardless of what the rules say, will try to avoid harm, do good, and look at the wider ramifications of what they are doing.

The upshot of all this is that in the heart of the law of confidentiality, where autonomy might expect a lot of bowing and scraping, it often plays second fiddle to other considerations.

---

[28] [2000] Lloyd's Rep Med 76.
[29] *Ibid*, 82.

From Principle to Practice:
Egdell, Genetic Counselling and *Axon*

W v Egdell

Take a fairly typical case—the cornerstone case of *W v Egdell.*[30] W was a very dangerous man. He had killed several people, and was detained in a secure hospital. His optimistic solicitors made an application to a Mental Health Review Tribunal, asking for him to be removed to a regional secure unit with a view to his eventual release. They commissioned a report from a psychiatrist, Dr Egdell, who concluded that W had a long standing and abnormal fascination with guns and explosives, and could pose a serious risk were he to be released. He strongly opposed the transfer. The solicitors, of course, decided not to rely on this report, and withdrew the application. Dr Egdell heard that they did not propose to rely on it. He was worried that the Tribunal might decide the application without the benefit of the full picture, and that the public might therefore be endangered. He therefore disclosed the report to the hospital, and it eventually found its way to the Tribunal. W heard about this unauthorised disclosure, and was outraged. He issued proceedings for breach of confidentiality.

The claim ended in the Court of Appeal. The court went through the usual steps. Was the information disclosed in circumstances of confidentiality? Of course. Almost all medical secrets are. Had the confidentiality in the disclosure evaporated for some reason—such as being made public in any event? No. There was therefore a duty to keep the information confidential. Was this duty breached? Of course. The real question was: was that breach of duty actionable? To decide that one had to weigh the public interest in disclosure against the public interest in non-disclosure. The balance in this case lay in favour of disclosure. Accordingly there was no actionable breach.

Today this claim would be analysed in rather different language. It would be said that W had an engaged Article 8(1) right, that there was a prima facie breach of that right, but that the wider considerations of Article 8(2) meant that the Article as a whole had not been violated. W's right not to have his confidences disseminated beyond the people to whom he had expressly authorised disclosure could be expressed in terms of autonomy, although, as noted above, it perhaps does less violence to language to describe it as a dignity right. But the trumping considerations of Article 8(2) owe nothing to autonomy, unless one asserts that Article 8(2) is really protecting the rights of the public not to be blown up or stabbed—and that this is really an autonomy interest. But this is trying rather too hard. Is it really right to say that Article 8(2) here is the guardian of the individual Article 2 and/or Article 3 and/or Article 8(1) rights of the members of the public

---

[30] [1990] 1 Ch 359.

who might have been affected by W's release? And that all these other rights are quintessentially autonomistic? Surely not, on both counts. What is plainly in view when we move from Article 8(1) to Article 8(2) is the idea of a society which is more than merely a collection of individuals. We see a wholly integrated societal corpus, not merely an archipelago of individuals. The legal rules that govern that nation—that corpus—are different from those that govern individuals. Individuals have to give way: they have to enter into a sometimes onerous social contract.

While sane societies will do their very best to maintain autonomy rights insofar as they are compatible with the existence of society, autonomy will sometimes have to give way. It is not a question of the autonomy of X giving way to the autonomy of A + B + C: it is a question of autonomy giving way to principles better adapted to the bigger scale. Autonomy can't rationally have its cake and eat it: it can't say 'I represent the individual as against society' (which is its legitimate and crucial function), and at the same time say 'I represent society and recognise that some of my individual clients sometimes need to be subdued.'

What principles are better adapted to the bigger scale? In a medical context the litany is now familiar. A decent law of confidentiality will not want to do harm: it will not want to be the cause of a killer being released to stalk the streets. It will want to do good: this will be another way in which it expresses its distaste at being a tunnel out of jail for the dangerous, but it will also think it a good thing for tribunals not to be misled, and for doctors to be able to sleep at night. And it will want to be just. Justice will recognise as its own work the balancing exercise at the core of the common law of confidentiality and the Article 8(2) determination.

Egdell was analytically easy. Do the same conclusions emerge from difficult cases?

Genetic Counselling[31]

X attends a genetic counselling service. Her child has a devastating genetic condition that will cause it to live a short and painful life. She is found to be a carrier of the gene. She has a sister, Y. The chances of Y being a carrier of the gene are very high. If Y is a carrier the chances of any baby born to Y having the condition are very high. X knows that Y is currently trying for a baby. Y has no idea that X's child has a genetic condition, and no idea that X has been investigated at all. X's genetic counsellor, Z, discovers all this. Z urges X to tell Y about the findings in her own case, and to suggest that Y attends for testing to see if she is a carrier. X refuses: she wants nothing to do with Y.[32] Z takes the initiative herself. She contacts Y and tells

---

[31] See too the discussion of the notion of 'reproductive autonomy' as a discrete right, and the consequences for genetic testing of that view, in chs 4 and 6 above.

[32] Based on an example given by Parker M and Lucassen AM (2001) *Lancet*, 357, and cited in Hope T (2004) *Medical Ethics: A Very Short Introduction* (Oxford, OUP) 95–6. See also Lucassen AM and Parker M (2004) 'Confidentiality and Serious Harm in Genetics—Preserving the Confidentiality of One Patient and Preventing Harm to Relatives' 12 *European Journal of Human Genetics* 93–7. Should

74

her about X's condition. X is outraged. She sues Z for breach of confidence, and reports her to the GMC.

This is a hypothetical case. Nothing comparable has found its way to the courts or to the GMC. What would be done? It is a finely balanced case. Z would point out that the GMC guidelines (which the court in the civil action would find to be powerfully persuasive) provide as follows:

> Disclosure of personal information without consent may be justified where failure to do so may expose the patient or others to risk of death or serious harm. Where third parties are exposed to a risk so serious that it outweighs the patient's privacy interest, you should seek consent to disclosure where practicable. If it is not practicable, you should disclose information promptly to an appropriate person or authority. You should generally inform the patient before disclosing the information.[33]

What, translated into legalese, are these guidelines saying? If you adopt the *Source Informatics* analysis, they are telling the court/the GMC, what the conscience of a reasonable doctor would do, and so (it is suggested above) how a reasonable balancing of the competing public interests would be carried out. If you adopt the Article 8 analysis, the guidelines suggest the process through which one should go in deciding whether the Article 8(2) criteria outweigh the Article 8(1) criteria. But in either event there are great problems. The guidelines urge the clinician (and so any tribunal) to consider whether failure to disclose the information 'may expose the patient or others to risk of death or serious harm.' Since we are fresh from a discussion of the legal personality of the foetus, one of the difficulties in wielding these guidelines in this context will be obvious: The 'person' who will suffer the risk of death or serious harm is not yet a person: it is a potential person. Also note that the law in other areas forbids, on compelling public policy grounds, arguments along the lines of 'My life is so miserable that it would have been better if I had not been born.'[34]

Does this mean that the law, in order to be consistent, should decline to identify the harm from the genetic condition as harm at all—since if it is so identified the result is likely to be that a person will not be brought into the world in the first place? As we have seen in the discussion of problems arising from reproductive technology, the law is blissfully untroubled by the inconsistency. Pre-implantation genetic testing is sanctioned by the Human Fertilization and Embryology Authority without even a puzzled glance at *McKay*.

---

one test without consent? See Lucassen AM and Kaye J (2006) 'Genetic Testing Without Consent: The Implications of the New Human Tissue Act 2004' 32 *Journal of Medical Ethics* 690–2.

[33] *Confidentiality: Protecting and Providing Information* (London, GMC, 2004) 14. These guidelines would no doubt feature in any modern case on the facts of *Egdell*. These guidelines are echoed in the context of disclosing prima facie confidential clinical information to the close contacts of patients with a serious transmissible disease: 'You may disclose information about a patient, whether living or dead, in order to protect a patient from risk of death or serious harm. For example, you may disclose information to a known sexual contact of a patient with HIV where you have reason to think that the patient has not informed that person, and cannot be persuaded to do so.' *Serious Communicable Diseases* (London, GMC, 1998) 9.

[34] See *McKay*, above.

The upshot is dictated by the *zeitgeist*, not by law or reason. For the purpose only of denying the potential foetus the possibility of existence, the potential foetus is likely to be invested with a privilege that the actual foetus does not have—namely legal personality. It has the privilege of being potentially legally able to suffer harm, so as to ensure that it will never suffer harm.

There are other interests in the melting pot, of course—notably those of Y. She will not suffer death as a result of a failure to disclose. She might suffer the harm of having a badly disabled child—but that is not 'serious harm' as understood by the guidelines in any other context. Any decision in favour of disclosure must rest primarily on the perceived possibility of the death or serious harm to the child. This is a classic illustration of the clash of autonomy interests. Autonomy cannot solve the problem that it has created itself. The solution must come from our other principles.[35]

Anyone who advises confidently in a case like this is a fool. There are few legal signposts in this ethical wilderness. But probably the doctor is likely to escape the censure of the GMC or the court.

If that is right, what principles have determined the conclusion? Autonomy can surely have no claim. X's autonomy rights have been unequivocally violated, and Y's autonomy rights cannot claim to have won the day. As we have seen, since Y was not at risk of death or serious harm, her rights were not part of the equation. What has happened is that X's autonomy rights have been outweighed by potential harm to a potential person. What rights of this potential person are engaged? Surely not autonomy rights? Existence is an important precondition of the exercise of autonomy. Autonomy cannot coherently unwish itself—at least not outside the sphere of end-of-life decision-making. In fact it is impossible coherently to identify any relevant rights possessed by the potential person other than rights which would be violated—not upheld—if the disclosure occurred. We have to conclude from this that a rights analysis gets us nowhere—and certainly not to the conclusion that we have tentatively decided is likely.

So what is going on? The answer is not really so difficult—nor so surprising. The tangled mess above is a consequence of trying to see everything in terms of autonomy. What is really happening is that Z is trying to avoid harm (as he intuitively and broadly defines it), do good (as he intuitively and broadly defines it), and be just and even-handed as between X and Y (and possibly as between X, Y and the potential foetus too).

---

[35] Charles Ngwena and Ruth Chadwick (1993) put it like this: 'What has to be taken into account is the fact that respecting the autonomy of one person may have implications for the autonomy of others. As the Royal College of Physicians argue, "blood relatives have an interest in knowing the truth which has nothing to do with influencing their behaviour towards affected individuals in their families, but as a necessary means to finding out the truth about themselves." . . . How is the choice between the autonomy of different people made? . . . What is clear is that the decision cannot be taken on autonomy grounds.': 'Genetic Diagnostic Information and the Duty of Confidentiality: Ethics and Law' 1 *Medical Law International* 73, 77.

The *Sue Axon* Case

The easiest and most representative example of a difficult case adjudicated on by the courts is *R (Axon) v Secretary of State for Health*.[36] Sue Axon thought that doctors should not give advice about contraception and abortion to girls under the age of 16 without notifying their parents. She brought judicial review proceedings, attacking a 2004 Department of Health document laboriously entitled 'Best Practice Guidance for Doctors and other Health Professionals on the provision of Advice and Treatment to Young People under 16 on Contraception, Sexual and Reproductive Health' ('the 2004 guidance'). The details of this document do not matter for present purposes.

The gist of her submission was that the 2004 guidance misrepresented the House of Lords' decision in the notorious case of *Gillick v West Norfolk and Wisbech Health Authority*,[37] which must now be read in the light of Article 8 of the ECHR. She contended that if the 2004 guidance was *Gillick*-compliant, then Article 8 itself rendered the guidance unlawful. Properly understood, she said, the law meant that 'a doctor was under no obligation to keep confidential advice and treatment he proposes to provide in respect of contraception, sexually transmitted infections and abortion, and must therefore not provide such advice and treatment without the parents' knowledge unless to do so would or might prejudice the child's physical or mental health so that it is in the child's best interest not to do so.' She had a second submission, which was more powerful. If this was not the position in relation to all these forms of advice and treatment, surely it must be correct at least in relation to abortion. Silber J rejected her contentions:

Gillick was not only the starting point: it was also the finishing point. *Gillick* related to the lawfulness of providing contraceptive advice or treatment to a girl under 16 with her parents' consent. Lord Fraser, in a speech with which Lord Scarman and Lord Bridge expressly agreed, said, at 174:

> [T]here may well be cases, and I think there will be some cases, where the girl refuses either to tell her parents herself or to permit the doctor to do so, and in such cases the doctor will, in my opinion, be justified in proceeding without the parents' consent or even knowledge, provided he is satisfied on the following matters: (1) that the girl (although under 16 years of age) will understand his advice; (2) that he cannot persuade her to inform her parents or allow him to inform her parents that she is seeking contraceptive advice; (3) that she is very likely to begin or to continue having sexual intercourse with or without contraceptive treatment; (4) that unless she receives contraceptive advice or treatment her physical or mental health or both are likely to suffer; (5) that her best interests require him to give her contraceptive advice, treatment or both without the parental consent.

Lord Fraser then fired a shot across the bows of doctors tempted to abuse the trust the court was reposing in them:

[36] [2006] QB 539.
[37] [1986] 1 AC 112.

That result ought not to be regarded as a licence for doctors to disregard the wishes of parents on this matter whenever they find it convenient to do so. Any doctor who behaves in such a way would be failing to discharge his professional responsibilities, and I would expect him to be disciplined by his own professional body accordingly.

These are stern words, but for obvious reasons the conduct of doctors in this area of practice is extremely difficult for the GMC to police effectively, even if it had the will.

The judgment in *Axon* can be summarised in a sentence: *Gillick* applies to the provision of all advice and treatment to children in relation to sexual matters, and that includes abortion (although the case for the disapplication of *Gillick* is stronger in relation to abortion). The route to that conclusion was a long and fascinating one.

The first possible way for Sue Axon to succeed was to enlist the help of *Gillick*. She contended that the 2004 guidance failed to emphasise, as she said *Gillick* did, that it would be unusual for a doctor to give relevant advice without parental consent or notification. She noted in particular that Lord Fraser hedged his famous guidelines round with caveats. One example makes the point:

[I]t points strongly to the desirability of her doctor being entitled in some cases, in the girl's best interests, to give her contraceptive advice and treatment.[38]

Lord Scarman, too, noted

Until the child achieves the capacity to consent, the parental right to make the decision continues save only in exceptional circumstances ... it has to be borne in mind that there is much that has to be understood by a girl under the age of 16 if she is to have legal capacity to consent to such treatment.[39]

Silber J gave this short shrift: the 2004 guidance adequately laid out Lord Fraser's guidelines. There was no need to go further and state that they would only exceptionally be satisfied.

But there were more fundamental issues than this. At the heart of the debate was the tension between a child's autonomy (which can be articulated in terms of Article 8 of the ECHR), the parents' (and the family's) right to family life, (which can also be articulated in terms of Article 8), and the parents' duty to make decisions in the child's best interests. It was common ground that an obligation of confidentiality was owed by clinicians to children under their care.[40] Sue Axon contended that the obligation to keep confidences was limited: it did not extend to keeping the child's secrets from her parents. Parents are different, she said: they are responsible for the welfare of their children. If the law imposes that duty on parents, it is only fair that it should allow parents the information necessary to allow them to discharge it. There is also a significant public interest in promoting

[38] [1986] AC 112, 174.
[39] *Ibid*, 189.
[40] See *Venables v News Group Newspapers Ltd* [2001] Fam 430; *Re C (A Minor: Wardship: Medical Treatment) (No 2)* [1990] Fam 39.

family life: the court can't do that if it sanctions secrecy. It is well recognised that duties of confidentiality are not absolute: disclosure is always permitted if it is in the public interest to disclose.[41] The public interest in disclosing information about proposed contraceptive, sexual health or abortion treatment is so strong that it should outweigh any interest in non-disclosure. If one analyses the obligation of confidentiality using the 'conscionability' test,[42] one gets the same result: Doctors with a properly adjusted conscience would always disclose the relevant information to the parents. No, said the Secretary of State: the duty is not limited in this way. To hold that it is would be to drive a coach and horses through the whole law of medical confidentiality. It is not clear from the judgment exactly how he put this. He did say, though, that the whole issue had already been decided (as Silber J found it was) by *Gillick.*

Silber J found on the evidence before him that, if a duty of confidentiality was not imposed, this

> would probably or might well deter young people from seeking advice and treatment on contraception, sexually transmitted diseases and abortion, and this would have undesirable and troubled consequences.[43]

This was enough to dispose of the contention that the public interest in disclosure outweighed the public interest in disclosure. It was also enough, in due course, to allow the Secretary of State to take refuge (although in fact he did not have to) in Article 8(2).

There was a good deal of argument about Article 12 of the United Nations Convention on the Rights of the Child, (ratified by the UK) which provides that

> State parties shall assure to the child who is capable of forming his or her own views the right to express those views freely in all matters affecting the child, the views of the child being given due weight in accordance with the age and maturity of the child.

This, thought Silber J, was inconsistent with Sue Axon's paternalistic submission as to how parental and children's rights should relate to one another. He agreed with Thorpe LJ in *Mabon v Mabon*[44] who, considering the UN Convention, had said:

> Unless we in this jurisdiction are to fall out of step with similar societies as they safeguard Article 12, we must, in the case of articulate teenagers, accept that the right to freedom of expression and participation outweighs the paternalistic judgment of welfare.

Sue Axon's arguments under Article 8 of the ECHR met the same fate. She contended that amongst the Article 8 rights was a right of parental authority (having regard to the corresponding parental responsibilities), that ensuring respect for family life may include enforcing those rights, and that ensuring respect for

---

[41] See, eg, *A-G v Guardian Newspapers (No 2)* [1990] 1 AC 109.
[42] See *R v Department of Health, ex p Source Informatics Ltd* [2001] QB 423. See above for discussion.
[43] [2006] QB 539, [66].
[44] [2005] 3 WLR 460.

family life will or may take precedence over avoiding any interference with the child's family life.[45]

Things had moved on since those cases, said the Secretary of State. We live in a braver and, if you are a child, freer world. And in any event they did not establish any parental rights to be informed about medical treatment. If anything the Article 8 arguments tended to support the right of children to have their medical confidences respected.[46] The gist of the Strasbourg jurisprudence was that parental authority dwindles as the child gets older. Put another way: as a child matures, the burden of showing ongoing family life, protected by Article 8, grows. There was no justification in ECHR authority or common sense, for holding that a parent retained an Article 8 right to parental authority in the context of medical advice about sexual matters where the child concerned understood and was able to deal adequately with the advice and its implications. Silber J agreed.

The final nail in Sue Axon's forensic coffin was the finding under Article 8(2). If the 2004 guidance did interfere with a parent's Article 8(1) rights, that interference was justified since it was 'in accordance with the law' and 'necessary in a democratic society . . . for the protection of health . . . or for the protection of the rights . . . of others', as well as proportionate.

Silber J concluded by reiterating and slightly expanding Lord Fraser's guidelines. His summary will be a much-quoted practitioner's *vade mecum*:

[A] medical professional is entitled to provide medical advice and treatment on sexual matters without the parent's knowledge or consent provided he or she is satisfied of the following matters:
(1) That the young person although under 16 years of age understands all aspects of the advice. (In the light of Lord Scarman's comments in Gillick at page 189C . . . he or she must 'have sufficient maturity to understand what is involved': that understanding includes all relevant matters and it is not limited to family and moral aspects as well as all possible adverse consequences which might follow from the advice).
(2) That the medical professional cannot persuade the young person to inform his or her parents or to allow the medical professional to inform the parents that their child is seeking advice and/or treatment on sexual matters. (As stated in the 2004 Guidance, where the young person cannot be persuaded to involve a parent, every effort should be made to persuade the young person to help find another adult, such as another family member or a specialist youth worker, to provide support to the young person.)
(3) That (in any case in which the issue is whether the medical professional should advise on or treat in respect of contraception and sexually transmissible illnesses) the young person is very likely to begin or to continue having sexual intercourse with or without contraceptive treatment or treatment for a sexually transmissible illness.
(4) That unless the young person receives advice and treatment on the relevant sexual matters, his or her physical or mental health or both are likely to suffer. (In considering this requirement, the medical professional must take into account all aspects of the young person's health.)

---

[45] Relying on *X v Netherlands* (1974) 2 DR 118 and *Nielsen v Denmark* (1988) 11 EHRR 175.
[46] See *Z v Finland* (1997) 25 EHRR 371 and *MS v Sweden* [1999] 28 EHRR 313.

(5) That the best interests of the young person require him or her to receive advice and treatment on sexual matters without parental consent or notification.[47]

He noted that 'the best judges of a young person's welfare are almost invariably his or her parents.'[48]

He concluded:

[T]hese guidelines have to be strictly observed and . . . if they are not, the medical professional concerned can expect to be disciplined by his or her professional body.[49]

Autonomy is very proud of the *Axon* case. It is one of the principal jewels in its crown. But glittering though it may be, *Axon* does not establish autonomy's absolute kingship. Other principles played a crucial and under-discussed part in the decision. In fact the decision highlighted graphically many of the drawbacks of relying solely on autonomy. The Silber guidelines reluctantly acknowledged that there may be circumstances in which the girl should have the treatment without her parents being notified, but they were quick to say that this was very much a last resort. The decision is not authority for the proposition that the evidently autonomous wish of a *Gillick* competent child about treatment without parental notification should simply be rubber-stamped without further inquiry. That is the result that autonomy wanted, and that is the result it signally failed to get. No, there is a duty to try to persuade the girl to discuss the matter with her parents (old-fashioned medical paternalism), and, apparently, an overriding obligation, even in the case of a *Gillick* competent patient, to consider whether treatment without the parents' knowledge is in her best interests (old-fashioned medical paternalism again). Autonomy would probably try to stigmatise as Victorian anachronism the presumption that it is in the girl's best interests to discuss the matter with her parents. If it failed, it would no doubt try to say that discussion with the parents was actually a way to try to guarantee that her decision was truly autonomous. But this is the special pleading that by now we are used to hearing and of which we should be profoundly sceptical. *Axon* is only an unmitigated triumph for autonomy if a *Gillick* competent child gets what she wants with no questions asked. And she does not. Why does she not? Because of the operation of notions other than autonomy. The more relaxed, discursive decision-making endorsed by the Silber guidelines is a process which obviously has as a possible outcome a decision by the child not to engage in sexual intercourse or not to have an abortion. To those decisions, as already discussed, beneficence, non-maleficence, and indeed justice as between the mother and a foetus, may have something to contribute.

All that said, though, it cannot be disputed that *Axon*'s bottom line is autonomistic. *Axon* breathed new life into *Gillick*. *Gillick* evidently extends beyond the

[47] [2006] QB 539, [154].
[48] *Ibid* [2].
[49] *Ibid* [156]. See now General Medical Council (2007) *0–18 Years: Guidance for all Doctors* <http://www.gmc-uk.org/guidance/ethical_guidance/children_guidance/contents.asp> accessed 25 Oct 2008.

provision of contraceptive services to the arena of abortion, where one might have thought it might have been less definitively authoritative. It has been the bridgehead for a new influx of children's rights jurisprudence into English law. Where that is going to end is anyone's guess.

Up until now the general message emerging from our survey of the English medico-legal scene is that while the ethicists are wildly and uncritically autonomistic, and the lawyers often parrot the ethicists' lines, the lawyers are, when you look at them closely, much less in thrall to autonomy than the ethicists. While this is still true when we look at *Axon*, there is much more straightforward autonomy there than we have been used to seeing. The reason for that is that *Axon* straddles the divide between the law of confidentiality and the law of consent. And consent is the fundamentalist heartland of traditional autonomy. It is there that we go next.

8

The Law of Consent

AT FIRST SIGHT an assault on autonomy in its traditional homeland of consent seems hopeless. The ramparts are high and apparently impregnable. Inside them, autonomy has grown complacent. Even if it can be persuaded to share influence outside the walls, here, at home, it is haughty.[1,2]

Miss B suffered a bleed into her cervical spinal cord. She was paralysed from the neck downwards, and was maintained on a ventilator. She was not only cognitively intact, but highly intelligent and articulate. She decided that she wanted to die. Her treating clinicians, who had formed a close emotional attachment to her, refused to stop the life-sustaining ventilation. She went to court to obtain a declaration that the continued ventilation was unlawful. It was decided that since she was plainly competent to make the decision that she had made, the ventilation was indeed unlawful. The ventilation was withdrawn, and she died.[3]

The important thing to note about this case is that there was no argument at all about philosophical fundamentals. The case, despite the high emotional temperatures, was legally a very boring and insignificant one. It turned on one basic question—a question determined every day by every clinician: was the patient competent to make the decision? Since the answer was yes, that was the end of the matter. The governing principle was uncontroversial. It was undiluted autonomy. Nobody dared to suggest that Miss B's right of self-determination should not extend to a right to withdraw the ventilation. Any such suggestion would have been hopeless.

In *Schloendorff v Society of New York Hospital*[4] Cardozo J promulgated the classic statement which is repeatedly cited in discussions about consent:

> Every human being of adult years and sound mind has a right to determine what shall be done with his own body; and a surgeon who performs an operation without his patient's consent commits an assault, for which he is liable in damages.

[1] Probably the best general survey of autonomy in the law of consent is in Brazier M (1992) *Protecting the Vulnerable: Autonomy and Consent in Healthcare* (London, Routledge).
[2] A fairly typical indication of the role of autonomy in the law of consent is in Elliott C and de Than C (2007) *The Case For a Rational Reconstruction of Consent in Criminal Law* 70(2) MLR 225, 231: 'The core value which consent should protect in a society which respects western liberal ideals is personal autonomy. This value can be sexual autonomy for the purposes of the sexual offences, physical autonomy for the purposes of the non-fatal and fatal offences and autonomy over one's property for the purposes of the property offences. This is the unifying principle that underpins the concept of consent, and both facilitates and requires a unitary response from the criminal law.'
[3] *B v An NHS Trust* [2002] 2 All ER 449; cf *Pearlmutter v Florida Medical Center* (1978) 129 NLJ 77.
[4] [1914] 211 NY 125, 126.

In *Airedale NHS Trust v Bland*, Lord Goff said:

First, it is established that the principle of self-determination requires that respect must be given to the wishes of the patient, so that, if an adult patient of sound mind refuses, however unreasonably, to consent to treatment or care by which his life might be prolonged, the doctors responsible for his care must give effect to his wishes, even though they do not consider it to be in his best interests to do so. . . . To this extent, the principle of the sanctity of life must yield to the principle of self-determination . . . and, for present purposes perhaps more important, the doctor's duty to act in the best interests of his patient must likewise be qualified.[5]

In *Re T (Adult: Refusal of Treatment)*, Lord Donaldson MR, considering the case of a pregnant young woman who had been injured in a car crash and was refusing a blood transfusion, said:

This situation gives rise to a conflict between two interests, that of the patient and that of the society in which he lives. The patient's interest consists of his right to self-determination—his right to live his own life how he wishes, even if it will damage his health or lead to his premature death. Society's interest is in upholding the concept that all human life is sacred and that it should be preserved if at all paramount. It is well established that in the ultimate the right of the individual is paramount.[6]

In *Malette v Shulman*, which concerned the administration of a life-saving blood transfusion to a Jehovah's Witness, the court said:

The state's interest in preserving the life or health of a competent patient must generally give way to the patient's stronger interest in directing the course of her own life . . . The right to determine what shall be done with one's body is a fundamental right in our society. The concepts inherent in this right are the bedrock upon which the principles of self-determination and individual autonomy are based. Free individual choice in matters affecting this right should, in my opinion, be accorded very high priority.[7]

Sometimes philosophers and judges, when they are talking about autonomy, are speaking about slightly different things. But not here. Lest there be any doubt that the judges think that they are talking about the same life-plan autonomy beloved of Ronald Dworkin, Peter Singer *et al*, consider this. Lord Steyn, in the context of a case about failure to obtain properly informed consent for a surgical procedure, expressly approved this passage from Ronald Dworkin:

Recognising an individual right of autonomy makes self-creation possible. It allows each of us to be responsible for shaping our lives according to our own coherent or incoherent—but in any case, distinctive—personality. It allows us to lead our lives rather than be led along by them, so that each of us can be, to the extent a scheme of rights can make this possible, what we have made of ourselves.[8]

---

[5] [1993] AC 789, 864.
[6] [1993] Fam 95, 112.
[7] (1990) 67 DLR (4th) 321, 333, 336.
[8] *Chester v Afshar* [2005] 1 AC 134, [18], citing *Life's Dominion: An Argument About Abortion, Euthanasia and Individual Freedom* (1993) (Knopf, New York) 224.

The principle expressed in these cornerstone cases—that when one is dealing with an adult competent patient, autonomy rules without question—has been repeatedly endorsed in the medico-legal context.[9] It is the nearest thing to a fundamental axiom of medical law that we can identify.[10] These passages, and others like them, lend vaulting judicial authority to the notion of the absolute hegemony of autonomy in medical ethics and law. The ethicists think that the judges are on their side: the judges think that the ruling autonomists are on their side.

But things are not always what they seem. In fact there are many exceptions to the fundamental axiom. There are many areas of the law of consent pertaining to competent adults where autonomy does not have a free hand. We need to look at those areas, as well as the special cases of children and incompetent adults, before moving on to ask the general questions: 'What is the law of consent trying to do?', 'How is it trying to do it?' and 'Is it possible for it to achieve its goal?'

Duty to Prevent Suicide: *Reeves v Commissioner of Police for the Metropolis*[11]

The deceased prisoner, Lynch, was detained in a police cell. He had been identified as a suicide risk. He had also been identified as being of sound mind. His judgment was not impaired. This was the basis on which the case was pursued and decided. He hanged himself in his cell. This was possible because the prison authority let down a flap on his cell door. It should not have been down. Lynch's cohabitee and administratrix brought a claim against the police. The police admitted that they owed Lynch a duty to prevent his suicide, and that that breach had enabled him to commit suicide. But that, they said, was not the end of the matter. There were two possible defences. First, a defence of *novus actus interveniens/volenti non fit injuria*. It was accepted that on the facts they came to the same thing. Second, a defence of contributory negligence, which the police contended should be 100%. This second point does not tell us much about the operation of the principle of autonomy, and will not be dealt with here.[12]

---

[9] See, eg, *Re MB (Adult: Medical Treatment)* [1997] 2 FLR 426; *St George's Healthcare NHS Trust v S* [1998] 3 All ER 673.

[10] It is not the same in all jurisdictions. Thus in Israel, the Patient's Rights Act allows ethics committees in some circumstances to override patients' informed refusal of treatment. Three conditions are necessary: (a) the clinicians must make every effort to ensure that the patient understands the risks of non-treatment; (b) the treatment proposed must offer a realistic chance of significant improvement; and (c) there is a reasonable expectation that the patient will consent retroactively. See Gross ML (2005) 'Treating Competent Patients By Force: The Limits and Lessons of Israel's Patient's Rights Act' 31 *Journal of Medical Ethics* 29–34. Whatever one thinks about this, it seems a more intellectually honest way to decide on, eg, one of the typical caesarean section refusal cases.

[11] [2000] AC 360.

[12] For further discussion, see Wheat K (2000), 'The Law's Treatment of the Suicidal' 8 *Medical Law Review* 182–209.

Lord Hoffmann, summarising and commenting on the arguments on the *novus actus/volenti* point, said this:

> On the first question, Mr Pannick [counsel for the defendant] relied upon the general principle stated in Hart and Honore, Causation in the Law, 2nd ed (1985) p 136: 'the free, deliberate and informed act or omission of a human being, intended to exploit the situation created by a defendant, negatives causal connection.' However, as Hart and Honore also point out, at pp 194–204, there is an exception to this undoubted rule in the case in which the law imposes a duty to guard against loss caused by the free, deliberate and informed act of a human being. It would make nonsense of the existence of such a duty if the law were to hold that the occurrence of the very act which ought to have been prevented negative causal connection between the breach of duty and the loss . . . Mr Pannick accepted this principle when the deliberate act was that of a third party. But he said that it was different when it was the act of the plaintiff himself. Deliberately inflicting damage on oneself had to be an act which negative causal connection with anything which had gone before.
>
> This argument is based upon the sound intuition that there is a difference between protecting people against harm caused to them by third parties and protecting them against harm which they inflict upon themselves. It reflects the individualistic philosophy of the common law. People of full age and sound understanding must look after themselves and take responsibility for their actions. This philosophy expresses itself in the fact that duties to safeguard from harm deliberately caused by others are unusual and a duty to protect a person of full understanding from causing harm to himself is very rare indeed. But, once it is admitted that this is the rare case in which such a duty is owed, it seems to me self-contradictory to say that the breach itself could not have been a cause of the harm because the victim caused it himself.[13]

Knowing the House of Lords' (and particularly Lord Hoffmann's) fondness for autonomy, counsel for the defendant tried to suggest that a decision against the police would be dangerously and widely repercussive. He got short shrift. Lord Hoffmann did not take the bait.

> Mr Pannick also suggested that the principle of human autonomy might be infringed by holding the commissioner liable. Autonomy means that every individual is sovereign over himself and cannot be denied the right to certain kinds of behaviour, even if intended to cause his own death. On this principle, if Mr Lynch had decided to go on hunger strike, the police would not have been entitled to administer forcible feeding. But autonomy does not mean that he would have been entitled to demand to be given poison, or that the police would not have been entitled to control his environment in non-invasive ways calculated to make suicide more difficult. If this would not infringe the principle of autonomy, it cannot be infringed by the police being under a duty to take such steps. In any case, this argument really goes to the existence of the duty which the commissioner admits rather than to the question of causation.[14,15]

[13] 367–8. For a comparable case, in which the British Columbia Court of Appeals rejected the *novus actus* defence, see *Funk Estate v Clapp* [1988] 54 DLR (4th) 512.

[14] [2000] AC 360, 369.

[15] As to the forcible feeding of hunger strikers, see *R v Home Secretary, ex p Robb* [1995] 1 All ER 677, in which Thorpe J declared that the situation fell within the bounds of the general law of capacity, and accordingly there was no obligation to feed artificially a hunger-striking prisoner of sound

This final sentence, and the previous passage cited, suggest that the police might have been running the wrong defence—that they would have been on firmer ground had they asserted that there was no duty of care at all, and therefore nothing that could be breached. The case would certainly have been more interesting and significant had this been the line taken. Lord Hoffmann thought, though, that the police were right to concede a duty. His reasons for saying this were in an almost throwaway line. If they are right, they have profound (and entirely undiscussed) consequences for the law of medical treatment decisions and the law of mental health:

> I think that the commissioner is right not to make [the distinction between a duty owed to a prisoner who is of sound mind and that owed to a prisoner who is not]. The difference between being of sound and unsound mind, while appealing to lawyers who like clear-cut rules, seems to me inadequate to deal with the complexities of human psychology in the context of the stresses caused by imprisonment.[16]

With the exception of Lord Hobhouse, who dissented, the other judges agreed with Lord Hoffmann's conclusion and reasoning on the question of *novus actus interveniens.*

If the distinction is blurred in the prison environment, how much more blurred will it be in the hospital environment, where the stresses are often far greater than in prison (people face death and disability rather than incarceration), and capacity fluctuates massively (with depression, pain and drugs). The whole law of medical consent is posited on the distinction. Indeed the whole rule of autonomy in the law of medical consent relating to 'competent' adults rests on the distinction. If the distinction evaporates, so does a lot of autonomy's authority.

Lord Hobhouse saw this. He rallied bravely to autonomy's side.

> [L]et me take two hypothetical situations, neither unduly fanciful. Suppose that the detainee is a political agitator whose primary motivation is to further a political cause. Such persons are liable to see self-destruction, in circumstances which they hope will attract as much publicity and media attention as possible, as an appropriate means of advancing their political cause. Can such a person, having taken advantage of a careless oversight by the police and carried out his purpose, vicariously bring an action against the police and recover damages from them? Or suppose a detainee who and whose family are in serious financial difficulties and who, knowing what the Court of Appeal decided in the present case, says to himself: 'the best way for me to help those I love is to commit suicide', and then carries out that purpose by taking advantage of the careless oversight. As Mr Pannick said in argument, he might even leave a suicide note for his wife telling her this. In cases such as this it would be surprising if the courts were to say that, notwithstanding the determinative, rational and deliberate choice of the deceased,

mind. See too *R v Collins and Ashworth Hospital, ex p Brady* [2000] Lloyd's Rep Med 355. Some have considered that forcible feeding in these circumstances might amount to a breach of Art 3 of the ECHR: see Livingstone S, Owen T and MacDonald A (2003) *Prison Law* (Oxford, OUP) para 6.17, although the Commission, in *X v Germany* (1984) 7 EHRR 152, thought that the Art 2 obligation trumped the Art 3 obligation.

[16] [2000] AC 360, 368–9.

that choice had not become the only legally relevant cause of the death. It would also in my judgment be contrary to principle. It certainly would be contrary to principle to resort to the fiction of saying that he was guilty of 100 per cent contributory negligence: if the responsibility for his death was his alone, the principled answer is to say that the sole legal cause was his own voluntary choice . . . [I]t is a basic rule of English law that a plaintiff cannot complain of the consequences of his own fully voluntary conduct—his own 'free, deliberate and informed' act: see Hart and Honore, *Causation in the Law*, p. 136. This principle, overlooked by the plaintiff, is to be found in a variety of guises in most branches of the law . . . Suicide is within the range of conduct lawfully open to a person: personal autonomy includes the right to choose conduct which will cause that person's death and the right to refuse to allow others to obstruct that choice: *Airedale NHS Trust v Bland* [1993] AC 789; *St George's Healthcare NHS Trust v S* [1999] Fam 26. Imprisonment does not deprive the prisoner of that autonomy: *Freeman v Home Office (No 2)* [1984] QB 524.[17]

Later in his judgment there is a passionate speech in favour of autonomy as the ruling principle, with, as what he rightly saw as the inevitable corollary of that rule, an assertion of the importance of the notion of capacity. The speech can be regarded as autonomy's CV.

Where a natural person is not under any disability, that person has a right to choose his own fate. He is constrained in so far as his choice may affect others, society or the body politic. But, so far as he himself alone is concerned, he is entitled to choose. The choice to commit suicide is such a choice. A corollary of this principle is, subject to the important qualification to which I will refer, the principle that a person may not complain of the consequences of his own choices. This both reflects coherent legal principle and conforms to the accepted use of the word 'cause': the person's choice becomes, so far as he is concerned, the cause. The autonomy of the individual human confers the right and the responsibility.

To qualify as an autonomous choice, the choice made must be free and unconstrained—ie voluntary, deliberate and informed. If the plaintiff is under a disability, either through lack of mental capacity or lack or excess of age, the plaintiff will lack autonomy and will not have made a free and unconstrained choice. Child plaintiffs come into this category. Both as a matter of causation and the attribution of responsibility, their conduct does not (without more) remove the responsibility of the defendant or transfer the responsibility to the child plaintiff: *Yachuk v Oliver Blais Co Ltd* [1949] AC 386. Similarly, plaintiffs suffering from a temporary or a more serious loss of mental capacity (*Kirkham v Chief Constable of the Greater Manchester Police* [1990] 2 QB 283; *Pallister v Waikato Hospital* [1975] 2 NZLR 725; *Pigney v Pointer's Transport Services Ltd* [1957] 1 WLR 1121), will not have made the requisite free and unconstrained choice. Where the plaintiff's lack of mental capacity has been caused by the defendant's breach of duty, the entitlement to recover is all the stronger. On the same basis choices made under constraint of circumstances, such as those made by rescuers or persons placed in immediate danger, will not carry with them the consequence that the choice was the sole cause of the subsequent injury to the plaintiff nor will it result in his bearing the whole responsibility for his injury: *Haynes v Harwood* [1935] 1 KB 146; cf *Cutler v United*

---

[17] [2000] AC 360, 387–8.

Dairies (London) Ltd [1933] 2 KB 297. The same applies if the plaintiff's choice was vitiated by misinformation or lack of information. In the context of employment, the question of the reality of the employee's assent and his acceptance of risk has been the subject of many decisions; perhaps the most illuminating discussion for present purposes is to be found in *Imperial Chemical Industries Ltd v Shatwell* [1965] AC 656, particularly per Lord Hodson, at pp. 680–681, where he stresses that the plaintiff's conduct cannot be described as voluntary unless he truly had a free choice . . . These qualifications are fundamental and are the basis of the decisions where a plaintiff has been held entitled still to sue notwithstanding his having made a choice which led to the event of which he complains.[18]

But Lord Hobhouse's counter-attack was hopeless.[19] The claimant won[20] and autonomy lost. Autonomy, even in the consideration of classic acts of self-determination by competent adults, has its limits. There will often be countervailing interests so powerful that they will outweigh autonomy interests. No one's autonomy right entitles them to be given poison, for instance. That is not only because the would-be-poison-giver's autonomy right is engaged, but also for wider reasons, which may be located in Article 2 of the ECHR, in the principle of the sanctity of life, in the distinction between acts and omissions, or on plain inarticulate and unarticulated decency—of which the common law has been a stout defender, even at the cost, sometimes, of visible internal coherence.

Those reasons of basic decency lay at the root of the House of Lords' decision in *Reeves*. Lord Hobhouse's speech was a legally impeccable one. But its weakness was precisely in its legal impeccability—in its inflexible devotion to the logical consequences of the governing theory. As we noted in chapter 1, the law is there to serve, not to be served. On one level there is no difference at all between the case of Miss B and the case of *Reeves*. Lord Hobhouse would have been obliged to say that had the police officers come into the cell and found Lynch hanging from the door, on the edge of death, it would have been an assault to cut him down. He would have had to award damages against the police officers, just as there were damages against the NHS Trust in the Miss B case. He would have been logical, and he would have been wrong. The reasoning of the majority in *Reeves* is logically insupportable (even where it is comprehensible), and wholly correct.

---

[18] *Ibid* 394–5.

[19] Another spirited counter-attack by autonomy is in Kottow M (2004) 'The Battering of Informed Consent' 30 *Journal of Medical Ethics* 565–9: 'Autonomy has been hailed as the foremost principle of bioethics, and yet patients' decisions and research subjects' voluntary participation are being subjected to frequent restrictions. It has been argued that patient care is best served by a limited form of paternalism because the doctor is better qualified to take critical decisions than the patient, who is distracted by illness. The revival of paternalism is unwarranted on two grounds: firstly, because prejudging that the sick are not fully autonomous is a biased and unsubstantial [*sic*]view; secondly, because the technical knowledge of healthcare professionals does not include the ethical qualifications and prerogative to decide for others.' The absent prerogative I understand. But I am not clear what 'ethical qualifications' would entitle clinicians to make such decisions in the absence of other justification.

[20] Although there was an element of contributory negligence, quantified at 50%.

Autonomy Over One's Genitalia?
R v Brown and Others[21]

The defendants were homosexual sado-masochists. They had engaged (with themselves and with others), in practices coyly described by the House of Lords as involving 'genital torture and violence to the buttocks, anus, penis, testicles and nipples. The victims were degraded and humiliated, sometimes beaten, sometimes wounded with instruments and sometimes branded. Bloodletting and the smearing of human blood produced excitement.'[22] All the injury was inflicted consensually. Had any criminal offence been committed? Yes, said the House of Lords, by a majority.[23] Although absence of consent had to be proved in order to secure a conviction for mere assault, the victim's consent was no defence to a charge of wounding or causing actual bodily harm[24] where there was no good reason for such wounding/actual bodily harm. Sado-masochistic pleasure did not constitute a good reason. There were circumstances where X, having intentionally used violence and caused actual bodily harm or a wound was entitled to be acquitted, but this was where 'the injury was a foreseeable incident of a lawful activity in which the person injured was participating.'[25]

What is a 'lawful activity'? Essentially it is one on which public policy smiles.[26] It does not smile on the practice of nailing one's genitalia to a board.

> Surgery involves intentional violence resulting in actual or sometimes serious bodily harm, but surgery is a lawful activity. Other activities carried on with consent by or on behalf of the injured person have been accepted as lawful notwithstanding that they involve actual bodily harm or may cause serious bodily harm. Ritual circumcision, tattooing, ear-piercing and violent sports including boxing are lawful activities.[27]

Lord Mustill, who is noted for taking forensic bulls firmly by the horns and being surprisingly ungored by them, dissented, but his observations on bodily injury in a surgical context are enlightening:

---

[21] [1994] 1 AC 212. The decision of the House of Lords was upheld by the European Court of Human Rights on the basis that, although the prosecution may have constituted an interference with the private lives of those involved, it was justified for the protection of public health: see *Laskey, Jaggard and Brown v UK* (1997) 24 EHRR 39.
[22] [1994] 1 AC 212, 236 (Lord Templeman).
[23] Lords Mustill and Slynn dissenting.
[24] Under ss 20 or 47 respectively of the Offences Against the Person Act 1861.
[25] [1994] 1 AC 212, 231 (Lord Templeman).
[26] And of course public policy is an inconstant arbiter. Note, eg, that in *Bravery v Bravery* [1954] 1 WLR 1169, 1180, Denning LJ condemned as criminal the conduct of a husband who, with his wife's consent, underwent a sterilisation operation to enable him 'to have the pleasure of sexual intercourse, without shouldering the responsibilities attached to it.' Such a procedure, said Denning LJ, was 'plainly injurious to the public interest'. This case is discussed by the Court of Appeal in *R v Dica* [2004] 1 QB 1257, 1269.
[27] [1994] 1 AC 212, 231 (Lord Templeman).

Many of the acts done by surgeons would be very serious crimes if done by anyone else, and yet the surgeons incur no liability. Actual consent, or the substitute for consent deemed by the law to exist where an emergency creates a need for action, is an essential element in this immunity; but it cannot be a direct explanation for it, since much of the bodily invasion involved in surgery lies well above any point at which consent could even arguably be regarded as furnishing a defence. Why is this so? The answer must in my opinion be that proper medical treatment, for which actual or deemed consent is a pre-requisite, is in a category of its own.[28]

What does the exception to the general rule in the case of surgery (or boxing, or ear piercing, or circumcision) signify?[29] Whether it is put in terms of 'lawfulness' or in a more descriptive way, it indicates that even when one is dealing with con-sensual acts between competent adults, autonomy is not the whole story. And why is it not the whole story? Because sometimes, unmoderated by other principles, it gives an answer that is plainly wrong. 'Plainly wrong', here, might cover a multi-tude of objections. It might mean that it makes the gorges of right-thinking and right-feeling people rise. It might mean that it endangers public safety or security. It might mean (since *Reeves* recognises what we all know—namely that capacity is not an all or nothing thing),[30] that people with slightly less capacity to resist an intrinsically undesirable activity might be sucked into it. And so on.

The Caesarean Section Cases

We have come across some of these already when discussing the notion of com-petition between a mother and a foetus. The comment was made there that in order (a) to keep in place the fig-leaf of intellectual consistency that covers the law of medical consent; and (b) to do what seemed to the judge to be right, the courts were willing to find incapacitate women who by the normal canons of capacity were perfectly competent to make a free decision.[31]

---

[28] [1994] 1 AC 212, 266.

[29] See Weait M (2005) 'Harm, Consent and The Limits of Privacy' 13(1) *Feminist Legal Studies* 97–122; Livings B (2007) 'A Different Ball Game: Why the Nature of Consent in Contact Sports Undermines a Unitary Approach' 71(6) *Journal of Criminal Law* 534–66.

[30] An elegant empirical demonstration of this is in Tan JOA, Stewart A, Fitzpatrick R and Hope T (2006) 'Competence to Make Treatment Decisions in Anorexia Nervosa' 13:4 *Philosophy, Psychiatry and Psychology* 267, 277: 'It is apparent that the difficulties with competence associated with anorexia nervosa, although clearly present, do not preclude the affected young women themselves from being able to perceive and discuss their own difficulties and decision-making processes. This differs signifi-cantly from the traditional "all-or-nothing" view of capacity.'

[31] See too Peart N, Campbell A *et al* (2000) 'Maintaining a Pregnancy Following Loss of Capacity' 8 *Medical Law Review* 275–99, and Herring J (2000) 'The Caesarean Section Cases and the Supremacy of Autonomy' in Freeman L and Lewis A (eds) *Law and Medicine* (Oxford, OUP); Annas GJ (1982) *Forced Caesareans: The Most Unkindest Cut of All* Hastings Center Report, 12, 16–17; Kluge EH (1988) 'When Caesarean Section Operations Imposed by a Court Are Justified' 14 *Journal of Medical Ethics* 206–11; Kolder VEB, Gallagher J and Parsons MT (1987) 'Court Ordered Caesarean Sections' (1987) 316 *New England Journal of Medicine* 1192–6; Nelson LJ and Milliken N (1988) 'Compelled Medical Treatment

The classic example is *Re MB (An Adult: Medical Treatment).*[32] This concerned a woman who was 40 weeks pregnant. She had needle phobia. It was found that the foetus was in a breech position. The woman was told that a vaginal delivery would pose a serious risk of death or brain damage to the baby. She agreed to have a caesarean section, and signed a consent form. At the last minute, though, she panicked because of her needle phobia, and withdrew her consent. When she was in labour, she again gave and then withdrew her consent. The health authority applied for and obtained a declaration that it would be lawful to operate on her, using reasonable force if necessary. What the Court of Appeal said on the issue of capacity has to be quoted almost in full, since it will be suggested that the court is forensically hoist with its own petard. It said:

(1) Every person is presumed to have the capacity to consent to or to refuse medical treatment unless and until that presumption is rebutted.

(2) A competent woman who has the capacity to decide may, for religious reasons, other reasons, for rational or irrational reasons or for no reason at all, choose not to have medical intervention, even though the consequence may be the death or serious handicap of the child she bears, or her own death. In that event the courts do not have the jurisdiction to declare medical intervention lawful and the question of her own best interests objectively considered, does not arise.

(3) Irrationality is here used to connote a decision which is so outrageous in its defiance of logic or of accepted moral standards that no sensible person who had applied his mind to the question to be decided could have arrived at it. As Kennedy and Grubb, *Medical Law,* (Butterworths, 2nd ed, 1994), point out, it might be otherwise if a decision is based on a misperception of reality (eg the blood is poisoned because it is red). Such a misperception will be more readily accepted to be a disorder of the mind. Although it might be thought that irrationality sits uneasily with competence to decide, panic, indecisiveness and irrationality in themselves do not as such amount to incompetence, but they may be symptoms or evidence of incompetence. The graver the consequences of the decision, the commensurately greater is the level of competence required to take the decision: *Re T (Adult: Refusal of Treatment)* [1993] Fam 95, *Sidaway v Board of Governors of the Bethlem Royal Hospital and the Maudsley Hospital* [1985] AC 871 and *Gillick v West Norfolk and Wisbech Area Health Authority And Another* [1986] AC 112, 169 and 186 . . .

(4)   A person lacks capacity if some impairment or disturbance of mental functioning renders the person unable to make a decision whether to consent to or to refuse treatment. That inability to make a decision will occur when:

>   (a) the patient is unable to comprehend and retain the information which is material to the decision, especially as to the likely consequences of having or not having the treatment in question;
>   (b) the patient is unable to use the information and weigh it in the balance as part of the process of arriving at the decision. If, as Thorpe J observed in *Re C (Refusal of*

---

of Pregnant Women' 259 *Journal of the American Medical Association* 1060–6; Wendy Savage (2002) 'Caesarean Section: Who Chooses—The Woman or Her Doctor?' in Dickenson D (ed) *Ethical Issues In Maternal-Fetal Medicine* (Cambridge, CUP) 263–83; Baylis F and Sherwin S (2002) 'Judgments of Non-Compliance in Pregnancy' in Dickenson D (ed) *Ethical Issues in Maternal-Fetal Medicine* (Cambridge, CUP) 285–301.

[32] [1997] 2 FLR 426: see too *Re L (Patient: Non-consensual treatment)* [1997] 2 FLR 837.

Medical Treatment) [1994] 1 FLR 31, a compulsive disorder or phobia from which the patient suffers stifles belief in the information presented to her, then the decision may not be a true one. As Lord Cockburn CJ put it in *Banks v Goodfellow* (1870) LR 5 QB 549, 569: '. . . one object may be so forced upon the attention of the invalid as to shut out all others that might require consideration.'

(5) The 'temporary factors' mentioned by Lord Donaldson MR in Re T (above) (confusion, shock, fatigue, pain or drugs) may completely erode capacity but those concerned must be satisfied that such factors are operating to such a degree that the ability to decide is absent.

(6) Another such influence may be panic induced by fear. Again, careful scrutiny of the evidence is necessary because fear of an operation may be a rational reason for refusal to undergo it. Fear may also, however, paralyse the will and thus destroy the capacity to make a decision.

Applying these principles to the facts of this case we find:

(1) Miss MB consented to a Caesarean section.

(2) What she refused to accept was not the incision by the surgeon's scalpel but only the prick of the anaesthetist's needle. Capacity is commensurate with the gravity of the decision to be taken.

(3) She could not bring herself to undergo the Caesarean section she desired because, as the evidence established, '. . . a fear of needles . . . has got in the way of proceeding with the operation . . . At the moment of panic, ...her fear dominated all . . . at the actual point she was not capable of making a decision at all . . . at that moment the needle or mask dominated her thinking and made her quite unable to consider anything else.'

On that evidence she was incapable of making a decision at all. She was at that moment suffering an impairment of her mental functioning which disabled her. She was temporarily incompetent. In the emergency the doctors would be free to administer the anaesthetic if that were in her best interests.[33]

This simply will not do. Paragraph (2) of the reasoning is a robust statement of the English law's historic and much proclaimed determination to allow even life-endangering eccentricity. It can only be read as forbidding a conclusion of incapacity on the grounds that the reasons given for a particular decision are irrational or non-existent. And yet that is precisely what the court in *MB* did.

The decision in *MB* was undoubtedly morally right. No doubt *MB* thanked the court devoutly whenever she cradled her child.[34] But it cannot be justified in the way that the court sought to do. What the *MB* court was trying to do was to hang onto the absolute sovereignty of autonomy while at the same time do the obviously just thing. It cannot be done. The fact that the court felt that it needed to be done is an important marker of the incantatory power of autonomy over the judicial mind. Like a cradle Catholic intellectually persuaded of the fallacy of the

---

[33] [1997] 2 FLR 426, 436–8.

[34] The judgement in the very similar case of *Re L (Patient: Non-Consensual Treatment)* [1997] 2 FLR 837, in which the judge ordered the compulsory treatment (caesarean section) of a woman with needle phobia, concluded: 'Before delivering this judgment today I was informed by Mr Francis that L had been delivered of a healthy baby, that she was delighted with the outcome, and that she had expressed apology that she had caused many people so much trouble.': at 840.

faith and yet still insistently calling herself a Catholic, the judges cannot bring themselves to say that they are no longer thoroughgoing autonomists, although what they actually do is justice, rather than autonomy. It would all be much simpler and more satisfactory if the lip-service were dropped. It seems particularly embarrassing or emotionally difficult to drop the lip-service within the confines of medical law. The House of Lords in *Reeves* were almost blithe about side-stepping autonomy. Autonomy enjoys particular status in medical law. This is presumably because medical law is about fundamentals more often and more obviously than, for example, contract is, and autonomy is the main fundamental principle that most philosophically unlettered lawyers know about.

One of the main problems faced by those who would like to demythologise autonomy and put it in its proper place, is the laughably artificial view that the medical law tends to have of capacity. It is a monolithic view: capacity is something that you either have or you do not have. On one level, of course, medical law acknowledges that this is not so. Look in any undergraduate textbook of medical law and you will see it plainly taught that one can have capacity for one thing but not for another. The capacity one needs to consent validly to a complex procedure like a triple coronary bypass is far greater than the capacity needed validly to consent to having your bedsore dabbed with surgical spirit. But this is so trite that it seems sometimes to be forgotten when we get away from the basic texts. When Lord Hoffmann, in *Reeves*, noted that

> the difference between being of sound and unsound mind, while appealing to lawyers who like clear-cut rules, seems to me inadequate to deal with the complexities of human psychology in the context of the stresses caused by imprisonment[35]

he was widely thought to be being daringly creative and impressively penetrating, and yet this is an axiom both familiar to anyone who has done an elementary medical law course and unaccountably elusive to the Court of Appeal in *Re MB*. *Re MB* was intellectually embarrassing for the Court of Appeal precisely because they started off with the dichotomy sound mind/unsound mind immovably fixed in their heads. If you start with a premise so plainly wrong, it is not surprising if, on your way to the obviously right conclusion, you go through some rough country and end up looking disreputable.

Autonomy is single-handedly responsible for this fossilisation of the idea of capacity. It suits autonomy's purposes well: it allows autonomy to stifle many of the questions in relation to the wholly notional, non-existent, perfectly capacitate adult. By asserting that everyone who is not obviously mad or a child falls into this category, autonomy acquires a very big constituency.

As well as producing ethically unacceptable results and asking us to accept premises about human psychology that are plainly untrue, autonomy has other allegations to face in its own homeland of 'competent' adults. One of the main allegations is that it sets a standard that, if it is meaningful at all, is wholly impos-

---

[35] [2000] AC 360, 368–9: discussed above.

sible to reach. It is to that allegation that we now go. It will involve examining two related issues. First, what does it mean when we say that we want something? And second, what information needs to be provided in order to ensure that a particular decision is freely made?

What Do We Mean When We Say 'I Want . . . '?

. . . or 'I don't want . . . '? While it is generally easier in practice for autonomy to defend its rule over 'I don't want . . . '-type assertions, the problem at the roots of both questions is the same.

Decisions about whether or not to undergo medical treatment are not made in the abstract. Nor are they made by individuals who have no feelings or obligations towards anyone but themselves. They are made by relational animals, at a particular time of day, in a particular place. They may be affected by what the patient has had for lunch, whether he has taken his medication, whether the sun is shining, whether he is getting on well with his wife, whether he trusts the advice he has had from the surgeon (which may itself be affected by the colour of the doctor's tie or his brand of aftershave), and whether he thinks the surgeon is good with his hands. They may be affected by religious belief or unbelief, by concerns about the burden that his post-operative care or his survival will place on his relatives, by the state of his bank balance or by doubts about the food at the nursing home. Relatives and carers, consciously or unconsciously, influence decision-making.

What then does it mean to say that 'X wants the procedure.'? I do not know. But surely the answer is not as simple as autonomy wants us to think it is—and needs us to think it is, if it is to retain its monopoly over the law in this area.

Sometimes, but not always, autonomy talks as if it acknowledges the difficulties inherent in the question. Then it will say: 'We live in a complex and imperfect world. The best anyone can hope for is a decision which approximates as nearly as possible to real autonomy. We need to ensure that undue influence is eliminated as far as we can. We need to give patients thinking time, where clinical circumstances permit it, so as to eliminate the fleeting influences on the patient's consideration, such as the weather and the state of his bowels. We need to ensure that the relevant information is provided, and that its import is explained. We need to ensure that the aftercare is of such a standard that it does not provide a disincentive to treatment.'

This is all laudable and desirable, but it leaves many questions unanswered. An important example is: Who is the person whose desire is being investigated? We come across this situation again in the context of patients with obviously compromised capacity, but it is pertinent for almost every patient. We are all schizophrenics. If X says that he does not want life-saving treatment, which X are we talking about? Is it the arthritic, slightly depressed man, anxious that his wife will discover that he has spent on the horses the money earmarked for their retirement? Is it the father and grandfather, with adoring children and grandchildren? Is it the little boy grown old, told by his drunken father that he is worthless and would be better off dead? Is it the Catholic who believes that life is intrinsically precious?

The problem arises in an acute, unavoidable form in life-threatening eating disorders. Who is the material patient, and what is the material desire there?[36]

The law has dealt with these issues using the very blunt intellectual instrument of capacity.[37] As we have seen, and as we will see again, it is very ready to be paternalistic by the only route it allows itself—namely by declaring that a person who appears to be doing something silly does not have the capacity to make decisions for himself. This, then, entitles the court to act in the patient's perceived best interests. What is really going on here is that the law, inevitably crediting itself with frankly clairvoyant insight, purports to be able to identify the real, fundamental part of a patient, listen to what it is saying, and distinguish between that and the competing suggestions made by the other, bogus personalities with which the person is possessed. Thus MB was not really herself when she was refusing the caesarean section. The real MB wanted to look after her baby. Indeed, perhaps the real MB was not frightened of needles at all.

This really will not do. Patients dubbed 'incompetent' by all the legal canons still have desires, and often have the ability to fulfil them. An 'incompetent' patient in a mental hospital may be highly sexed and perfectly capable of enjoying a mutually satisfactory sexual relationship with a similarly 'incompetent' patient. It may be one of their only joys. Autonomy and the law tend to frown on such liaisons, even if a judge has endorsed the compulsory sterilisation of one or both of them. But why? Surely the liaison is perfectly autonomous? If you want a reason to proscribe it you have to search in prurient public policy, not autonomy. Beneficence and non-maleficence will find it hard to prise the couple apart.

Onora O'Neill has suggested that what we want more than anything else in our encounters with doctors is to be able to trust them.[38] While that assertion tends to

[36] See: Tan JOA, Stewart A, Fitzpatrick R and Hope T (December 2006) 'Competence to Make Treatment Decisions in Anorexia Nervosa' 13:4 *Philosophy, Psychiatry and Psychology* 267–82; Vollmann J (December 2006) '"But I Don't Feel It." Values and Emotions in the Assessment of Competence in Patients with Anorexia Nervosa' 13:4 *Philosophy, Psychiatry and Psychology* 289–91; Tan JO, Hope T and Stewart A (2003) 'Anorexia Nervosa and Personal Identity: The Accounts of Patients and Their Parents' 26(5) *International Journal of Law and Psychiatry* 533–48; Foddy B and Savulescu J (2007) 'Addiction Is Not an Affliction: Addictive Desires Are Merely Pleasure-Oriented Desires' 7:1 *American Journal of Bioethics* 29–32; Foddy B and Savulescu J (2006) 'Addiction and Autonomy: Can Addicted People Consent to the Prescription of Their Drug of Addiction?' 20(1) *Bioethics* 1–15.

[37] It is a blunt instrument even when it is properly understood and applied. But lawyers, clinicians and ethicists often understand the idea very differently. See Schneider PL and Bramstedt K (2006) 'When Psychiatry and Bioethics Disagree About Patient Decision Making Capacity' 32 *Journal of Medical Ethics* 90–93; Szasz T (2005) '"Idiots, Infants and the Insane": Mental Illness and Legal Incompetence' 31 *Journal of Medical Ethics* 78–81; Tan JOA and McMillan JR (2004) 'The Discrepancy Between the Legal Definition of Capacity and the British Medical Association's Guidelines' 30 *Journal of Medical Ethics* 427–9.

[38] O'Neill O (2002) *Autonomy and Trust in Bioethics* (Cambridge, CUP).

conflate several of the issues that we have dissected out above, it is probably more accurately descriptive than any other single statement of the attitude a typical patient takes into the consultation room. Conversely, how many patients really confront their doctor thinking, at any level, 'My real desire is to ensure that I retain control, and that that life-plan of mine isn't frustrated'? While such thoughts may indeed be an element of the thinking of some patients—and particularly highly educated patients who have read books about autonomy and are consequently over-realised, probably the overwhelming thought even in such patients is 'I want a doctor whom I can trust to process all the disparate elements which go to make up my desires, and sympathetically and with technical expertise bring about the holistic result that I want.' If that is autonomy speaking, it is autonomy speaking with a very disguised voice. In fact it is old fashioned benevolent paternalism.[39]

These conjectures are supported strongly by empirical studies. A recent study in Canada of twelve different patient populations concluded that

> Despite consumerist rhetoric among some bioethicists, very few respondents wish an autonomous role. Most wish to share [decision making] with their providers. . . . These results are not what one would expect in a health care environment that is strongly influenced by advocates of healthcare consumerism; however they are consistent with a growing body of literature that suggests that a shared model of the doctor-patient relationship is desirable. These results help to shed light on what is meant by the 'autonomous patient'[40]

A Dutch study concluded that

> support was clearly found for other concepts of autonomy than the liberal individualist . . . This concept does not fit very well the paradigm of evidence based patient choice.[41]

---

[39] See Perry CB and Applegate WB (1985) 'Medical Paternalism and Patient Self-Determination' 33(5) *Journal of the American Geriatric Society* 353–9.

[40] Deber RB, Kraetscher N, Urowtiz S and Sharpe N (2007) 'Do People Want to Be Autonomous Patients? Preferred Roles in Treatment Decision-Making in Several Patient Populations' 10(3) *Health Expectations*, September 2007, 248–58, 248, 256. Other studies supporting these conclusions include Deber RB (1994) 'Physicians in Health Care Management: 7. The Patient-Physician Relationship: Changing Roles, and the Desire for Information' 151 *Canadian Medical Association Journal* 171–6. Elwyn G Edwards A, Mowle S *et al* (2000) 'Measuring The Involvement of Patients in Shared Decision-Making: A Systematic Review of Instruments' 1406 *Patient Education and Counselling* 1–19; Charles CA, Gafni A, Whelan T (1997) 'Shared Decision Making in the Medical Encounter: What Does It Mean?' 44 *Social Science and Medicine* 681–92; O'Connor AM, Rostom A, Fiset V *et al* (1999) 'Decision Aids for Patients Facing Health Treatment or Screening Decisions: Systematic Review' 319 *British Medical Journal* 731–35 (all cited Deber *et al*, above); El-Wakeel H, Taylor GJ, Tate JJT (2006) 'What Do Patients Really Want to Know in an Informed Consent Procedure? A Questionnaire-Based Survey of Patients in the Bath Area, UK' 32 *Journal of Medical Ethics* 612–16. See, however, Schattner A, Rudin D and Jellin N (2004) 'Good Physicians from the Perspective of their Patients' 12: 4(1) *BMC Health Services Research* 26, and Andereck W (2007) 'From Patient to Consumer in the Medical Marketplace' 16(1) *Cambridge Quarterly of Healthcare Ethics* 109–13.

[41] Stiggelbout AM, Molewijk AC, Otten W *et al* (2004) 'Ideals of Patient Autonomy in Clinical Decision Making: A Study on the Development of a Scale to Assess Patients' and Physicians' Views' 30 *Journal of Medical Ethics* 268–74.

Until recently the English law, by and large, and despite its tendency to use the language of autonomy, has been sympathetic to Onora O'Neill's view. The very existence of elaborate regulatory machinery to ensure that doctors are trustworthy is perhaps some sort of acknowledgment of this. The tautology is pleasing: you need trustworthy doctors so that they can be trusted. There are signs, however, that this sympathetic attitude is changing, and that autonomy is regaining some of the ground that it lost. To understand this, we need to look at what the law thinks that patients should be told about medical treatment, and why it thinks this.

What is 'Relevant Information'?

However 'competent' someone is, and however well integrated and uncoerced they are, a bare minimum of information about the proposed procedure and its pros and cons is needed if the decision about the procedure is to be in any sense the patient's own. This is not to say that it is necessarily a bad thing if the decision is not the patient's own: we will return to this later.

The foundational case is of course *Sidaway v Board of Governors of the Bethlem Royal Hospital and the Maudsley Hospital.*[42] The ratio of *Sidaway* is notoriously elusive. There were five judges, and five very dissimilar speeches. *Sidaway* used to be cited most commonly as authority for the proposition that in deciding for the purposes of civil litigation whether or not a clinician has given adequate information about a proposed procedure, the *Bolam* test should be applied. That construction emerges most clearly from the speech of Lord Diplock, and has been repeatedly endorsed by subsequent courts.[43] But the other speeches are being gradually rediscovered. Thus in *Pearce v United Bristol Healthcare NHS Trust*,[44] a decision which embodied some of the judicial excitement about the new scrutiny of the *Bolam* test in *Bolitho*,[45] Lord Woolf MR appeared to import Lord Scarman's 'prudent patient' test into mainstream medical law.[46] But even if Lord Diplock remains uncontradicted, and *Bolam* reigns supreme in the law relating to the appropriate standard of counselling, the fact that the General Medical Council has issued authoritative guidelines on the procedure that should be adopted when counselling patients.[47] Those guidelines appear to embody the 'prudent patient'

---

[42] [1985] 1 AC 871.

[43] Eg, *Gold v Haringey Health Authority* [1987] 2 All ER 888.

[44] [1999] PIQR P 53.

[45] *Bolitho v City and Hackney Health Authority* [1998] AC 232; see discussion above.

[46] Lord Woolf MR said, at 59: 'If there is a significant risk which would affect the judgment of the reasonable patient, then in the normal course it is the responsibility of the doctor to inform the patient of that significant risk, if the information is needed so that the patient can determine for him or herself as to [*sic*] what course he or she should adopt.' This formulation does not appear to differ very significantly from that of the High Court of Australia in the notorious case of *Rogers v Whittaker* (1992) 175 CLR 479.

[47] See General Medical Council (1999) *Seeking Patients' Consent: The Ethical Considerations* (London, GMC).

test or even to go beyond it.[48] Because of the ostensible authority of the body from which they emanate, it will be hard to assert that counselling done other than in accordance with these guidelines is *Bolam* defensible.[49]

Autonomy, of course, did not like the *Bolam* analysis at all. It is hard to say that a right (such as autonomy) is in any meaningful sense absolute if the availability or nature of that right is determined by the quintessentially relativistic view of a responsible body of medical opinion. Autonomy likes to think of itself as inalienable and absolute. The traditional reading of *Bolam* forbids the boast.

But Lord Scarman seems to be resurgent. He, along with the GMC, is increasing the status of status of autonomy in the law of consent. He thought that it would be 'disturbing' if

medical judgment . . . [determined] whether there exists a duty to warn of risk and its scope. . . . It would be a strange thing if the courts should be led to conclude that our law, which undoubtedly recognises a right in the patient to decide whether he will accept or reject the treatment proposed, should permit the doctors to determine whether and in what circumstances a duty arises requiring the doctor to warn his patient of the risks inherent in the treatment which he proposes.[50]

He went on:

The right of 'self-determination'—the description applied by some to what is no more and no less than the right of a patient to determine for himself whether he will or will not accept the doctor's advice—is vividly illustrated when the treatment recommended is surgery. A doctor who operates without the consent of his patient is, save in cases of emergency or mental disability, guilty of the civil wrong of trespass to the person: he is also

[48] They state, eg, at 4–5: 'When providing information you must do your best to find out about patients' individual needs and priorities. For example, patients' beliefs, culture, occupation or other factors may have a bearing on the information they need in order to reach a decision. You should not make assumptions about patients' views, but discuss these matters with them, and ask them whether they have any concerns about the treatment or the risks it may involve. You should provide patients with appropriate information which should include an explanation of any risks to which they may attach particular significance. Ask patients whether they have understood the information and whether they would like more before making a decision.' So, there is a duty to find out what an individual patient wants to know, a duty to tell the patient that and, further and more frighteningly, a duty to ensure that that individual patient has actually understood. The difficulties are not merely practical clinical difficulties (how on earth to find the time to take the psychological and cultural inside leg measurements of patients in order to provide this bespoke consenting service), but fundamental legal difficulties too. Under *Sidaway* a doctor who, it is said, should have told a patient about a ridiculously small risk of a small complication would be able to say: 'There is a responsible body of medical opinion which would not have given that warning.' Under the new guidelines a patient will be able to say: 'The risk you should have warned about might not have been sufficiently large or of such a nature to dissuade most, or oven any other, people from the procedure. But I wanted to know about it for personal reasons, and you should have found out that I wanted to know and told me.' And it will be difficult, given the way the guidelines are framed, to contradict that patient.
[49] They followed *The Surgeon's Duty of Care: Guidance for Surgeons on Ethical and Legal Issues* (1997) published by the Senate of Surgery of Great Britain and Ireland, which, together with *Sidaway*, was the real bridgehead into the UK of the full-blooded doctrine of 'informed consent'. The Department of Health has produced some rather more moderate guidelines on consent which are (for doctors) encouragingly non-committal on the issue of the 'prudent patient' test. They appear to consolidate the common law position, and are interestingly silent about the GMC guidelines.
[50] [1985] 1 AC 871, 882.

guilty of the criminal offence of assault. The existence of the patient's right to make his own decision, which may be seen as a basic human right protected by the common law, is the reason why a doctrine embodying a right of the patient to be informed of the risks of surgical treatment has been developed in some jurisdictions in the USA and has found favour with the Supreme Court of Canada. Known as the 'doctrine of informed consent', it amounts to this: where there is a 'real' or a 'material' risk inherent in the proposed operation (however competently and skilfully performed) the question whether and to what extent a patient should be warned before he gives his consent is to be answered not by reference to medical practice but by accepting as a matter of law that, subject to all proper exceptions (of which the court, not the profession, is the judge), a patient has a right to be informed of the risks inherent in the treatment which is proposed. The profession, it is said, should not be judge in its own cause: or, less emotively but more correctly, the courts should not allow medical opinion as to what is best for the patient to override the patient's right to decide for himself whether he will submit to the treatment offered him.[51]

Having reviewed authorities from the US and Canada, he concluded:

To the extent that I have indicated I think that English law must recognise a duty of the doctor to warn his patient of risk inherent in the treatment which he is offering: and especially so, if the treatment be surgery. The critical limitation is that the duty is confined to material risk. The test of materiality is whether in the circumstances of the particular case the court is satisfied that a reasonable person in the patient's position would be likely to attach significance to the risk. Even if the risk is material, the doctor will not be liable if upon a reasonable assessment of his patient's condition he takes the view that a warning would be detrimental to his patient's health.[52]

We return later to the significance of that last sentence.

Nothing in this came as any surprise to lawyers over the other side of the Atlantic.

The growth of the US doctrine of informed consent is easy enough to map.[53] Although its roots go back considerably further, a convenient starting point is *Salgo v Leland Stanford Jr University Board of Trustees*,[54] where Bray J, of the California Court of Appeals, held that:

a physician violates his duty to the plaintiff and subjects himself to liability if he withholds any facts which are necessary to form the basis of an intelligent consent by the patient to the proposed treatment.

In 1960 the Supreme Court, in *Natanson v Kline*,[55] stated that:

Anglo-American law starts with the premise of thoroughgoing self-determination. It follows that each man is considered to be master of his own body, and he may, if he be of sound mind, expressly prohibit the performance of life-saving surgery or other medical

[51] [1985] 1 AC 871, 882.
[52] *Ibid* 889–90.
[53] For a good comparative survey of the position re informed consent in various jurisdictions, including New Zealand, France, Germany and Japan, see de Cruz P (2001) *Comparative Healthcare Law* (London, Cavendish) 323–57.
[54] (1957) 317 P 2d 170 (Cal).
[55] (1960) 186 Kan 393; (1960) 350 P 2d 1093.

treatment. A doctor might well believe that an operation or form of treatment is desirable or necessary but the law does not permit him to substitute his own judgment for that of the patient by any form of artifice or deception.

So far as American law is concerned, the first sentence was something of an understatement. Not only does the American law start with that premise, it tends to end with it too. And so far as English law was concerned, the statement was not then true, but may prove to have been prophetic.

Note that this formulation doesn't distinguish between the tests for battery and negligence. Informed consent generally is bad at making this distinction. It can be a dangerous conflation.

By 1966 the notion of 'informed consent' was a requirement for all research work funded by the State.[56]

In 1972 came *Canterbury v Spence*[57] a decision of Robinson J in the District Court. Despite its lowly status, it has been enormously influential. It subsequently metastasised throughout the US law of medical consent, and Lord Scarman, in *Sidaway*, adopted it without caveat. Robinson J said:

> [(a)] We reject the thought that the patient should ask for information before the physician is required to disclose. Caveat emptor is not the norm for the consumer of medical services. Duty to disclose is more than a call to speak merely on the patient's request or merely to answer the patient's questions: it is a duty to volunteer, if necessary, the information the patient needs for intelligent decision.
>
> [(b)] [T]o bind the disclosure obligation to medical usage is to arrogate the decision on revelation to the physician alone. Respect for the patient's right to self-determination on particular therapy demands a standard set by law for physicians rather than one which physicians may or may not impose on themselves. The patient's right of self decision shapes the boundaries of the duty to reveal.
>
> (c)   [Since consent is the informed exercise of a choice, there must be an opportunity to evaluate knowledgeably the available options and the risks inherent in each. Accordingly the doctor must disclose all 'material risks'. A risk is material when] a reasonable person, in what the physician knows or should know to be the patient's position, would be likely to attach significance to the risk or cluster of risks in deciding whether or not to forgo the proposed therapy.
>
> (d)   [The doctor has, however, a] therapeutic privilege [– the privilege not to disclose information if a reasonable medical assessment would have shown that disclosure would have posed a serious threat of psychological detriment to the patient].[58]

These principles were endorsed in Canada in *Reibl v Hughes*[59] and in Australia where, in *Rogers v Whittaker*,[60] the High Court of Australia held that:

[56] See the Surgeon General's Memorandum *Clinical Investigation Using Human Subjects* (1966).
[57] (1972) 464 F 2d 772.
[58] This principle is acknowledged in the GMC guidelines, *Seeking Patients' Consent: The Ethical Considerations* (London, GMC, 1999) 6: 'You should not withhold information necessary for decision making unless you judge that disclosure of some relevant information would cause the patient serious harm. In this context serious harm does not mean the patient would become upset, or decide to refuse treatment.'
[59] (1980) 114 DLR (3d) 1 (Laskin CJC).
[60] (1992) 67 ALJR 47.

The law should recognise that a doctor has a duty to warn a patient of a material risk inherent in the proposed treatment; a risk is material if, in the circumstances of the particular case, a reasonable patient in the patient's position, if warned of the risk, would be likely to attach significance to it or if the medical practitioner is or should be reasonably aware that the particular patient, if warned of the risk, would be likely to attach significance to it.[61]

Thus we have in US, Canadian, Australian and, arguably, English law, a 'reasonable patient' test. But although this purports to be generated by a passionate concern for patient autonomy, is it really? It is only really protecting the autonomy of the entirely hypothetical patient whose characteristics and desire to be informed are exactly that of the reasonable patient who exists only inside the judge's head. This is entirely inevitable. It is an acknowledgment by the law of the impossibility of achieving truly autonomistic patient counselling. It is an acknowledgment, in fact, that the whole job of devising an ethically sound and practically workable law of consent to treatment is, although it was conceived as autonomy's project, a project that autonomy itself cannot do. Would we really get a law that looked any different if we allowed beneficence and non-maleficence to write the law books? I doubt it. Note that last-cited sentence of Lord Scarman—specifically allowing the non-disclosure of a material risk where the disclosure would be harmful. That is non-maleficence speaking, and what it says is wholly antithetical to what autonomy says. But surely it is right, and surely it is the only practicable way forward.

The true doctrine of 'informed consent' is easy enough for lawyers to articulate, but its implementation is nightmarish. The nightmares are vividly illustrated by the GMC guidelines, which appear to be a genuine attempt to get to grips with the objection that the 'reasonable patient' does not exist.[62]

What should patients be told? Autonomy would like them to be told everything. It realises that the 'reasonable patient' test is a rather shabby compromise. The life-plan of patient X may require the disclosure of information that would be entirely irrelevant or actively harmful to the notional reasonable patient. But even if autonomy were given its desire, how could that desire possibly be satisfied? There is a theoretically almost infinite amount of information about any proposed course of treatment. There is a vast and terrifying literature setting out the vanishingly rare side-effects of even the simplest and commonest over-the-counter drugs. Should the prescription of paracetamol be unlawful unless the whole corpus of its esoteric literature has been summarised by the clinician, and steps taken to ensure that the patient has understood sufficiently for the decision to take the drug to be classified as sufficiently autonomous?

What about the right not to know? Sometimes more information enslaves and confuses, rather than frees. Lord Scarman acknowledged that, if information would do harm, there was a right not to disclose it. Possibly, and hopefully, there is also a duty not to disclose it. But yet autonomy is keen to press the information

---

[61] (1992) 67 ALJR 52. In *Rogers v Whittaker* it was held to be negligent to fail to warn of a risk of blindness of 1 in 14,000.
[62] See n 59 above: Some of the difficulties are commented on in n 49 above.

on even a reluctant patient—a patient who would be happier to let the doctor he trusts do what he thinks best. The GMC guidelines say:

> No-one may make decisions on behalf of a competent adult. If patients ask you to with-hold information and make decisions on their behalf, or nominate a relative or third party to make decisions for them, you should explain the importance of them knowing the options open to them, and what the treatment they may receive will involve. If they still insist they do not want to know in detail about their condition and its treatment, you should still provide basic information about the treatment. If a relative asks you to withhold information, you must seek the views of the patient. Again, you should not withhold relevant information unless you judge that this would cause the patient serious harm.[63]

This is undiluted Kant. You are not really free if you do not have the information. You are not free if you do not want the information. You are going to be free whether you like it or not. We will ram your freedom down your throat.[64]

This is legally curious. You can waive your rights in just about every other corner of law: why not here? It is yet another example of the law (through the GMC) saying that autonomy is so fundamental a part of the human description that to delegate it or otherwise alienate it is for some reason unacceptable? Childress and Beauchamp,[65] recognising the danger of such thinking for mainstream autonomists, are at pains to say that they have no difficulty with the truly autonomous delegation of decision-making power.[66] But your decision to delegate is hardly autonomous if you don't know, at least roughly, what sorts of decisions you are delegating. If you delegate all power to X in the expectation that all X will have to decide about is who cleans the house, and in fact X will be making decisions about life-sustaining medical treatment, it is hard to see how the decision about life-sustaining medical treatment is remotely autonomous. But if you do know that X will be making decisions about life-sustaining medical treatment, you will often necessarily have forfeited your right not to know. It's an uncomfortable cleft stick—a cleft stick cut from the tree of old-fashioned autonomy. The tree must not be cut down, but it must be prevented from leaning dangerously over into areas required for the safe passage of lots of limping patients.

Here, as ever, autonomy is not up to the job. Of course some sort of doctrine of informed consent is vital. But we must keep in mind what it is there for. The best reason for requiring informed consent is that it protects against deception and coercion. After all the convoluted unreality of *Sidaway, Canterbury v Spence* and the GMC, it is an immense relief to read the pragmatism of Onora O'Neill. Informed consent is not really about autonomy, she says:

---

[63] *Seeking Patients' Consent: The Ethical Considerations* (London, GMC, 1999) 7.
[64] The tone in which autonomy insists on patients being told the truth appears well in Vince T and Petros A (2006) 'Should Children's Autonomy Be Respected by Telling Them of Their Imminent Death?' 32 *Journal of Medical Ethics* 21–3, and Godkin D (2006) 'Should Children's Autonomy Be Respected by Telling Them of Their Imminent Death?' 32 *Journal of Medical Ethics* 24–5.
[65] *Principles of Biomedical Ethics* (OUP, 2001) 63.
[66] See too Andorno R (2004) 'The Right Not to Know: An Autonomy Based Approach' 30 *Journal of Medical Ethics* 435–40.

Informed consent procedures protect choices that are timid, conventional and lacking in individual autonomy (variously conceived) just as much as they protect choices that are self assertive, self knowing, critically reflective and bursting with individual autonomy (variously conceived).[67]

What patients really want is to trust their clinicians, as discussed above. In the case of someone with a finely scripted life-plan, that will include trust that the doctor knows the life-plan and will act in accordance with it. That notion is much more realistic than anything we see in the thinking of the ruling autonomists. It is a notion which rests far more firmly on beneficence, non-maleficence (both in themselves and as pillars of the doctor-patient relationship), than it does on autonomy.

Patient Responsibility

The role of the doctor in ensuring patient autonomy is often over-emphasised.[68] This is rather ironic. It has occurred largely because autonomy tends to be discussed in the context of medico-legal liability. One might think, on first principles, that the person whose autonomy we are talking about should, by definition, have the primary responsibility for ensuring that they have the information necessary to make appropriate decisions. Isn't that what being autonomous means? But one searches the English authorities in vain for much of a trace of this. Yes, there are occasional medical negligence cases where patients have been found to have been contributorily negligent (for example in failing to return for follow-up, or by failing to tell the clinician the full history of their condition), but there has never been a reported case in which a court has found that the onus lay on the patient to discover a material fact—perhaps by asking the doctor, or by researching themselves. Patients are certainly much better informed about the risks and benefits of their treatment than they ever were: we have the internet to thank for that. And yet both law and medicine persist in the paradoxical view that in order to protect autonomy interests doctors must be stoutly paternalistic, treating their patients like ignorant children.[69]

---

[67] O'Neill O (2003) 'Some Limits of Informed Consent' 29 *Journal of Medical Ethics* 4, cited Herring J (2006), *Medical Law and Ethics* (Oxford, OUP) 131.

[68] See, eg, Brazier M (2006) 'Do No Harm—Do Patients Have Responsibilities Too?' 65 *Cambridge Law Journal* 397, which makes the case that its title suggests, and questions the notion that there is nothing to be said about medical ethics than 'autonomy rules'. Also Evans HM (2007) 'Do Patients Have Duties?' 33 *Journal of Medical Ethics* 689–94.

[69] For a detailed discussion of the impact of patients' own inquiries on the autonomicity of their decisions, see Kukla R (2007) 'How Do Patients Know?' 37;5 *Hastings Center Report* 27–35. She concludes, at 34: 'We have legal and professional norms in place designed to ensure that health professionals play an appropriate role in providing patients with the informational resources they need to be autonomous managers of their own health care. As laypeople's practices of medical inquiry and information collection change, we must ask how we can institutionalize norms that will adequately reflect

The Limits of Consent

One of the (many) problems about writing generally on the law of consent is that failure to obtain consent can have different consequences (criminal, civil—both assault and negligence, and regulatory), and each of these means something different when it talks about adequate consent.[70] This is appropriate: in the civil law it is right that negligence should be easier to prove than assault, and of course crime should be more demanding that the civil law. The different demands do not in themselves tell us much about the view that the law has of autonomy. That is well illustrated, though, by three examples from different areas of the law. First, the question of when consent is vitiated in cases of the transmission of disease by sexual intercourse; second, the question of how far the consent to a surgical procedure can stretch; and third, the issue of the use to which human tissue deposited in a biobank can be put.

A doctor inserted an instrument into a woman's vagina. He was motivated only by a desire for sexual gratification. The woman consented because she thought it was diagnostically justified. The Supreme Court of Victoria held that there was no assault: there was no fraud as to the nature and quality of the act.[71]

This result seemed bizarre to many.[72] It was a consequence of the twisted philosophy of *R v Clarence*.[73] Clarence had gonorrhoea, and knew it. His wife did not know of his infection. He slept with her, and she got infected. He was prosecuted under sections 47 and 20 of the Offences Against the Person Act 1861—causing

the real character of patients' needs and abilities as active inquirers. . . . While I have warned that clinicians should not expect their patients to hear them as unilateral and automatically authoritative sources of information, I have also argued that clinicians have moral as well as technical expertise to offer their patients, and a crucial role to play in enabling their patients to function as autonomous knowers and choosers. The increasingly active role that laypeople are taking—and indeed, are asked by our culture to take—as medical inquirers and as participants in collaborative knowledge-building is riddled with both empowering possibilities and the danger for distortion and peer pressure. This essay . . . calls for sensitivity to how such changes alter the physician-patient relationship, inflect the meaning of patient autonomy, and put new pressures on the clinical encounter that may call for some changes to its structure.'

[70] Thus in *Chatterton v Gerson* [1981] QB 432, 443, Bristow J said: 'Once a patient is informed in broad terms of the nature of the procedure which is intended, and gives her consent, that consent is real, and the cause of action on which to base a claim for failure to go into risks and implications is negligence, not trespass.' See also *Davis v Barking, Havering and Brentwood Health Authority* [1993] 4 Med LR 85.

[71] *R v Mobilio* [1991] 1 VR 339.

[72] (1888) 22 QBD 23. See too *R v Richardson* [1998] 2 Cr App R 200, where a dentist suspended from practice performed dental procedures on patients who assumed that he was properly registered. They said that they would not have consented had they known about the suspension. The dentist's conviction for assault occasioning actual body harm was quashed, the Court of Appeal saying that there was nothing tantamount to a mistake of identity, and that the patients knew perfectly the nature and quality of the acts they were subjected to. But in *R v Tabassum* [2000] 2 Cr App R 328, the appellant was convicted of indecently assaulting women who allowed him to examine their breasts, mistakingly believing that he was medically qualified. Here, said Rose LJ, 'there was no true consent'. That view had to wait until *R v Dica* [2004] 1 QB 1257 for its full expression. See also *R v Cort* [2004] QB 388.

[73] (1888) 22 QBD 23.

actual (section 47) and grievous (section 20) bodily harm. At the time (the law has since changed) it was thought necessary to establish an assault, and consent is of course a defence to assault. He said that his wife had consented to the act of sexual intercourse, which indeed she had. The prosecution rejoined that there had been no true consent: that if she had been told about his infection (a fact clearly material to the decision whether or not to sleep with someone), she would have withheld her consent. Clarence was convicted. He appealed. The appeal court allowed his appeal, saying that valid consent was consent to an act of the 'nature and quality' of that which was done. Mrs Clarence had consented to an act of the 'nature and quality' of that which was done—namely sexual intercourse. She knew perfectly well what sexual intercourse was, and had said yes to it.

Ever since its promulgation, *Clarence* has had academic obloquy poured over it.[74] The main objection was the obvious one: sexual intercourse with an infected person is not an act of the same nature and quality as sexual intercourse with an uninfected one. That is particularly obviously so when the disease concerned is a dangerous one such as HIV. There is now another objection. Assault is no longer an element of section 47 or section 20[75]: why then should consent be a defence?

Those, more or less, were the arguments which ushered *Clarence* into legal history. Mohammed Dica was HIV positive, and knew it. He had unprotected sexual intercourse with two women. The women did not know that he was HIV positive, and said that they would not have slept with him if they had known. Both became HIV positive themselves. *Dica* was convicted by a jury of causing grievous bodily harm. He appealed. The Court of Appeal said that *Clarence* was no longer good law, at least in the context of sexually transmitted disease.[76] There was no true consent here.

Dica was clarified and consolidated by the Court of Appeal in *R v Konzani*.[77] The analysis adopted there was explicitly based on the autonomy of the victim. Judge LJ said:

> For the complainant's consent to the risks of contracting the HIV virus to provide a defence, it is at least implicit from the reasoning in *R v Dica*, and the observations of Lord Woolf CJ in *R v Barnes* confirm, that her consent must be an informed consent. If that proposition is in doubt, we take this opportunity to emphasise it. We must therefore examine its implications for this appeal. The recognition in *R v Dica* of informed consent as a defence was based on but limited by potentially conflicting public policy considerations. In the public interest, so far as possible, the spread of catastrophic illness must be avoided or prevented. On the other hand, the public interest also requires that the principle of personal autonomy in the context of adult non-violent sexual relationships should be maintained. If an individual who knows that he is suffering from the HIV

---

74 See, eg, Glanville Williams (1984) 'Alternative Elements and Included Offences' 43 *CLJ* 290.
75 *R v Wilson* [1984] AC 242: see too *R v Burstow; R v Ireland* [1997] 3 WLR 534.
76 *R v Dica* [2004] QB 1257.
77 [2000] 1 WLR 910. The defendant was convicted of inflicting grievous bodily harm (s 20 of the Offences Against the Person Act 1861) on three women. He knew that he was HIV positive, and was aware of the risk of infecting partners with whom he had unprotected sex. He nonetheless had unprotected sex with the complainants without telling them of his HIV status.

virus conceals this stark fact from his sexual partner, the principle of her personal autonomy is not enhanced if he is exculpated when he recklessly transmits the HIV virus to her through consensual sexual intercourse. On any view, the concealment of this fact from her almost inevitably means that she is deceived. Her consent is not properly informed, and she cannot give an informed consent to something of which she is ignorant. Equally, her personal autonomy is not normally protected by allowing a defendant who knows that he is suffering from the HIV virus which he deliberately conceals, to assert an honest belief in his partner's informed consent to the risk of the transmission of the HIV virus. Silence in these circumstances is incongruous with honesty, or with a genuine belief that there is an informed consent. Accordingly in such circumstances the issue either of informed consent, or honest belief in it will only rarely arise: in reality, in most cases, the contention would be wholly artificial.[78]

Surely all right-thinking people, as well as autonomy, will have welcomed the demise of *Clarence* and its substitution by *Dica/Konzani*.[79] But autonomy should not crow too loudly. It is hardly a very big victory. Any half-decent principle would have decreed the same result, and the judgment itself contains no great rhapsodies to autonomy. *Clarence* was outrageous: *Dica* was simply commonsensical. Of course one should have a choice about whether or not one sleeps, life-threateningly, with someone who is HIV positive. One hardly has to be a thoroughgoing Millian autonomist in order to think that one should have a choice about whether or not to play Russian roulette. Even under the principle in *Clarence* one might have thought that there was a fair chance of a conviction: having unprotected sexual intercourse with someone who is HIV positive is arguably an act very different in nature from having it with someone who is not.

But perhaps there is some real comfort for autonomy in *Dica* . There was discussion about the extent to which one can consent at all to serious bodily injury.[80] While noting the general principle that one could not consent to such serious injury, the court was not impressed with the submission that, simply because there was a known risk of serious injury in many acts of consenting sexual intercourse, that intercourse was unlawful. To extrapolate the general principle so that it had that conclusion would be to interfere more significantly than the judges could properly do with personal autonomy. Where there was true consent, only Parliament could write the laws of the bedroom:

---

[78] *Ibid* [41]–[42].

[79] The decision in *Dica* was welcomed in, eg, Rogers J (2005) 'Criminal Liability for the Transmission of HIV' [2005] *CLJ* 20; Spencer J (2004) 'Liability for Reckless Infection: Part 1' 154 *NLJ* 384; and Spencer J (2004) 'Liability for Reckless Infection: Part 2' 154 *NLJ* 448. Where it was not, this was often because it was thought that Parliament, not the judges, should have decided criminal liability in these circumstances (eg, Smith ATH (2004) *Criminal Law: The Future* [2004] *Crim LR* 971, 977). Others had doubts about the practicality of the *Dica* solution, rather than with the principle behind it: see, eg, Weait M (2005) 'Criminal Law and the Sexual Transmission of HIV' 68(1) *MLR* 121–34. The principles of *Dica* and *Konzani* do indeed have some critics (see, eg, Weait M (2005) *Knowledge, Autonomy and Consent* [2005] Crim LR 763), but the criticism is rarely framed in terms of outright support of *Clarence*.

[80] Discussed in detail above.

The problems of criminalising the consensual taking of risks like these include the sheer impracticability of enforcement and the haphazard nature of its impact. The process would undermine the general understanding of the community that sexual relationships are pre-eminently private and essentially personal to the individuals involved in them. And if adults were to be liable for prosecution for the consequences of taking known risks with their health, it would seem odd that this should be confined to risks taken in the context of sexual intercourse, while they are nevertheless permitted to take the risks inherent in so many other aspects of everyday life, including, again for example, the mother or father suffering a serious contagious illness, who holds the child's hand, and comforts or kisses him or her goodnight. In our judgment, interference of this kind with personal autonomy, and its extent and level, may only be made by Parliament.[81]

It is not clear where *Dica* will lead, other than to more doctors being prosecuted and struck off for fondling their patients' breasts on clinically implausible pretexts.

Incidental Findings on Operation

The standard UK NHS consent form has a catch-all clause in it:

I understand that any procedure in addition to those described on this form will only be carried out if it is necessary to save my life or to prevent serious harm to my health.[82]

Autonomy would presumably have few doubts about the 'save my life' element (it would presumably recognise that life is a pre-requisite to the exercise of autonomy),[83] but would frown at the 'prevent serious harm to my health.' It is indeed very broad. If effective, it could permit the clinicians to do many things to the patient that they believed were necessary to prevent serious harm, but which had not even been raised with the patient, let alone sufficiently discussed.

The boundaries of acceptability are not easy to sketch, although it is often easy to tell which side of the boundary a particular case falls on. In the Canadian case of *Murray v McMurchy*,[84] fibroids were found during a caesarean section. The gynaecologist was concerned about the risk that they would pose in any future pregnancy, and therefore, without the patient's consent, sterilised her by ligating her fallopian tubes. There was no defence to the claim of battery, and quite rightly. But in another Canadian case, *Marshall v Curry*,[85] a surgeon was found to be justified when he removed a life-threateningly gangrenous testicle discovered during a hernia operation. That was obviously right too. But it is often not that easy.

Imagine that a patient gives her specific consent to a laparotomy to determine the cause of her pelvic pain, and to deal with that cause if possible. An ovarian

[81] *R v Dica* [2004] QB 1257, [51].
[82] Department of Health, 2002.
[83] See Tait K and Winslow G (1977) 'Beyond Consent: The Ethics of Decision-Making in Emergency Medicine' 126(2) *Western Journal of Medicine* 158–9.
[84] Unreported, 1949.
[85] Unreported, 1933.

tumour is found. It has not contributed in any way to her pain. The tumour is life-threatening, but not immediately life-threatening. What should the surgeon do? Can he safely take refuge in the words of the consent form? After all, removal of the tumour will be necessary to prevent serious harm to the patient's health. Indeed, if the tumour is not removed then and there, the patient, if she consents to subsequent surgical treatment for the tumour, will have to undergo another general anaesthetic, and that is hardly good for her health.

Here we have a classic clash of our principles. Autonomy says: 'Wake her up and consent her properly for the ovariectomy. She has a right to be involved in the decision about whether or not to invade her body in this particularly traumatic and life-changing way.' Beneficence and non-maleficence say: 'Almost certainly she will want the ovariectomy. Why trouble her with the additional general anaes-thetic and the emotionally burdensome wait for the next theatre slot, in the know-ledge that she has a tumour inside her that might metastasise at any moment? Far better to do the procedure now. Other patients will also benefit from the proce-dure being done now: it will be quicker to get it over with rather than having to book another slot. Most of the traumatic invasion to her body has been done already. To do the procedure now will involve much less invasion than she will have to undergo if the ovariectomy is deferred. Deferment would involve sewing her up and then re-opening the original wound.'

The last points made by beneficence and non-maleficence (regarding the addi-tional invasion that deferment would entail) indicate that sometimes they can be better guardians of the really core autonomy interests (such as the right not to have your body invaded) than traditional autonomy itself.

The outcome of this case in the present climate of English law is uncertain. Certainly the defendant would be at real risk. And yet surely the arguments on the side of immediate intervention are overwhelming. In contrast to the concrete ben-efits conferred by beneficence and non-maleficence, autonomy promises nothing solid. It is often so. Patients are too often asked to trade their real welfare, includ-ing their peace of mind, for the entirely theoretical and unasked-for advantage of being able to determine their own medical destiny—when in practice they would have wanted that destiny to be decided by the clinician anyway. Doctors, too, are victims of the autonomy cult. They should not have to lose sleep over a case like this one. In one of the most corrosive of ironies, autonomy often proves tyrannical.

Consent, Biobanks and the Effect of Analysing Consent Questions in ECHR Terms

There are now many repositories of human biological specimens (biobanks) in many countries. They have many potential uses. They can be used for genotyping and other analyses, and can help to identify rare mutations in large populations, to follow the medical history of individuals with particular genotypes, and to correlate drug responses with genotype.[86] The legal and ethical problems involved in the regulation of biobanks vary widely—often according to the nature of the bank,[87] but a common issue is the extent of the consent that has been given or can be implied for the use of the tissue.

Imagine that 10 years ago a patient, X, donated a tissue sample to a biobank. X was told that the tissue would be used for genetic research relating to the sole research interest of the biobank at the time: muscular dystrophy. Time marched on, and so did researchers. The funding of the biobank changed, and eventually none of the tissue held by the biobank was used for muscular dystrophy work. It emerged, however, that in a way wholly unforeseeable at the time that the tissue was donated, the tissue was crucial for a promising new line of work connected with myasthenia gravis. It has proved impossible to trace X to get specific authority for this new work. What should be done? Can one imply consent to the new use from the fact of consent to the old use? How should one approach the question? As any market researcher knows, one can determine the answer by framing the question carefully. Should one ask, for instance: 'Is it really likely that if we had asked X if he minded the sample being used for other potentially life-saving purposes he would have refused?' The answer to this question is that he would probably not have refused. After all, it makes no obvious practical difference to him what is done to a dead lump of tissue sitting in a bottle of formalin.

But the thoroughgoing autonomist is not happy with this slanted question and the almost inevitable answer to it. The point for the autonomist is not that there would probably not have been an objection. That is the sort of causation argument seen in clinical negligence cases, which are notoriously fought out in ethical deserts. Something as important as what is done with one's body should not turn on something as crude as the burden or standard of proof. What is important is that, as a matter of fact, X has been denied the right even to comment on what is done with a bit of him. And as for 'implied consent'? Well, if the law of consent isn't specific, it is no law at all. In any event, how can one possibly imply consent

---

[86] See Rothstein MA and Knoppers BA (2005) 'The Regulation of Biobanks: Introduction' 33 *Journal of Law, Medicine and Ethics* 1, 6; Gibbons SMC and Kaye J (2007) 'Governing Genetic Databases: Collection, Storage and Use' 18 *King's Law Journal* 201–8; Caulfield T (2007) 'Biobanks and Blanket Consent: The Proper Place of Public Good and Public Perception Rationales' 18 *King's Law Journal* 209–26; Campbell AV (2007) 'The Ethical Challenges of Genetic Databases: Safeguarding Altruism and Trust' *King's Law Journal* 18.

[87] Rothstein and Knoppers (see n 87 above), comment: 'For example, in classical biobanking, reanalyzing stored pathology specimens, for which consent may never have been given for any research, raises important issues of the necessity and feasibility of retroactively obtaining informed consent. Population banking raises the different issue of prospectively obtaining informed consent, including opt-in versus opt-out provisions and the additional ethical issues of conducting research in culturally discrete or minority subpopulations. Commercial biobanking may raise issues of technology transfer, intellectual property and information and benefit sharing. Virtual banking involves yet another variation on obtaining informed consent as well as concerns about the privacy and security of the information, and the public and private accountability of the biobank.'

10 years down the line? The older the biobank is, the more strained the arguments about implied consent will become. X may, for all we know, have loathed myaesthenics all his life, and been pledged to do everything he could to make their lives even harder. That was a view X was entirely entitled to hold. He would be outraged to learn that he was helping them now.

We could multiply the arguments on both sides *ad nauseam*. It would serve no purpose here. Suffice it to say that although the legal issues that arise in such situations are easy to identify, the answers that the courts would give are not.[88]

The problem of X's consent is likely to be analysed in terms of Article 8 of the ECHR. We saw the language of Article 8 when discussing the law of confidentiality. Article 8 provides a convenient framework for discussing consent questions too, but although Article 8 appears inevitably in all barristers' skeleton arguments in consent cases, traditional consent cases have never been decided in the UK on the basis of Article 8. But here, Article 8 is likely to be central to the law's analysis. There is no compelling legal reason for this: it is simply that the lawyers will think 'What interests are in play? Surely the public interest in the myasthenia gravis research going ahead? Doesn't Article 8 have something to say about public interests?' The same thinking should determine the mode of analysis in other consent cases too, but since lawyers are conservative, and like to run in the ruts in which they have always run, they tend not to think of public interest in the context of consent unless it is completely unavoidable. Here, and unusually, it is unavoidable even for the most myopic of traditional common lawyers.

Usually the result under Article 8 will be the same as the result that the traditional analysis gives. But X's case is one of the few sorts in which the Article 8 analysis might produce an answer materially different to the traditional one. Once Article 8(2) is allowed to speak on behalf of wider societal interests, it is strangely compelling. Normally, in a conspiracy engineered by autonomy, it is silenced.

Once Article 8(2) gets a real foothold in the law of consent (which it is likely to do through a case like this), it is likely to loosen the stranglehold that autonomy has on some issues. Article 8(2) declares that no man is an island unto himself. When that is pointed out, and it is noted that the roof of the world doesn't fall in at the declaration, the law of consent looks a good deal more common-sensical and realistic.

Autonomy can draw little comfort from the outcome of consent cases in Strasbourg framed in Article 8 terms. Compulsory treatment cases have relied on many of the cited interests under Article 8(2) to justify interference with the basic Article 8(1) right. Examples include public safety (for vaccination and screening programmes[89]), the prevention of disorder or crime (for compulsory blood tests

---

[88] Medical Research Council (2001) *Human Tissue and Biological Samples for Use in Research: Operational and Ethical Guidelines* (London, MRC, 2001); Nuffield Council on Bioethics (1995) *Human Tissue: Ethical and Legal Issues* (London, Nuffield Council on Bioethics, 1995); Furness PN and Nicholson ML (2004) 'Obtaining Explicit Consent for the Use of Archival Tissue Samples: Practical Issues' 30 *Journal of Medical Ethics*, 561–4.

[89] *Acmanne* v *Belgium* (1984) 40 DR 251.

for drunk drivers[90] and drug tests for prisoners[91]), and the protection of the rights and freedoms of others (for compulsory blood tests in a paternity suit[92]).

The court's trumping of parental decisions about children's treatment is one area where one might expect Article 8 to be vocal. In practice the courts have said that the English law's overriding concern for the welfare of the child satisfies Article 8, just as it satisfies the UN Convention on the Rights of the Child.[93]

On the face of it Article 3 might seem to be a better advocate for autonomy than Article 8 is. Article 3 provides, baldly, that:

No-one shall be subjected to torture or to inhuman or degrading treatment or punishment.

There are none of the qualifying caveats of Article 8.

Is this autonomistic? It can certainly be read that way. But it can also be read as a product of beneficence, non-maleficence, any other worthwhile philosophical principle one can think of, or simply plain decency. Whatever its philosophical origins, it is plainly right. If autonomy can claim it, though, the claim hardly bolsters its profile in the law of consent.

Perhaps this is not surprising. Article 3 seems a very long way from medicine. But the Strasbourg court's legal geography is not everybody's. The court has held that the Article can be invoked in medical contexts, but then, having got the excited attention of medical lawyers, has gone on to say that in fact it probably will have little practical effect. The route to this profoundly unsatisfactory conclusion is convoluted. In a lot of anxious consideration in Strasbourg, 'degrading' has been held to have its natural meaning.[94] Generally, of course, bona fide medical treatment, even given without valid consent, is unlikely to be degrading. This was acknowledged in *Herczegfalvy v Austria*,[95] where it was held that 'as a general rule, a measure which is a therapeutic necessity cannot be regarded as inhuman or degrading.'

This begs two questions: (a) what constitutes therapeutic necessity?; and (b) when does the general rule not apply?

What does 'therapeutic necessity' mean? The opinion in *Herczegfalvy* refers both to treatment which is 'necessary from the medical point of view and carried out in conformity with standards accepted by medical science',[96] and to treatment which 'could reasonably be considered to be justified by medical considerations'.[97] These are not obviously identical.

[90] *X v Netherlands* (1974) 2 DR 118.
[91] *Peters v Netherlands* (App 21132/93) (1994), unreported.
[92] *X v Austria* (App 5591/73) (1973) 43 CD 161.
[93] Art 3(1) of the Convention says: 'In all actions concerning children, whether undertaken by public or private social welfare institutions, courts of law, administrative authorities or legislative bodies, the best interests of the child shall be a primary consideration.' See too *Garcia v Switzerland*, App No 10148/82.
[94] *Ireland v UK* (1978) 2 EHRR 25, [167]: *East African Asians Cases* (1973) 3 EHRR 76, 80.
[95] (1993) 15 EHRR 437, [82].
[96] *Ibid* 468.
[97] *Ibid* 469.

But one must not get too lawyerly about all this. Whatever 'therapeutic necessity' is, treatment outside Dr Mengele's surgery, even without consent, is unlikely to be therapeutically unnecessary. And if it is, doing it will be actionable in the domestic law of negligence and/or assault. So the Article adds nothing.

When will the general rule not apply? The type of departure from the general rule that seems to be envisaged in *Herczegfalvy* is where the force used to administer otherwise necessary treatment renders the whole process inhuman or degrading.[98] It is not clear from *Herczegfalvy*, though, whether it matters whether the patient is capable of consenting or not. *Herczegfalvy* was a hunger strike case. The 'treatment' concerned was force-feeding. There were doubts there about the patient's capacity. One would have thought on first principles that one did not need much capacity to make a decision as basic as that. The patient certainly seemed capable of indicating pretty decisively that he did not want to be fed, as the ribs broken and teeth lost in his struggles with the feeders showed. There was muted disapproval of the amount of force used, but it was held that there had been no breach of Article 3.[99] It is a rather undemanding Article.

It is difficult to imagine things becoming more messy than this. But they do. The few certainties about the construction of Article 3 that staggered out of *Herczegfalvy* took a brutal beating in *X v Denmark*.[100] There it was held that medical treatment, even with consent, could be a breach of Article 3 if it was 'experimental'. In X new and fairly untested equipment was used to carry out the operation consented to. In fact it carried a greater risk to the patient than the conventional equipment. This, however, was not considered to be 'experimental'. It was further held that experimental treatment would only constitute a breach 'under certain circumstances', but it was not indicated what those circumstances might be. X raises more questions than it answers. 'Experimental' was and remains undefined.

Article 3, then, proves to be either wholly irrelevant or not demonstrably relevant to cases in a medical context involving competent patients.

One might have thought, however, that Article 3 might genuinely have had something new to say about the treatment of unconscious patients. But as the English law presently stands, it is not clear that it does. This issue is considered further below.

Autonomy is happier in English domestic law than it is in Strasbourg. The public interest caveats of the Convention are antithetical to the spirit of autonomy. Yet even on English shores, enthroned in its castle of consent, autonomy proves to be less secure than a first look suggests.

---

[98] This emerges from the opinion rather than from the judgment of the court.

[99] Interestingly, it was also held that there had been no breach of Art 8, on the grounds that he did not have the capacity to consent. However, the consideration of Art 8 can be politely described as skimpy.

[100] (1983) 32 DR 282.

The Notion of Capacity

Capacity has hovered phantasmally behind all the discussions about consent. We have been talking so far about the 'competent' patient: the one who has capacity. We will shortly move on to talk about the 'incompetent' patient. We have already commented on the unreality of the distinction, citing approvingly the comments of Lord Hoffmann in *Reeves*, and noting that one's capacity is dependent on the complexity of the decision one is facing: one has to ask 'competent for what?' And yet the distinction not only persists, but determines the entire architecture of the law of consent. In analysing any examination problem relating to consent, the first question that the candidate is told to ask is: 'Is the patient competent?' If yes, corpus of law X applies. If no, corpus of law Y applies. Autonomy is keen to maintain the illusion of a clear distinction between the two states, because its rule, with the exceptions that we have examined, tends to be unquestioned in relation to competent patients. If the boundary between capacity and incapacity is blurred, autonomy's hold on the law generally is weakened.

As we will see, there is an important presumption that a patient has capacity unless and until incapacity is shown. This presumption is entirely theoretically correct. Any alternative is terrible to contemplate. But autonomy has perfused medical thinking so completely that capacity is often presumed over-hastily.

Raymont *et al* surveyed patients on medical wards. 50 of them were found to be incompetent to consent to treatment. Only 12 of them had been acknowledged to be incompetent by their treating clinicians.[101] It is difficult to believe that this represents slipshod clinical practice. It is more likely to represent a reluctance to realise that one is outside the legal and ethical reach of undiluted autonomy. Partly this is due to the great propaganda war that autonomy has fought and won. Partly it is because a presumption of patient autonomy is comforting for the clinician: if the patient is in control and has total responsibility for what happens to him, the burden on the clinician is less. Best interests determinations are onerous. There is a prevailing, politically correct nervousness about medical paternalism, fuelled by the General Medical Council. Patient welfare is often the casualty of that political correctness.

What does the law mean by incapacity? For this one has to go to the Mental Capacity Act 2005, which has consolidated the common law which previously governed this area.[102] As consolidating Acts go, it did a good job.

By section 3(1) of the 2005 Act, a person lacks capacity if he is unable:

(a) to understand the information relevant to the decision,
(b) to retain that information,

---

[101] Raymont V, Bingley W, Buchanan A *et al* (2004) 'Prevalence of Mental Incapacity in Medical Inpatients and Associated Risk Factors: Cross-Sectional Study' 364, 9443 *The Lancet* 1421–7.

[102] See Johnston C and Liddle J (2007) 'The Mental Capacity Act 2005: A New Framework for Healthcare Decision Making' 33 *Journal of Medical Ethics* 94–7.

(c) to use or weigh that information as part of the process of making the decision, or

(d) to communicate his decision (whether by talking, using sign language or any other means).[103]

The 'information relevant to the decision' includes information about the reasonably foreseeable consequences of deciding one way or the other and of failing to make the decision.[104]

The Act warns, as do the cases,[105] against the danger of concluding that someone lacks capacity simply because the decision they make or propose to make is eccentric, or contrary to the values held by the doctor or judge.

> a lack of capacity cannot be established merely by reference to . . . (b) a condition of his, or an aspect of his behaviour, which might lead others to make unjustified assumptions about his capacity.[106]

Although incapacity deprives autonomy of jurisdiction, autonomy can surely have little argument with the definition in section 3(1)(a), (b) or (c). These criteria are collectively the antithesis of autonomy. But section 3(1)(d) is rather different. Someone is deemed incapacitate if they cannot communicate. Practically, of course, such a provision is inevitable. If a patient has locked-in syndrome, the continued activity of their mind or the specificity of their life-plan will, absent an applicable advance directive, be irrelevant. But nonetheless autonomy is legitimately offended. The offence is unavoidable. The disease, rather than any competing principle, has prevented autonomy from doing its job.

If an adult patient has lost capacity, then and then only are we in the territory of 'best interests'. Decision-making on behalf of children raises slightly different issues. We discuss those separately. What follows relates only to incompetent adults.

Best Interests and Incompetent Adults

The common law has been coherently codified in section 4 of the Mental Capacity Act 2005. Section 4 is a checklist. It has to be used by any assessor of best interests.[107] It provides that the assessor:

— Must consider all the relevant circumstances, and in particular take the following steps;[108]

---

[103] This is drawn substantially from In *Re C (Adult: Refusal of Medical Treatment)* [1994] 1 All ER 819, where the court said that a patient has the necessary capacity if he has the ability to: (a) receive and retain information; (b) believe the information; and (c) weigh the information, balancing the risks against the benefits. The court in *Re C* noted that a compulsive disorder or phobia may stifle belief in the information presented, annihilating capacity.

[104] Mental Capacity Act 2005 ss 3(4), 4(1).

[105] Eg, *B v An NHS Trust* [2002] 2 All ER 449, above.

[106] Mental Capacity Act 2005 s 2(3).

[107] It is supplemented by a long, detailed and genuinely practical Code of Practice.

[108] Mental Capacity Act 2005 s 4(2).

— Must consider whether it is likely that the person will at some time have capacity in relation to the matter in question, and if it appears likely that he will, when that is likely to be.[109]
— Must, so far as reasonably practicable, permit and encourage the person to participate, or to improve his ability to participate, as fully as possible in any act done for him and any decision affecting him.[110]
— Where the determination relates to life-sustaining treatment he must not, in considering whether the treatment is in the best interests of the person concerned, be motivated by a desire to bring about his death.[111]
— Must take into account, if it is practicable and appropriate to consult them, the views of:
  (a) anyone named by the person as someone to be consulted on the matter in question or on matters of that kind;
  (b) anyone engaged in caring for the person or interested in his welfare;
  (c) any donee of a lasting power of attorney granted by the person; and
  (d) any deputy appointed by the court, as to what would be in the person's best interests and, in particular, as to the matters dealt with in the previous bullet point.[112,113]
— Must consider, so far as is reasonably ascertainable:
  (a) the person's past and present wishes and feelings (and in particular any relevant written statement made by him when he had capacity);
  (b) the beliefs and values that would be likely to influence his decision if he had capacity; and
  (c) the other factors that he would be likely to consider if he were able to do so.[114]

This last provision, which is section 4(6), raises some crucial and fascinating issues which are highly pertinent to the issue of which principles are being honoured by the Act. They are, however, best illustrated in the context of end-of-life decision-making, which is the subject of the next chapter. Their discussion is deferred to that chapter.

Generally these 'best interests' determinations are made by those responsible for performing or not performing the suggested action. They should take account of all the evidence available to them, and consult with others who may be able to give information as to where the best interests lie.

[109] Mental Capacity Act 2005 s 4(3).
[110] *Ibid* s 4(4).
[111] *Ibid* s 4(5).
[112] *Ibid* s 4(7).
[113] Although this is an intelligently drafted list, it raises many questions which will have to be litigated sooner rather than later: what does 'reasonably ascertainable' mean?; when is it 'practicable and appropriate to consult'? An assessor who has worked his way diligently through the list can then (but only then), take refuge in the provision that 'there is sufficient compliance with [s 4] if [having worked through the list] he reasonably believes that what he does or decides is in the best interests of the person concerned.': s 4(9).
[114] Mental Capacity Act 2005 s 4(6).

It is commonly and wrongly said that the 2005 Act ushered into English law a brand new idea—that of proxy-decision-making. This is wrong: every best interests determination is necessarily an exercise in proxy decision-making.[115] But the Act does erect a new and elaborate proxy scheme of a sort familiar to the Scots.

Under the Act a donor can confer on a donee authority to make decisions about (amongst other things)

> personal welfare or specified matters concerning [the donor's] personal welfare . . . which includes authority to make such decisions in circumstances where [the donor] no longer has capacity.[116]

There are, of course, restrictions on the extent to which a donee can force a donor to undergo an act that the donor resists, or restrict the donor's liberty of movement.[117] These restrictions will quite often be relevant in medico-legal practice. A donee can only do or authorise these things if: (a) he reasonably believes the donee to lack capacity in relation to the matter in question[118]; (b) he reasonably believes that it is necessary to do the act to prevent harm to the donee[119]; and (c) the act is a proportionate response to the likelihood of the donor suffering harm, and to the seriousness of that harm.[120]

A lasting power of attorney which permits decisions about a donor's personal welfare is subject to the provisions of the Act relating to advance refusals of treatment,[121] does not extend to decisions relating to circumstances other than those where the donor lacks capacity (or the donee reasonably believes that he does),[122] but does extend to

> giving or refusing consent to the carrying out or continuation of a treatment by a person providing healthcare for [the donor].[123]

An instrument creating a lasting power of attorney relating to personal welfare matters cannot authorise impliedly the giving or refusing of consent to the carrying out or continuation of life-sustaining treatment. This can only be done expressly.[124]

The court has power to appoint a 'deputy' to make decisions on behalf of a person.[125] Any decision by a court about what is in a person's best interests trumps

---

[115] Also proxy decision-making is permitted under the Medicines for Human Use (Clinical Trials) Regulations 2004 SI 2004/1031, which came into force in the UK in May 2004. The Regulations permit proxy consent to the participation of incompetent adults in medical research. An early report of the way these Regulations worked in practice suggested that the decisions of the proxies did not necessarily reflect those of the patients themselves: see Mason S, Barrow H, Phillips A *et al* (2006) 'Brief Report on the Experience of Using Proxy Consent for Incapacitated Adults' 32 *Journal of Medical Ethics* 61–2.

[116] Mental Capacity Act 2005 s 9(1).

[117] *Ibid* s 11.

[118] *Ibid* s 11(2).

[119] *Ibid* s 11(3).

[120] *Ibid* s 11(4).

[121] *Ibid* s 11(7)(b). The advance refusal provisions are ss 24, 25 and 26, and are discussed in ch 5.

[122] *Ibid* s 11(7)(a).

[123] *Ibid* s 11(7)(c).

[124] *Ibid* s 11(8).

[125] *Ibid* s 16.

a decision by a deputy.[126] A court appointed deputy can extend to 'giving or refusing consent to the carrying out or continuation of a treatment by a person providing health care'[127] and to 'giving a direction that a person responsible for ... health care allow a different person to take over that responsibility.'[128] Similar restrictions apply to the exercise of a deputy's power as apply to a donee under a lasting power of attorney.[129] A deputy 'may not refuse consent to the carrying out or continuation of life-sustaining treatment.'[130]

The Act does nothing to change the law. It is truly a consolidating Act. But, like much consolidating legislation, the facts of its enactment and the associated scrutiny have succeeded in raising legal awareness of some ideas that have long been present in the common law, but have been occluded beneath a mass of case-specific detail.

Before looking in general at the principles behind the Act it is necessary to look at one important element in the cases. That is the relevance of the *Bolam* test to the ascertainment of best interests.

The starting point is the decision of the House of Lords in *Re F (Mental Patient: Sterilisation)*.[130]

The issue at stake there was how one decides whether or not it is in the best interests of a incapacitated patient to undergo sterilisation. Lord Goff said this:

> [T]he doctor has to act in the best interests of the assisted person. In the case of routine treatment of mentally disordered persons, there should be little difficulty applying this principle. In the case of more serious treatment, I recognise that its application may create problems for the medical profession; however, in making decisions about treatment, the doctor must act in accordance with a responsible and competent body of relevant professional opinion, on the principles set down in *Bolam v Friern Hospital Management Committee* [1957] 1 WLR 582. . . . Mr Munby . . . [deployed] the argument that, in the absence of any *parens patriae* jurisdiction, sterilisation of an adult woman of unsound mind, who by reason of her mental incapacity is unable to consent, can never be lawful. He founded his submission upon a right of reproductive autonomy or right to control one's own reproduction, which necessarily involves the right not to be sterilised involuntarily.[132]

That impassioned plea on behalf of reproductive autonomy failed. The *Bolam* test was imported into the law of medical consent, to cheers of relief from doctors and howls of disbelief from almost everyone else.

Re F left some important questions unanswered. What was the role of the court? Was it simply to satisfy itself that the clinicians concerned had assessed best interests in a way that would be endorsed by a responsible body of clinicians? What if

---

126 Mental Capacity Act 2005 s 16(4).
127 *Ibid* s 17(1)(d).
128 *Ibid* s 17(1)(e).
129 See generally *Ibid* s 20.
130 *Ibid* s 20(5).
131 [1990] 2 AC 1.
132 *Ibid* 78. See too *Ibid* 52 (Lord Bridge), 66–8 (Lord Brandon) and 69 (Lord Griffiths). See also *Airedale NHS Trust v Bland* [1993] AC 789, 884 (Lord Browne-Wilkinson).

there were conflicting views, each representing a responsible body of opinion? Should the operation be done or not? Re F offered no way out of that impasse.

It took the pragmatism of *Re S (Sterilisation: Patient's Best Interests)*[133] to show the way.

> I would suggest that the starting point of any medical decision would be the principles enunciated in the *Bolam* test, and that a doctor ought not to make any decision about a patient that does not fall within the broad spectrum of the *Bolam* test. The duty to act in accordance with responsible and competent professional opinion may give the doctor more than one option since there may well be more than one acceptable medical opinion. When the doctor moves on to consider the best interests of the patient he/she has to choose the best option, often from a range of options. As Mr Munby has pointed out, the best interests test ought, logically, to give only one answer.
>
> In these difficult cases where the medical profession seeks a declaration as to lawfulness of the proposed treatment, the judge, not the doctor, has the duty to decide whether such treatment is in the best interests of the patient. The judicial decision ought to provide the best answer, not a range of alternative answers. There may, of course, be situations where the answer may not be obvious and alternatives may have to be tried. It is still at any point the best option of that moment which should be chosen.[134]

The Court of Appeal in *Re S* was as near to irreverent dismissal of a ruling decision of the House of Lords as the Court of Appeal ever gets. Here is Thorpe LJ, in anarchic mood:

> The *Bolam* test was, of course, developed in order to enable courts to determine the boundaries of medical responsibility for treatment that has gone wrong, and usually disastrously wrong. So at first blush it would seem an unlikely import in determining the best interests of an adult too disabled to decide for him or herself. . . . I would therefore accept Mr Munby's submission that in determining the welfare of the patient, the *Bolam* test is applied only at the outset to ensure that the treatment proposed is recognised as proper by a responsible body of medical opinion skilled in delivering that particular treatment. That may be a necessary check in an exercise where it would be impossible to be over-scrupulous. But I find it hard to imagine in practice a disputed trial before a judge of the division in which a responsible party proposed for an incompetent patient a treatment that did not satisfy the *Bolam* test. In practice, the dispute will generally require the court to choose between two or more treatments both or all of which comfortably pass the *Bolam* test.[135]

Practically, therefore, the evaluation of best interests is akin to the sort of welfare appraisal that is the bread and butter of the Family Division.[136] *Re F* has been quietly sidelined as a decision that could only have been made by judges a long way from the coal face.

So *Bolam* itself has been nudged into the background. Both autonomy and common sense are happy about this. *Bolam* only ever entered the picture to calm down

[133] [2000] 2 FLR 389.
[134] *Ibid* 400 (Butler-Sloss P).
[135] *Ibid* 402–3.
[136] See *Ibid* 402 (Thorpe LJ), and *Re A (Male Sterilisation)* [2000] 1 FLR 549.

doctors and their insurers, and because of a realisation that medicine (and there-fore the assessment of best interests), is not an exact, mathematical business. Once *Bolam* has ensured that doctors making best interests determinations can sleep at night, it has done its job. It must surely give way to the notion that best interests are: (a) theoretically objectively ascertainable; and (b) as intrinsic to the patient (and extrinsic to the doctor) as the colour of the patient's eyes. Autonomy screams 'paternalism' at *Bolam*, and the scream is just. That is not to say that the doctor has no legitimate role in decisions about treatment and the withdrawal of treatment—far from it: but the doctor's role in the ascertainment of best interests is akin to looking at and noting down the eye colour rather than to doing anything that requires the exercise of clinical judgment. That is the theory, and it is vital to the proper relationship of doctor to incompetent patient that this theoretical under-standing is maintained. Of course on the ward it is all much more messy than this. *Bolam* mops up the mess.

With the possible exception of the reference to advance directives (which we deal with later) there can be no principled objection to the best interests criteria in sec-tion 4 of the 2005 Act. They attempt bravely to grope towards a humane, respectful decision about treatment, exhorting the decision-maker to involve the incapacitate patient as much as possible, and to take into account all the relevant information from whatever source. The point for our purposes is that autonomy cannot lay sole claim to these principles. It can truly claim to have supplied much of the language in which the Act expresses the need to let the patient make the decision insofar as possible,[137] but that is not at all the same thing as establishing sole authorship. Any and all of our competing principles would have drafted identical legislation.

We ought at this stage to grapple with an objection that autonomy can make. It could say that the other principles—beneficence, non-maleficence and so on—are hopeless by themselves, because they do not prescribe the content of any moral duty. It is all very well saying: 'Do good', or 'Do no harm', autonomy would go on. But what is meant by that? Only autonomy is bold enough (the submission would go) to say that the good consists in allowing and facilitating free choice. In the case of incapacitated patients it has been asserted that beneficence and non-maleficence would produce the same result as autonomy. While autonomy will of course be gratified by that conclusion, autonomy would no doubt contend that beneficence and non-maleficence by themselves can force no conclusion at all: in agreeing with autonomy's conclusion they are wholly parasitic on autonomy. Not only are they parroting autonomy's words, they are relying totally on autonomy for the very principles that decree their conclusion.

The objection has a superficial attraction. In one form or another it appears whenever autonomy makes a bid for the ethical Presidency. Both the attraction and the error lie in its simplicity. Autonomy is assuming that 'goodness' itself (for instance) needs and can have a one-line definition. It is very quick to supply that definition. Beneficence (for example) acknowledges its dependence on other

---

[137] Notably in ss 4(3) and 4(4).

principles: it is not sufficiently explicit by itself. Hence its catholicity. It is naive and unfair to call that catholicity ethical inadequacy. Beneficence and non-maleficence are far more useful than autonomy precisely because they act as convenors. They gather many delegates round the table before listening and adjudicating. Listening to many points of view before one makes up one's mind is not at all the same thing as moral destitution. Beneficence and non-maleficence have distinct moral content, but it is moral content derived from a survey and an evaluation of many sources, including autonomy.

Any attempt by autonomy to rule in the arena of incompetent patients is of course perverse. By definition incompetent patients have truncated autonomy.[138] With the important exception of the issue of advance directives,[139] autonomy has little to say about incompetent patients, and should have the humility to back off and leave the discussion to others.

Children

Autonomy flounders, too, when it comes to the question of the treatment of and withdrawal of treatment from children.[140] A child in English law is someone under the age of 18. Assuming that one is not demonstrably incompetent, on one's 18th birthday one is magically invested by the English law with the power to consent to and to refuse all treatment—even life-saving treatment. One moves from a realm of partial dependence on the judgment of others to a realm of almost complete autonomy.[141]

Up until the 18th birthday the position is fairly complex and, at first blush, anomalous. The notion of *Gillick* competency is important. It has been discussed

---

[138] They still have desires, though, and often the ability to act on them, as we noted in discussing the position of incompetent patients having sexual intercourse with each other.

[139] Discussed in detail in ch 11.

[140] Although non-*Gillick*-competent children are legally incapacitate, the Mental Capacity Act 2005 does not apply to them.

[141] See Anderson P (1990) *Choosing For Children: Parents' Consent To Surgery* (Oxford, OUP); Alderson P, Hawthorne J and Killen M (2005) 'The Participation Rights of Premature Babies' 13 *International Journal of Children's' Rights*, 31–50; Anderson P (2007) 'Competent Children? Minors' Consent to Health Care Treatment and Research' 65 *Social Science and Medicine* 2272–83; Shenoy S, Archdeacon C, Kotecha S and Elias-Jones A (2003) 'Current Practice for Obtaining Consent in UK Neonatal Units' 188 *Bulletin of Medical Ethics* 17–19; Nicholson R (1986) *Medical Research with Children: Ethics, Law and Practice* (Oxford, OUP); British Medical Association (2001) *Consent, Rights And Choices In Healthcare For Children And Young People* (London, BMA); Royal College of Paediatrics and Child Health (2000) 'Guidelines For The Ethical Conduct of Medical Research Involving Children' 82 *Archives of Disease in Childhood* 117–82; Burke TM, Abramovitch R, Zlotkin S (2005) 'Children's Understanding Of The Risks And Benefits Associated With Research' 31 *Journal of Medical Ethics* 715–20. Street K, Ashcroft R, Henderson J *et al* (2000) 'The Decision-Making Process Regarding the Withdrawal or Withholding of Potential Life-Saving Treatments in a Children's Hospital' 26 *Journal of Medical Ethics* 346–52. See also General Medical Council (2007) *0–18 Years: Guidance for all Doctors* <http://www.gmc-uk.org/guidance/ethical_guidance/children_guidance.contents.asp> accessed 25 Oct 2008.

earlier in the context of the *Axon* case.[142] The expression comes from *Gillick v West Norfolk and Wisbech Area Health Authority*[143] The facts of the case are well known and in any event do not matter for present purposes. At the heart of the decision is the notion that the competence of a child to consent to treatment should not rest on some artificial legal presumption—for example that a person becomes capable of consenting for all purposes at the age of 14—but instead that a child should be able to consent to treatment when she 'achieves a sufficient understanding and intelligence to enable . . . her to understand fully what is proposed.'[144] This is a tall order: has anyone ever understood anything fully? In practice what is meant by complete understanding is a sufficient understanding (sufficiency as determined, ultimately, by the court[145]) of the risks and benefits of treatment and non-treatment.[146]

Consent to treatment can validly be obtained from a *Gillick* competent child of any age, or a 16 or 17 year old, or from a person with parental responsibility, or from the court.

The specific reference to 16 and 17 year olds is a consequence of section 8 of the Family Law Reform Act 1969. This provides that:

(1) The consent of a minor who has attained the age of 16 years to any surgical, medical or dental treatment which, in the absence of consent, would constitute a trespass to his person, shall be as effective as it would be if he were of full age; and where a minor has by virtue of this section given an effective consent to any treatment it shall not be necessary to obtain any consent for it from his parent or guardian.

(2) In this section 'surgical, medical or dental treatment' includes any procedure undertaken for the purposes of diagnosis, and this section applies to any procedure (including, in particular, the administration of an anaesthetic) which is ancillary to any treatment as it applies to that treatment).

(3) Nothing in this section shall be construed as making ineffective any consent which would have been effective if this section had not been enacted.

Note that this does not apply to refusals of treatment.[147] Where a 16 or 17 year old (or of course anyone under the age of 16) refuses treatment, that refusal can be trumped by anyone with parental responsibility, or by the court. The court can override the decision of someone with parental responsibility.

Why this distinction between consent to treatment and refusal of treatment? It grafts into the law a presumption in favour of treatment, and accordingly a presumption that the doctors know best. If the child or her parents want what the doctor proposes, there is no problem. If the child or her parents do not want what the doctor proposes, the court can (and is likely to) say that the doctors should

---

[142] *R (Axon) v Secretary of State for Health* [2006] QB 539, above.

[143] [1986] 1 AC 112.

[144] *Ibid* 185 (Lord Scarman).

[145] For the criteria that the court will apply, see *Re MB (an adult: medical treatment)* [1997] 2 FLR 426.

[146] See Lord Donaldson MR in *Re R (a Minor) (Wardship: Medical Treatment)* [1991] 4 All ER 177, at 187: see too Mental Capacity Act 2005 s 3(4).

[147] Confirmed in *W (A Minor) (Medical Treatment: Court's Jurisdiction)* [1993] Fam 64.

have their way. The test to be applied in deciding whether treatment should or should not go ahead is of course the 'best interests' test. The law is cautiously, but appropriately paternalistic. The child's view of where its best interests lie should of course be ascertained, and the older the child is, the greater the weight that they will have, but best interests, say the courts, are an objective matter: the child's views are pertinent but certainly not determinative. A good working guide for judges engaged in ascertaining best interests in child treatment cases was given by Balcombe LJ in *Re W (A Minor) (Medical Treatment: Court's Jurisdiction)*[148]:

> Since Parliament has not conferred complete autonomy on a 16 year old in the field of medical treatment, there is no overriding limitation to preclude the exercise by the court of its inherent jurisdiction and the matter becomes one for the exercise by the court of its discretion. Nevertheless, the discretion is not to be exercised in a moral vacuum. Undoubtedly, the philosophy . . . is that, as children approach the age of majority, they are increasingly able to take their own decisions concerning their medical treatment. In logic there can be no difference between an ability to consent to treatment and an ability to refuse treatment . . . Accordingly the older the child concerned the greater the weight the court should give to its wishes, certainly in the field of medical treatment. In a sense this is merely one aspect of the application of the test that the welfare of the child is the paramount consideration. It will normally be in the best interests of a child of sufficient age and understanding to make an informed decision that the court should respect its integrity on such a personal matter as medical treatment, all the more so if that treatment is invasive. In my judgment, therefore, the court exercising the inherent jurisdiction in relation to a 16 or 17 year old child who is not mentally incompetent will, as a matter of course, ascertain the wishes of the child and will approach its decision with a strong predilection to give effect to the child's wishes. . . . Nevertheless, if the court's powers are to be meaningful, there must come a point at which the court, while not disregarding the child's wishes, can override them in the child's own best interests, objectively considered. Clearly such a point will have come if the child is seeking to refuse treatment in circumstances which will in all probability lead to the death of the child or to severe permanent injury.

Philosophers will want to take violent issue with Balcombe LJ's assertion that it is Parliament that confers autonomy. Parliament and many lawyers, including myself, will want to take violent issue with his assertion that 'in logic there can be no difference between an ability to consent to treatment and an ability to refuse treatment.' But if he is right on this last point, the law is definitively and defiantly illogical.

A good example of the court using its trumping power is *Re M (Child: Refusal of Medical Treatment)*,[149] where the court authorised a heart transplant in a 15½ year old child who refused her consent. Probably in most such cases the child will look back gratefully on the court's decision.

Parental decisions about their children's treatment are, again, important considerations, but will give way to the court's determination of where the best interests of the child lie. Francis and Johnston observe that

[148] [1993] Fam 64, 88.
[149] [1999] FCR 577.

there may be a form of rebuttable presumption that the parents' views should be respected, particularly when their rights to a family life under Article 8 of the European Convention on Human Rights are taken into account.[150]

The presumption is often rebutted—typically in Jehovah's Witness and similar cases. Judges are slow to allow parents to sacrifice their children on the altar of their own religious principles.[151]

There are rare occasions when, although the court decides that treatment would be in the child's best interests, the parental refusal of consent may persuade the court that the treatment should not go ahead. This is likely to be on purely practical grounds, where the parental attitude means that the child will not get the support for the treatment or its aftermath which is necessary to ensure that the treatment is effective,[152] or possibly where the proposed intervention, although objectively in the child's medical best interests, is only marginally so.[153]

The Strasbourg jurisprudence has not changed the way the English courts view these questions. Parents undoubtedly have an Article 8 right to be involved in decisions about the treatment of their children, although those rights will diminish as the child gets older.[154] Article 9 similarly comes into play where religious objections to treatment are raised.[155] But both Articles have crucial caveats: the basic right protected in the first part of each Article is subject to wider societal considerations: in particular it can be interfered with insofar as necessary 'for the protection of health or morals, or for the protection of the rights and freedoms of others.' The 'others' relevant in this equation are primarily the child patients themselves, as well as, arguably, other child patients in similar situations whose treatment decisions may be affected by the judicial decision in question.

What principles are at play in the law relating to consent to treatment and non-treatment by and on behalf of children? Reading the judgments it is easy to see, and be dazzled by, all the talk about autonomy. At one level the whole ratio of *Gillick* is that autonomy should rule the roost if it can safely do so. But this is hardly the

[150] Francis R and Johnston C (2001) *Medical Treatment: Decisions and the Law* (London, Butterworths) 40–41.
[151] Eg, *Re E (A Minor)* [1993] 1 FLR 386. Similar attitudes hold in other jurisdictions. Thus, eg, in *Prince v Massachusetts* (1944) 321 US Reports 158 the court said: 'Parents may be free to become martyrs themselves, but it does not follow that they are free in identical circumstances to make martyrs of their children before they have reached the age of full and legal discretion when they can make choices for themselves.'
[152] See, eg, *Re T (A Minor) (Wardship: Medical Treatment)* [1997] 1 WLR 242. In Jehovah's Witness-type cases the effect of otherwise beneficial treatment on the child might be exclusion from the community. In such cases it may be concluded that the treatment is not in the child's overall best interests.
[153] See Mercurio MR (2007) 'Parental Refusal of Transfusion on Religious Grounds: An Exception to the Standard Approach' 2 *Clinical Ethics* 146–8.
[154] See the *Axon* case, above.
[155] Art 9 of the ECHR provides: '(1) Everyone has the right to freedom of thought, conscience and religion; this right includes freedom to change his religion or belief and freedom, either alone or in community with others and in public or in private, to manifest his religion or belief, in worship, teaching, practice and observance. (2) Freedom to manifest one's religion or beliefs shall be subject only to such limitations as are prescribed by law and are necessary in a democratic society in the interests of public safety, for the protection of public order, health or morals, or for the protection of the rights and freedoms of others.'

real rule. The position is that children can autonomously agree to treatment which it has already been decided is good for them: that is hardly autonomy. They cannot refuse treatment which it has been decided is good for them: that is the antithesis of autonomy. As has already been pointed out in the discussion of *Axon*,[156] the tone of the guidelines for parental involvement laid down by *Gillick* is stoutly paternalistic.

Kant can help us to see more clearly what is going on here. The law, on its face, says that children in some situations are truly free. But freedom consists in compliance with the universal law. The universal law in the area of treatment decision-making decrees that the doctors (whom the court will almost always endorse) have rightly assessed the child's best interests in coming to the conclusion that treatment should be carried out. If the child does not agree with the doctors' conclusion it is not free, and the principle of personal autonomy is accordingly not affronted if the child is compelled to have the treatment. If that is a victory for autonomy, it is the hollowest of all conceivable victories.

The truth is that autonomy does not rule in this arena, and it is right that it does not. The children of Jehovah's Witnesses should not be allowed to bleed to death because they or their parents think that they should. Even if such a child could be said to have come to her decision autonomously it would still be wrong to allow her decision to prevail. Using autonomy's own criteria many of the treatment decisions made by children and subsequently overridden by the courts are strictly autonomous. It is still right that they are overridden. That is because autonomy's perspective is too narrow. Autonomy makes a judgment at time X based on the information then available. The law sees the broader picture: it bases its judgment on what it knows about how human beings change over time and what the general criteria for human happiness are, as well as on its knowledge of and respect for the individual preferences and situation of the patient. When the law trumps a child's decision, it is wisdom trumping impulse. Wisdom, as we have seen, is catholic in her choice of counsellors. In the topic that we look at in Chapter 11—end-of-life decision-making—she needs all the help she can get.

---

[156] Above.

9

Litigation, Rights and Duties

T HE LAW OF clinical negligence may seem to have little to do with autonomy. But there are some important connections.
    Autonomy rightly insists on the right to litigate, and is opposed to the
sort of blanket immunities from suit, generally based on public policy, that have
been such an important part of the English law of tort. But it is justice, rather than
autonomy, that heads the campaign for freedom to litigate about anything. It was
considerations of justice, under Article 6 of the ECHR, that compelled the
European Court of Human Rights to frown on blanket immunities[1] and made
the modern English law of negligence more elastic and more open to new causes
of action than it has been at any time since the early Middle Ages.

Issues of autonomy often feature in the course of clinical negligence claims—
most notably in claims based on *Sidaway*-type allegations that a procedure has
been done without adequate counselling having been given and without appropriate consent having been taken. Those issues are dealt with in detail in the chapter on consent.

But autonomy's most deep seated interest in the business of litigation is in the
form in which claims are expressed. It likes the idea of rights. It dislikes the idea of
duties except as servants of rights.

The notion of duty has been at the root of the law of tort. 'Who is my neighbour?' Lord Atkin famously asked.[2] The purpose of asking the question was to
identify the person to whom a duty was owed. It is still an important question.
There is still a lot of live law about the limits of the class of persons to whom a professional relationship is owed, and about the nature of that relationship. But while
that law still needs to be read, the focus of the analysis of cases in tort has shifted
dramatically. Previously the claimant came into court and said: 'The defendant
owes me a duty. He has breached it. I have suffered loss. I want compensation.'
Now the claimant can say instead: 'I have a right. It has been violated by you. You

---

[1] See *Osman v UK* [1999] 1 FLR 193, [151]: 'The Court would observe that the application of the
rule in this manner without further inquiry into the existence of competing public interest considerations only serves to confer a blanket immunity on the police for their acts and omissions during the
investigation and suppression of crime and amounts to an unjustifiable restriction on an applicant's
right to have a determination on the merits of his or her claim against the police in deserving cases.';
cp *Z v United Kingdom* [2001] 2 FLR 246, *TP and KM v United Kingdom* [2001] 2 FLR 289, and *Barrett
v Enfield London Borough Council* [1999] 3 All ER 193.
[2] *Donoghue (or McAlister) v Stevenson* [1932] AC 562.

should not have violated it. I may or may not have suffered real loss, but I want compensation.'[3]

The important thing to note here is that the new analysis does not start with a neighbour relationship such as a doctor-patient relationship. Relationship may in fact be an element later down the road (for example, in determining whether or not the defendant should not have violated the right)—but it is not foundational. Human rights claims start by an individual saying: 'my territorial waters have been invaded'. That presupposes a view of individuals as islands, which is precisely the view that autonomy has.

That, at any rate, is the theory. It looks like a complete takeover by autonomy. But as we have repeatedly seen, this is not how things really work. The formulation above overstates things in several ways. The European Convention on Human Rights can only be invoked as against public authorities—out-pouchings of the State. Most importantly, in clinical negligence practice in the UK, this includes NHS bodies. And of course autonomy, so excited by the promises of the first part of many of the Articles under the Convention, is frequently frustrated by the caveats in the second.[4] In most workaday clinical negligence practice the 'old' analysis still prevails, and the requirement to prove 'real' loss is still an important one in practice. The House of Lords has recently emphasised that the European Convention on Human Rights is not a tort statute,[5] but the mere fact of a violation can itself ground a claim.

With the keen eye of philosophical faith one can see autonomy and other principles at work in the law relating to clinical negligence claims, but the outlines are misty and the laws they have generated are sufficiently old and sufficiently certain to render more or less irrelevant in daily forensic combat the principles that birthed them. One obvious example is the law of limitation, which balances the autonomous right of a litigant to recover compensation for a loss against the defendant's autonomous right to be able to sleep at night after the expiry of the limitation period, and the wider societal interests in certainty and finality in litigation. If one is trying to score points, which of course this book is, one might make the rather cheap and obvious point that this is yet another example of autonomy failing to get the upper hand, despite all the rhetoric with which it promotes itself.

We have seen already, in the context of reproductive rights, that there are limits to the healthcare treatment that one can demand. And in fact the real situation is that one cannot insist on an individual doctor doing anything whatever. So far as the law of tort is concerned a doctor can choose whether or not to enter into a doctor-patient relationship with any particular patient. The only apparent exception to that is not a true exception at all. It is the case of a general practitioner who

---

[3] See *Chester v Afshar* [2005] 1 AC 134, in which the normal rules of causation in tort were relaxed in order to compensate a claimant whose right to be fully informed had been violated.

[4] The best example, and the one most commonly relevant in medical law, is Art 8. Art 8(1) is drafted by autonomy: Art 8(2) has many other draftsman, and Art 8(2) often prevails.

[5] *R (Greenfield) v Secretary of State for the Home Department* [2005] 1 WLR 673.

comes upon a person in his geographical practice area who needs medical attention. The GP's contract with the health authority or Primary Care Trust requires the GP to give the required medical attention: the law of tort does not. The English law of tort compels no-one to be a Good Samaritan. The situation is no different within an NHS hospital. Patients there have a right to expect to be given the care reasonably to be expected of competent doctors, but the duty to provide it is a duty of the NHS Trust concerned. The individual clinician has a contractual duty to his employer—the Trust—to provide the medical services for which he is paid, but if he decides for good, bad or no reason not to treat a patient, then the law of tort will have nothing to say to him. The Trust will, of course, and so will the General Medical Council; but the patient's tortious redress is against the Trust.

Autonomy should smile on this result in this case.[6] In a culture that has a healthcare system which is obliged to provide free and reasonable care to all, the autonomy interests of the patient are (at least theoretically) unaffected by such a rule, and the autonomy interests of the doctor are protected. The operation of the principle is well illustrated by the Miss B case[7]—although that concerned clinicians' unwillingness to stop treatment, rather than an unwillingness to treat. Miss B wanted her life-sustaining ventilation to be stopped. Her treating clinicians were (entirely appropriately) emotionally involved with her case, and did not feel that they could help in bringing about her death. The court decided that they did not have to do so, but that the treating NHS Trust[8] should find other clinicians willing to stop the treatment and give the ancillary palliative care.

Appearing to rely mainly on the principle of clinician autonomy,[9] the courts have repeatedly refused to order doctors to do things.[10] That is the judicial orthodoxy. In *Re R (A Minor) (Wardship: Consent to Treatment)*[11] Lord Donaldson MR said: 'No doctor can be required to treat a child, whether by the court in the exercise of its wardship jurisdiction, by the parents, by the child or anyone else. The decision whether to treat is dependent upon an exercise of his own professional

---

[6] Although one of autonomy's principal spokesmen, Julian Savulescu, would not: see ch 3, above.
[7] *B v An NHS Trust* [2002] 2 All ER 449; see ch 8, above.
[8] Or possibly the conscientiously objecting doctors themselves: this would accord with the General Medical Council's new rules on conscientious objection, discussed in ch 3 above. In *R (Burke) v General Medical Council* [2005] QB 424, [191], Munby J, at first instance, said: 'An NHS Trust or other health authority, being a public authority for the purposes of the Human Rights Act 1998, can be required to arrange for the treatment to be commenced or continued by other doctors willing to do so where this is necessary in order to prevent what would otherwise be a breach of the patient's Convention rights.'
[9] There are other practical reasons too. They were identified by Lord Donaldson MR, in *Re J (A Minor) (Child in care: medical treatment)* [1992] 3 WLR 507, at 517, and Munby J in *Burke*, above, at [180]–[194]: (a) the difficulty of specifying with sufficient precision just what the Trust would be required to do; (b) even if a judge could tell the Trust what to do, since the courts would not grant a mandatory injunction to enforce a contract of employment the Trust's ability to make a similarly enforceable demand on its staff would be highly doubtful; and (c) an order might fail properly to take into account the availability of the necessary human, financial and other resources.
[10] Another good example is in *An NHS Trust v MB and Mr and Mrs B* [2006] EWHC 507 (Fam), [90] where Holman J expressed the view that it was in the best interests of a child with spinal muscular atrophy to continue being ventilated, but noted that: 'Although that is my opinion, I cannot and do not make any order or declaration to that effect. I merely state it.'
[11] [1992] Fam 11, 26.

judgment, subject only to the threshold requirement that, save in exceptional cases usually of emergency, he has the consent of somebody who has authority to give that consent.' In *Re J*, both Balcombe LJ and Leggatt LJ agreed:

> The court is not, or certainly should not be, in the habit of making orders unless it is prepared to enforce them. If the court orders a doctor to treat a child in a manner contrary to his or her clinical judgment it would place a conscientious doctor in an impossible position. To perform the court's order could require the doctor to act in a manner which he or she genuinely believed not to be in the patient's best interests: to fail to treat the child as ordered would amount to a contempt of court.[12]

> [T]he essential distinction remains: whether the court should positively order treatment to be given or not to be given, or whether it should do no more than consider whether or not to authorise it, where authority is needed. I can myself envisage no circumstances in which it would be right directly or indirectly to require a doctor to treat a patient in a way that was contrary to the doctor's professional judgment and duty to the patient. A court can give or withhold consent or authority such as might be given or withheld by a patient or a child's parent. But no reported case has been cited to the court in which any judge in any jurisdiction has ever purported to order a doctor to treat a patient in a particular way contrary to the doctor's will until Waite J made his order in the present case.[13,14]

Although the language of medical self-determination is used as a shorthand by the courts in coming to such conclusions, when they are forced to expound the reasons for it is plain that other principles are at work. Those principles have been explored in chapter 2.

We live in a world of infinite suffering and limited healthcare resources. Several reasons why patients should not be allowed to stamp their feet and demand whatever they want have already been discussed. They have all been located in principle. But there is a brutally practical reason too: there is not the money in a state-financed healthcare system for all the medical and surgical intervention that everyone will want. One man's dialysis is another man's denial of dialysis.

How does one choose whom to treat?[15] It is a massive debate, but some of it touches on our issues.[16] There is an understandable desire to use objectively verifiable criteria in healthcare resource allocation. One of the most popular methods

[12] [1992] 3 WLR 507, 519 (Balcombe LJ).

[13] *Ibid* 520 (Leggatt LJ).

[14] See too *Brophy v New England Sinai Hospital* NE 2d 626, at 639 (Mass 1986): The Massachusetts Supreme Judicial Court stated that there 'is nothing in the law which would justify compelling medical professionals . . . to take active measures which are contrary to their view of their ethical duty towards their patients.' There have been occasional examples of US courts not following this principle, however. See, eg, *In the Matter of Baby K* 832 F Supp 1022 (ED Va 1993), where the court ordered a hospital to continue the ventilation of an anencephalic child, although the hospital thought that this was not clinically indicated. Cited in Price D, Samanta J, Harvey B and Healey P (2007) 'Clinician Autonomy: Doctor's Orders?' 2 *Clinical Ethics* 124–8.

[15] For an outline of the law, see Foster C (2007) 'Simple Rationality? The Law of Healthcare Resource Allocation in England' 33 *Journal of Medical Ethics* 404–7.

[16] For instance: To what extent is it legitimate for a clinician's own beliefs to impinge on resource allocation decisions? See ch 3 above, and Polder JJ and Jochemsen H (2000) *Professional Autonomy in the Healthcare System* 21(5) *Medicine and Bioethics* 477–91.

is the rampantly utilitarian one of calculating how many Quality Adjusted Life Years (QALYs) one can buy per dollar. The 'Year' part is unexceptional. The problem of course comes in the assessment of 'Quality'. In practice autonomy tends to dictate the criteria by which Quality is judged. 'How mobile will he be?' 'Will he be able to look after himself?' 'Will he be able to think as keenly as he did before the operation?', and so on. This is not a criticism: it is merely an observation. Autonomistic language is likely to be prominent in the drafting of any sensible objective criteria. Hopefully, though, other principles will contribute: 'He may not be as sharp as he was, but he appears to enjoy looking at the garden': 'He'll be in a wheelchair, but he'll get a lot of reading done.' 'He'll need a carer, but he's really looking forward to seeing his first grandchild, who is due in the summer.'

Pertinent to this debate is the growing acknowledgment that autonomy needs to be reconnected to social responsibility. Patients' autonomistic demands for the new medication they have heard about on the TV and read about on the internet needs to be put into the context of limited resources. That context is unlikely to have been helpfully explained by the pharmaceutical company sponsoring the advertising. Graber and Tansey comment:

One reason that healthcare reform has failed in the USA is that patients and providers have a strong defensive reaction to solutions that encroach on self-determination. Providers want the freedom to make choices that they believe are in patients' best interests and patients want to make choices without any proscriptions. However, this freedom is financially costly to the healthcare system. A poignant example is the manner in which drug costs continue to rise, in part because of patient demands for medications 'as seen on TV' or in other media . . . .doctors may feel pressure to allow the consumer to drive the decision-making process to maintain what is perceived as good doctor-patient relationships . . . .Even though the doctor-patient relationship and respect for doctor and patient autonomy represent moral goods in themselves, the compelling good of social responsibility, or the principle of justice, may suffer when costly medications are prescribed.[17]

They suggest that patients should sign the following document:

I, as the patient, am requesting that my provider prescribe drug _____ for me. I understand there are less expensive medications that are also effective. I understand that by requesting this more expensive medication I am increasing healthcare costs to others, increasing the cost of insurance, using resources that could be used elsewhere in the healthcare system and may be taking an additional risk to my health as all of the side effects of new drugs may not be known. The reason that I am asking for this medication is _____. I believe that the benefit to me outweighs the potential risks and resultant harms to others.[18]

Autonomy cannot possibly object to such a document. It helps to educate the patient; it helps to increase the patient's autonomy; it may help to conserve

---

[17] Gruber MA and Tansey JF (2005) 'Autonomy, Consent and Limiting Healthcare Costs' 31 *Journal of Medical Ethics* 424–6, 424.
[18] *Ibid* 425.

resources useful in maintaining the autonomy of others. But autonomy would sign it with a scowl. It is a document from the files of beneficence and justice.

Does autonomy approve at all of a state healthcare system? The ultimate self-made man, of whom autonomy is so proud, bridles at the idea. Autonomy is an extreme political conservative, and believes so potently in the good of individual choice and the illegitimacy of the state that it dislikes the idea of the state taking from the citizen who has made good economic choices (and can so afford to pay his own medical insurance premiums) to provide for the citizen who has not. On the other hand, a destitute patient, denied potentially life-saving healthcare because of his poverty, is itself an affront to autonomy. Autonomy recognises that without healthcare the patient is profoundly non-autonomous. It regrets the poor choices that brought the patient to the position where he needs the state, but sometimes the autonomy-recovering and autonomy-preserving power of health-care might triumph over the basic political distaste for free healthcare. In resolving dilemmas like this, which autonomy has created itself, autonomy really does the help of our other principles.[19]

[19] Rice T (2001) 'Individual Autonomy and State Involvement in Health Care' 27(4) *Journal of Medical Ethics* 240–44; Cohen J (2000) 'Patient Autonomy and Social Fairness' 9(3) *Cambridge Quarterly of Healthcare Ethics* 391–9; Menzel PT (1992) Equity, Autonomy and Efficiency: What Healthcare System Should We Have? 17(1) *Journal of Medicine and Philosophy* 33–57.

10

Medical Research on Humans

ALTHOUGH MEDICAL RESEARCH on humans poses many difficult and important ethical questions, they are not questions which are of much interest to this chapter.[1] That is because in relation to the law of the United Kingdom:

(a) in the context of research autonomy reigns supreme (with some caveats to which we will come), and no one who has peered inside Mengele's laboratory can or decently should question that supremacy; and
(b) most of the caveats have already been dealt with in discussing the general law of consent.

The UK law relating to medical research is found in many places. In relation to incompetent adults it is now more or less consolidated in the Mental Capacity Act 2005: the relevant provisions are outlined below. The common law still has a substantial influence,[2] and many of the detailed rules are strewn confusingly around the statute book.[3] But the immediate origin of many of the principles that ground and inspire the domestic law are international instruments.

In 1964 the Declaration of Helsinki was adopted by the World Medical Association. It continues to have a profound effect on the international regulation of research. It has been revised five times since its adoption. The revisions (and particularly the last two, in 1996 and 2000), have been highly controversial and bitterly contested. Although in the original 1964 draft the distinction between 'therapeutic' and 'non-therapeutic' research was said to be fundamental, reference to the distinction was removed completely in 2000, amid howls of protest from many.

Helsinki is woolly but profoundly influential. It has considerable rhetorical (although no technical legal) force when wielded in the courts,[4] and, most importantly, it has informed the codes of professional conduct in many states. In

---

[1] There are accessible accounts of the relevant ethical difficulties in McNeill P (1998) 'Experimentation on Human Beings' in Kuhse H and Singer P (eds) *A Companion to Bioethics* (Oxford, Blackwell) 369–78; and De Castro LD (1998) 'Ethical Issues in Human Experimentation' *Ibid* 379–89.

[2] Eg *R v Brown*, above, in relation to the limits of valid consent to personal injury.

[3] Eg in the Health and Social Care Act 2001, the Human Fertilisation and Embryology Act 1990, and the Medicines for Human Use (Clinical Trials) Regulations 2004 SI 2004/1031 (which gives effect to EC Directive 2001/20/EC).

[4] As it has been on many occasions, particularly in the US; most notably in *Abdullahi v Pfizer Inc* 2002 WL 31082956. For a fuller list of citations and discussion of exactly how US judges have viewed the Helsinki Declaration, see Plomer *Ibid* 5.

England, as we have seen, that is a potent and very direct way to make substantive law.

Helsinki emphasises the need to see research on human subjects as a last resort, the need for the inherent risks to be proportionate to the possible benefit, the need for consent from all competent participants, and the rights of all subjects to withdraw from the project. Most importantly for our purposes, paragraph 5 provides that:

> In medical research on human subjects, considerations related to the well-being of the human subject should take precedence over the interests of science and society.

There is accordingly no room within the Helsinki Declaration for the balancing of societal benefits against personal benefits that we have previously seen in (for instance), the structure of Article 8 of the European Convention on Human Rights.[5]

There was a brave attempt to state international biomedical norms in the Council of Europe's Convention on Human Rights and Biomedicine (CHRB), opened for ratification in Orviedo in 1997. It built on the foundations laid by the Helsinki Declaration as well as many other international instruments.[6] Article 2 of the Convention repeats paragraph 2 of the Helsinki Declaration, asserting:

> The interests and welfare of the human being shall prevail over the sole interest of society or science.

Consent is dealt with in what looks at first blush like considerable detail:

Article 5—General rule

An intervention in the health field may only be carried out after the person concerned has given free and informed consent to it.

This person shall beforehand be given appropriate information as to the purpose and nature of the intervention as well as on its consequences and risks.

The person concerned may freely withdraw consent at any time.

Article 6—Protection of persons not able to consent

Subject to Articles 17 and 20 below, an intervention may only be carried out on a person who does not have the capacity to consent, for his or her direct benefit.

Where, according to law, a minor does not have the capacity to consent to an intervention, the intervention may only be carried out with the authorisation of his or her representative or an authority or a person or body provided for by law.

The opinion of the minor shall be taken into consideration as an increasingly determining factor in proportion to his or her age and degree of maturity.

Where, according to law, an adult does not have the capacity to consent to an intervention because of a mental disability, a disease or for similar reasons, the intervention

---

[5] With the autonomistic demands of Art 8(1) mitigated by the wider societal concerns of Art 8(2).

[6] Notably the Universal Declaration of Human Rights (1948), the European Convention on Human Rights (1950), the European Social Charter (1961), the International Covenant on Civil and Political Rights (1966), the Convention for the Protection of Individuals with regard to Automatic Processing of Personal Data (1981) and the Convention of the Rights of the Child (1989).

may only be carried out with the authorisation of his or her representative or an authority or a person or body provided for by law.

The individual concerned shall as far as possible take part in the authorisation procedure.

The representative, the authority, the person or the body mentioned in paragraphs 2 and 3 above shall be given, under the same conditions, the information referred to in Article 5.

The authorisation referred to in paragraphs 2 and 3 above may be withdrawn at any time in the best interests of the person concerned.

Article 7—Protection of persons who have a mental disorder

Subject to protective conditions prescribed by law, including supervisory, control and appeal procedures, a person who has a mental disorder of a serious nature may be subjected, without his or her consent, to an intervention aimed at treating his or her mental disorder only where, without such treatment, serious harm is likely to result to his or her health.

Article 8—Emergency situation

When because of an emergency situation the appropriate consent cannot be obtained, any medically necessary intervention may be carried out immediately for the benefit of the health of the individual concerned.

Article 9—Previously expressed wishes

The previously expressed wishes relating to a medical intervention by a patient who is not, at the time of the intervention, in a state to express his or her wishes shall be taken into account.

Research itself is the subject of Articles 15, 16, 17 and 18. They provide as follows:

Article 15—General rule

Scientific research in the field of biology and medicine shall be carried out freely, subject to the provisions of this Convention and the other legal provisions ensuring the protection of the human being.

Article 16—Protection of persons undergoing research

Research on a person may only be undertaken if all the following conditions are met:
(i)   there is no alternative of comparable effectiveness to research on humans;
(ii)   the risks which may be incurred by that person are not disproportionate to the potential benefits of the research;
(iii) the research project has been approved by the competent body after independent examination of its scientific merit, including assessment of the importance of the aim of the research, and multidisciplinary review of its ethical acceptability;
(iv)   the persons undergoing research have been informed of their rights and the safeguards prescribed by law for their protection;
(v)   the necessary consent as provided for under Article 5 has been given expressly, specifically and is documented. Such consent may be freely withdrawn at any time.

Article 17—Protection of persons not able to consent to research

Research on a person without the capacity to consent as stipulated in Article 5 may be undertaken only if all the following conditions are met:
(i)   the conditions laid down in Article 16, sub-paragraphs i to iv, are fulfilled;

(ii)   the results of the research have the potential to produce real and direct benefit to his or her health;

(iii)   research of comparable effectiveness cannot be carried out on individuals capable of giving consent;

(iv)   the necessary authorisation provided for under Article 6 has been given specifically and in writing; and

(v)   the person concerned does not object.

Exceptionally and under the protective conditions prescribed by law, where the research has not the potential to produce results of direct benefit to the health of the person concerned, such research may be authorised subject to the conditions laid down in paragraph 1, sub-paragraphs i, iii, iv and v above, and to the following additional conditions:

(i)   the research has the aim of contributing, through significant improvement in the scientific understanding of the individual's condition, disease or disorder, to the ultimate attainment of results capable of conferring benefit to the person concerned or to other persons in the same age category or afflicted with the same disease or disorder or having the same condition;

(ii)   the research entails only minimal risk and minimal burden for the individual concerned.

Article 18—Research on embryos in vitro

Where the law allows research on embryos in vitro, it shall ensure adequate protection of the embryo.

The creation of human embryos for research purposes is prohibited.

The Convention states that most of the rights it details may be restricted by states insofar as prescribed by law and necessary in a democratic society in the interest of public safety, for the prevention of crime, for the protection of public health or for the protection and freedoms of others, but this ability to derogate is specifically excluded for (inter alia, and insofar as relevant to our subject), research on competent and incompetent subjects.[7]

This restriction on derogation sounds impressive, but the definition of 'consent' in Articles 6, 7, 8 and 9 (upon which the Articles specifically dealing with research depend) is so vague that the restriction can be easily circumvented by any half-competent domestic draftsman. More significant than the dangerous malleability of the text, however, (malleability demanded by the need to accommodate many different legal systems), is the fact that despite the liberal drafting a disappointingly small number of states have signed the Convention. The UK is amongst the non-signatories. The Convention is in any event toothless: it contains no right of petition to any court. Any infringement of a Convention right would have to be framed as a breach of the ECHR in order to be justiciable.[8] In practice that is not difficult to do, particularly given the extraordinary elasticity of Article 8 of the ECHR. This makes one wonder, though, if the CHRB serves any purpose at all. The answer is that it does. Although both the CHRB and the Helsinki Declaration

---

[7]   See Art 26: There can be no such restriction placed on Arts 11, 13, 14, 16, 17, 19, 20 or 21.

[8]   As was done, eg, in *Glass v UK* [2004] 1 FLR 1019.

are inevitably drafted loosely, there is no room whatever to read anything anti-autonomistic between their lines. One might want 'consent' to be buttressed with a tighter definition, but the fact that it is not does not begin to dethrone autonomy. Any lawyer seeking to argue that anything akin to Article 8(2) of the ECHR should allow autonomy to take second place would face an impossible battle. Both the CHRB and the Helsinki Declaration are profoundly persuasive, and have infiltrated and influenced UK legislation and national professional codes of conduct.

In relation to research on incompetent adults, the law is now consolidated in the Mental Capacity Act 2005.[9] Section 31 provides, inter alia, that such projects will not be approved by 'the appropriate body' (and accordingly will not be lawful), unless the following requirements are met:

(2) The research must be connected with—

(a) an impairing condition affecting [the proposed patient]; or
(b) its treatment.

(3) 'Impairing condition' means a condition which is (or may be) attributable to, or which causes or contributes to (or may cause or contribute to), the impairment of, or disturbance in the functioning of, the mind or brain.

(4) There must be reasonable grounds for believing that research of comparable effectiveness cannot be carried out if the project has to be confined to, or relate only to, persons who have capacity to consent to taking part in it.

(5) The research must—

(a) have the potential to benefit [the patient] without imposing on P a burden that is disproportionate to the potential benefit to [the patient] or
(b) be intended to provide knowledge of the causes or treatment of, or of the care of persons affected by, the same or a similar condition.

(6) If the research falls within paragraph (b) of subsection (5) but not within paragraph (a), there must be reasonable grounds for believing—

(a) that the risk to [the patient] from taking part in the project is likely to be negligible, and
(b) that anything done to, or in relation to, [the patient] will not—

(i) interfere with [the patient's] freedom of action or privacy in a significant way, or
(ii) be unduly invasive or restrictive.

Section 33 provides, inter alia and insofar as relevant, that:

(2) Nothing may be done to, or in relation to, [the patient] in the course of the research—

(a) to which he appears to object (whether by showing signs of resistance or otherwise) except where what is being done is intended to protect him from harm or to reduce or prevent pain or discomfort, or
(b) which would be contrary to—

(i) an advance decision of his which has effect, or

⁹ There is also specific provision in the Medicines for Human Use (Clinical Trials) Regulations 2004 SI 2004/1031 for clinical trials involving incompetent adults.

(ii) any other form of statement made by him and not subsequently withdrawn, of which [the researcher] is aware.

(3) The interests of the person must be assumed to outweigh those of science and society.

(4) If he indicates (in any way) that he wishes to be withdrawn from the project he must be withdrawn without delay.

All this material will now be familiar. The origins of each clause in the principles of Helsinki and the CHRB are clear. They are rather less clear in the law relating to research on children, but that is mainly because the UK law in that area is itself unclear. The details of that law are not relevant for our purposes: they would obfuscate rather than clarify. It suffices to say that the philosophy of the law, if not its effect, is identical to the philosophy of the law relating to competent and incompetent adults.[10]

The relevant professional advice for UK doctors is the General Medical Council's *Research: The Role and Responsibilities of Doctors*.[11] It emphasises that

research involving people directly or indirectly is vital in improving care for present and future patients and the health of the population as a whole,[12]

and that

doctors involved in research have an ethical duty to show respect for human life and respect people's autonomy. Partnership between participants and the health care team is essential to good research practice and such partnerships are based on trust. You must respect patients' and volunteers' rights to make decisions about their involvement in research. It is essential to listen to and share information with them, respect their privacy and dignity, and treat them politely and considerately at all times.[13]

'Research' is defined very broadly as

any experimental study into the causes, treatment or prevention of ill health and disease in humans, involving people or their tissues or organs or data. It includes toxicity studies, clinical trials, genetic studies, epidemiological research including analyses of medical records, and other collections and analyses of data about health and illness, whether anonymised or not. It covers clinical research which may be therapeutic, that is of potential benefit to patients who participate, and non-therapeutic, where no immediate benefit to those patients or volunteers who participate is expected.[14]

---

[10] See Hunter D and Pierscionek BK (2007) 'Children, Gillick Competency and Consent for Involvement in Research' 33 *Journal of Medical Ethics* 659–62, which criticises the deployment of the notion of *Gillick* competence in most cases of research involving children. Also Medical Research Council (2004) *Medical Research Involving Children* (London, MRC); Nicholson R (1986) *Medical Research with Children: Ethics, Law and Practice* (Oxford, OUP); and Royal College of Paediatrics and Child Health (2000) 'Guidelines for the Ethical Conduct of Medical Research Involving Children' 82 *Archives of Disease in Childhood* 117–82.

[11] General Medical Council, London, February 2002.

[12] *Ibid* para 1.

[13] *Ibid* para 2.

[14] *Ibid* para 3: so following the 2000 re-draft of the Declaration of Helsinki in abolishing the distinction between therapeutic and non-therapeutic research.

It does not apply to clinical audit which involves no experimental study, or to 'innovative therapeutic interventions designed to benefit individual patients'.[15]

It follows Helsinki and the CHRB in requiring researchers to be satisfied that the research is not contrary to their interests, and that, in relation to therapeutic research, the foreseeable risks will not outweigh the potential benefits to the patients. It again emphasises that 'The development of treatments and furthering of knowledge should never take precedence over the patients' best interests'. So far as non-therapeutic research is concerned,

> you must keep the foreseeable risks to participants as low as possible. In addition the potential benefits from the development of treatments and furthering of knowledge must *far* outweigh any such risks.[16]

Recognising that researchers may sometimes lose objectivity in their enthusiasm to break new ground, the GMC stipulates that ethical approval must be obtained from a properly constituted and relevant research ethics committee, and 'you must conduct research in an ethical manner and one that accords with best practice'.[17] Predictably there is heavy emphasis on appropriate consent: the GMC's own consent guidelines, which we have already looked at, are specifically referred to, and some of the principles there are tailored specifically to the research situation.[18] Payment is not prohibited, but payment must not be offered

> at a level which could induce research participants to take risks that they would otherwise not take, or to volunteer more frequently than is advisable or against their better interests or judgment.[19]

The UK ethos, then, is identical to the ethos of Helsinki and the CHRB. It is straightforwardly autonomistic. Your body is your own. Nobody can make you do anything with it by way of research even if that research would benefit mankind massively. It is no different for incompetent adults or children: however medically or socially useful even entirely non-invasive research might be, it cannot be started if there is a whisper of protest, and has to be stopped if the person gives the slightest indication that he or she does not want it to continue.

---

[15] *Ibid* para 4.
[16] *Ibid* para 5. The word 'far' makes the UK test particularly stringent. Para 18 of the Helsinki Declaration simply says that research should only be conducted 'if the importance of the objective outweighs the inherent risks and burdens to the subject', commenting that 'This is especially important where the human subjects are healthy volunteers.' Art 6(2) of the European Protocol to the CHRB provides that in the case of research which does not have the potential to produce results of direct benefit to the subject, it can only be undertaken if it 'entails no more than acceptable risk and acceptable burden.' For discussion of what amounts to acceptable risk in this context, see Hope T and McMillan J (2004) 'Challenge Studies of Human Volunteers: Ethical Issues' 30 *Journal of Medical Ethics* 110.
[17] General Medical Council (2002) *Research: The Role and Responsibilities of Doctors* (London, GMC) para 5. See too Royal College of Physicians (2007) *Guidelines on The Practice Of Ethics Committees in Medical Research With Human Participants*, 4th Edition (London, Royal College of Physicians).
[18] General Medical Council (2002) *Research: The Role and Responsibilities of Doctors* (London, GMC) paras 15–22.
[19] *Ibid* para 14.

It does not follow from this that you can do anything with your body that you want to. We discussed this issue in detail when grappling with *R v Brown*.[20] Some of the damage that might be consensually incurred in the course of medical research might be serious damage that on the face of it falls within the prohibition in *Brown*. Indeed, surely there is a risk (however small) in most medical research, of serious injury. Since medical research is regularly endorsed by the courts there is evidently nothing wrong with accepting the *risk* of such serious injury. But what about the probability or the certainty of such injury? The ratio of *Brown* is elusive, but probably it is something along the lines of the semi-tautology: 'You cannot lawfully accept serious bodily injury if it is incurred in the course of an activity that is not lawful.' And what is not lawful is determined by public policy. In practice what happens is the judges delegate to ethics committees the job of arbiters of public policy. If the ethics committee says that the risk of injury or the injury itself is acceptable, then no court, applying *Brown* is going to say that the doctors conducting the clinical trial are guilty of causing actual or grievous bodily harm. That is because the ethics committee (no doubt without beginning to realise that that was what it was doing), has said that the research is in the same analytic category as boxing or wrestling.

The prohibition on substantial payment is interesting. We meet it again when we deal with the question of organ donation. What does it have to say about the rule of autonomy? One might say that a truly autonomous man should be allowed to sell his body or any of its parts if he wants to. Why should he not? Surely there are echoes of Kant here. The prohibition is hinting at an internal war between the sensual man (who wants the money and the things he can buy with it), and the intellectual man (who may not want his body to be interfered with). The law is concerned with enabling the intellectual man to hold out against the siren voices of the sensual man. The implication is that there is an objectively correct decision to be made, and that can only be made by the intellectual man, acting in obedience to the universal law. Only by resisting the sensual man can the individual be truly free—truly autonomous. By subduing the voice of the sensual man the law is helping freedom: the prohibition is actually helping real autonomy, not hindering it.

It is easy to state the principles. It is fairly easy to apply them in the west. But what seems simple in London is often much more complex in Nairobi. Much of the debate about the scope of the CHRB and the Helsinki Declaration has concerned work by western researchers abroad. Anyone who has read John Le Carre's novel *The Constant Gardener* will have had a taste of the ethical flavour of the debates about conducting clinical trials in the third world. Pharmaceutical companies need to test the efficacy of their drugs. Given the legal and ethical constraints of research in the west (and often the relative infrequency in the west of the target diseases—eg HIV/AIDS), it is often in the interests of such companies to conduct their trials in less tightly regulated (and more highly infected) places. The ethics are not easy. Suppose a destitute Kenyan mother is HIV positive. A western

[20] See ch 8, above.

drug company asks her if she would like to try a drug which might arrest the infection. The potential hazards of the drug are such that the company would never get permission to conduct the trial in the west, and if it did, the potential cost of litigation would be prohibitively colossal. The woman is told that it is believed that there is a good chance that the drug will increase her life span, and that it is believed that there is a low chance of significant side-effects. Notwithstanding the impossibility of obtaining clearance for the trial in the west, both these statements are true. The woman has no money to buy alternative anti- retroviral drugs. If she does not enter the trial, she will certainly die of AIDS. What do ethics say? What does autonomy say? What should the law say?[21]

Autonomy, the Helsinki Declaration and the CHRB are all profoundly uneasy about this. Without the drug the woman will soon be dead, and dead people are not autonomous at all. How should we characterise her choice? Is it really different from any of the choices that any of us make? All of our choices have context: hers is simply more stark and brutal than the ones westerners have to make in most comparable situations. Most, but not all. The approach of death has a way of mutating choices in a way that sounds blasphemous to healthy people who love the language of freedom. It does that in the west too. In *Simms v Simms*[22] an 18 year old boy and a 16 year old girl both suffered from variant CJD—a progressive neurodegenerative disease caused by prions. The disease had robbed them of capacity. There was no recognised cure and no drugs were recognised as being effective at prolonging life. Japanese researchers had experimented with infusion into the cerebral ventricles of a drug called pentosan polysulfate in rodents and dogs infected with scrapie, another disease caused by prions. It appeared to prolong life. This work had been presented at various conferences, but at the time of the determination had not been published in any peer-reviewed journal. It had never been used in this context on human patients. It was classic experimental treatment. Because it involved intraventricular infusion it was necessarily invasive, and would have to be administered under general anaesthesia. There was a 2 per cent risk of infection, and a 5 per cent risk of a cerebral haemorrhage. The judge found that the treatment might not confer any benefit at all. On the other hand 'the chance of improvement is slight but not non-existent'. The most that could be hoped for was some prolongation of an already badly compromised life:

Each patient is entitled under Article 2 of the European Convention to the right to life. Article 8 gives to each patient the right to respect for his family life. Is a prolongation of

---

[21] For a discussion of the ethics of this type of situation see, eg, Angell M (1988) 'Ethical Imperialism? Ethics in International Collaborative Clinical Research' 16 *New England Journal of Medicine* 1081–3; Angell M (1997) 'The Ethics of Clinical Research in the Third World' 337(12) *New England Journal of Medicine* 847–9; Glantz L, Annas G, Grodin M and Mariner W (1998) 'Research in Developing Countries: Taking Benefit Seriously' 28(6) *Hastings Center Report* 38–42, cited by Plomer A (2007) in *The Law and Ethics of Medical Research: International Bioethics and Human Rights* (London, Cavendish) 4; see also Newton SK and Appiah-Poku J (2007) 'Opinions of Researchers Based in the UK on Recruiting Subjects from Developing Countries into Randomized Controlled Trials' 7: 3 *Developing World Bioethics* 149–56.

[22] [2003] 1 All ER 669.

life as it is led worthwhile for [the patients]? The parents of each say emphatically Yes. There is undoubtedly evidence that there is some value to their lives. A reduced enjoyment of life even at quite a low level is to be respected and protected. . . . I consider that even the prospect of a slightly longer life is a benefit worth having for each of these two patients. There is sufficient possibility of unquantifiable benefit for me to find that it would be in their best interests to have the operations and the treatment subject to an assessment of the risks.[23]

The only difference between this situation and that of the Kenyan woman is that the drug company in the hypothetical Kenyan case has a profit motive (it wants to be able to say that it has a properly tested drug), whereas the only motive considered in the *Simms* case was the desire to keep the patients alive. No doubt the Japanese researchers and the treating clinicians, as well as the wider community, were passionately interested too in whether the drug could be used in this way on other patients: it is hard to say that that was illegitimate, but it was not the focus of the judicial inquiry. If one is really concerned about the Kenyan woman, though, should one deprive her of her only chance of living on the basis of some sanctimonious quibble about motive? It presumably doesn't matter to her why her potential saviour is acting in the way he is.[24]

Autonomy dislikes *Simms*, and autonomy, if it is being consistent, would probably withhold the anti-retrovirals from the Kenyan woman—thinking it better that she died (and so became wholly non-autonomous) than that the principle of autonomy became diluted.

The other principles are more pragmatic, but not less principled for all that. *Simms* was straightforward common sense, but common sense with roots deep in beneficence. Non-maleficence sounded an appropriate caution in *Simms*, but rightly recognised that its job there was simply to sound caution rather than to have the final say. The cited passage from the judgement of Butler-Sloss P is important for another reason, though: it is the first obvious appearance so far of another principle which has a good claim to rule in the shadowlands between life and death: the principle of the sanctity of life. We now move to those shadowlands.

[23] [2003] 1 All ER 683 (Butler-Sloss P). Her reference to there being 'some value to their lives' does not sit easily with the jurisprudence either of Strasbourg or the UK, but we all know what she meant.
[24] Allmark P and Mason S (2006) 'Should Desperate Volunteers Be Included in Randomised Controlled Trials?' 32 *Journal of Medical Ethics* 548–53. Minogue BP, Palmerfernandez G, Udell L *et al* (1995) 'Individual Autonomy and the Double-Blind Controlled Experiment—The Case Of Desperate Volunteers' 20 *Journal of Medicine and Philosophy* 43–55.

11

The End of Life

T
HE STRONG TEMPTATION when writing about the law of the end of life is to start with grand statements of principle. It is best to resist it, and to start instead with some cruel facts.

Jodie and Mary were Siamese twins. They shared an aorta. Mary was parasitic on Jodie; she relied on Jodie's heart. This put a great strain on Jodie. If they were not separated, both would die. If they were separated, Mary would die but Jodie would have a good chance of a relatively normal life. The surgeon contemplating the separation was worried. He knew that he would be killing Mary in order to let Jodie live. Was that lawful?[1]

The case found its way to the Court of Appeal.[2] The court decided that the separation was lawful. There were two stages in its consideration: the first involved the consideration of 'family law' questions; the second involved criminal law questions. The criminal law questions do not concern us here.[3]

There were three 'family law' questions: (1) was it in Jodie's best interests to be separated from Mary?; (2) was it in Mary's best interests to be separated from Jodie?; (3) if there was a conflict between the interests of Jodie and Mary, how was that conflict to be resolved?

Question (1) was easy: of course it was in Jodie's interest to be separated from her sister. One might have thought that (2) was easy too. Indeed two of the three judges, Ward and Brooke LJJ, found it easy. If Mary were not separated from Jodie, Mary would have a few months of life, possibly in pain, and certainly profoundly compromised. But this was still a lot better than nothing: the court should hesitate long before taking it away. The value of a life does not consist in its duration or even in its objective quality: it is intrinsically valuable. That, as we will see, is the reassuring orthodoxy.

The real interest for our purposes is in the judgment of Robert Walker LJ, who dissented from the other two judges on the issue of question (2). It was in Mary's best interests to die, he said. What she had was not worth keeping. But the fatal

---

[1] For ethical discussions, see Bratton MQ, Chetwynd SB (2004) 'One Into Two Will Not Go: Conceptualising Conjoined Twins' 30 *Journal of Medical Ethics* 279–85 and Kaveney MC (2001) 'The Case of Conjoined Twins: Embodiment, Individuality and Dependence' 62 *Theological Studies* 753–86; Harris J (2002) 'Human Beings, Persons and Conjoined Twins: An Ethical Analysis of the Judgment In Re A' 9(3) *Medical Law Review* 221–36.

[2] *Re A (Children) (Conjoined Twins: Surgical Separation)* [2001] Fam 147.

[3] I have discussed them in detail in Foster C (2007) *Elements of Medical Law* (London, Claerhout) 101–6.

operation would not merely remove a detriment (her miserable life): it would actually confer a benefit:

> By a rare and tragic mischance, Mary and Jodie have both been deprived of the bodily integrity and autonomy which is their natural right. There is a strong presumption that an operation to separate them would be in the best interests of each of them . . . In this case the purpose of the operation would be to separate the twins and so give Jodie a reasonably good prospect of a long and reasonably normal life. Mary's death would not be the purpose of the operation, although it would be its inevitable consequence. The operation would give her, even in death, bodily integrity as a human being.[4]

Finally, Mary would have the autonomy that nature had denied her. The act of effecting the autonomy would have killed her, but the autonomy itself would be a benefit. This is the sort of forensic *Alice in Wonderland* that autonomy can write.

Ward LJ, in the Jodie and Mary case, began his consideration of the medical law issues with a heading: 'The fundamental principle'.[5] That principle was the straightforward autonomy of *Schloendorff*[6] and *Re T.*[7] It is rather ironic that one of the most robust assertions of the principle is in a case where, by definition, there was no question at all of any autonomy rights being in play—*Airedale NHS Trust v Bland*,[8] which concerned a patient with an undisputed diagnosis of Permanent Vegetative State (PVS). Assuming the diagnosis to be correct, Tony Bland could not and would never feel anything at all. He had no pains and no pleasures. He was assumed to have no mental life at all, and even if he had he had no way of communicating anything to anyone. He could breathe unaided, but had to be tube-fed. It is impossible to imagine anyone less autonomous. But was it lawful to stop his artificial nutrition and hydration?

What, here, is the starting principle? It is one that hovers behind all discussions of all medico-legal questions. Usually it does not have to be invoked explicitly. It is the principle of the sanctity of life. Judges generally seem to be rather less embarrassed about using the term 'sanctity' than many ethicists.[9] In the philosophical world it seems to be rather out of fashion, and as we have already noted, philosophers are much more fashion-conscious than lawyers. All the judges in *Bland*

---

[4] *Re A (Children) (Conjoined Twins: Surgical Separation)* [2001] Fam 147, 259.

[5] *Ibid* 176.

[6] *Schloendorff v Society of New York Hospital* (1914) 105 NE 92, which contains Cardozo J's classic formulation: 'Every human being of adult years and sound mind has a right to determine what shall be done with his own body.' (p 93).

[7] In *Re T (Adult: Refusal of Treatment)* [1993] Fam 95, 102, where Lord Donaldson of Lymington MR noted that 'This right of choice [about what shall be done with one's own body] is not limited to decisions which others might regard as sensible. It exists notwithstanding that the reasons for making the choice are rational, irrational, unknown or even non-existent.'

[8] [1993] AC 789.

[9] Thus Jean Davies notes, 'The sanctity of human life is no longer advanced as an overriding principle by most of those who want voluntary euthanasia to remain a crime. Presumably this is because sanctity is a religious concept and they recognize that few people in contemporary Britain think in those terms. The alternative wording is now "respect for human life". Of course everyone agrees that this is a fundamentally important principle.': Davies J (1995) 'The Case for Legalizing Voluntary Euthanasia' in Keown J (ed) *Euthanasia Examined: Ethical, Clinical and Legal Perspectives* (Cambridge, CUP) 88.

acknowledged the importance of the principle, and they all acknowledged that it was not absolute. Two citations make the point:

Lord Keith of Kinkel:

[I]t remains to consider whether the principle of the sanctity of life, which it is the concern of the state, and the judiciary as one of the arms of the state, to maintain, requires this House to hold that the judgment of the Court of Appeal was incorrect. In my opinion it does not. The principle is not an absolute one.... In my judgment it does no violence to the principle to hold that it is lawful to cease to give medical treatment and care to a PVS patient who has been in that state for over three years, considering that to do so involves invasive manipulation of the patient's body to which he has not consented and which confers no benefit upon him.[10]

Lord Goff of Chieveley

[T]he fundamental principle is the principle of the sanctity of human life—a principle long recognised not only in our own society but also in most, if not all, civilised societies throughout the modern world, as is indeed evidenced by its recognition both in Article 2 of the European Convention for the Protection of Human Rights and Fundamental Freedoms (1953) (Cmd. 8969) and in Article 6 of the International Covenant of Civil and Political Rights 1966. But this principle, fundamental though it is, is not absolute.... First, it is established that the principle of self-determination requires that respect must be given to the wishes of the patient, so that if an adult patient of sound mind refuses, however unreasonably, to consent to treatment or care by which his life would or might be prolonged, the doctors responsible for his care must give effect to his wishes, even though they do not consider it to be in his best interests to do so.... To this extent, the principle of the sanctity of life must yield to the principle of self-determination.[11,12]

We shall return to Lord Goff's comment about the sanctity of life yielding to self-determination in considering the question of advance directives, but so far the articulation by the *Bland* judges of the circumstances in which the principle of the sanctity of life has to give way to autonomy is nothing new: we saw it clearly in chapter 8 when looking at the case of Miss B, who sought to have declared unlawful her continued artificial ventilation.

Bland allowed us an unusually clear look at the sanctity of life—unclouded by any considerations of autonomy. It is not always clear what the judges mean when they talk about sanctity of life (sometimes they talk as if what is sacred about a life is the bundle of rights which a person has, or the faculties—including autonomy—which a person has[13]), but in general sanctity and autonomy are spoken of as

[10] [1993] AC 789, 859.

[11] *Ibid* 863–4.

[12] Being either unable to see that Tony Bland had any interests at all, or perceiving that his persisting interests were in not being violated by invasive treatment, the House of Lords held that the life-sustaining treatment could stop—indeed that because it was essentially assaultative it had to stop. The removal of the feeding tube was intended to cause his death, but if it were removed, and he died, there would be no murder because the removal was an omission, not an act, and one needed an act for murder.

[13] For a detailed survey of what is meant by the sanctity of life when it is invoked by judges in many jurisdictions, see Foster C (2005) 'What Is Man, That the Judges Are Mindful of Him?' *Journal of Philosophy, Science and Law* 5. <http://www6.miami.edu/ethics/jpsl/archives/all/pvs.html> accessed 27 December 2007.

distinct ideas. The distinction becomes very clear (and loud) when we come to the debate about euthanasia.

Although couched in rather different (and more explicit) language than that used by the judges, the philosopher-autonomists skirt the principle of the sanctity of life in much the same way. There are two main (and very closely related) devices used. The first is the bluff, straightforward way, used by John Harris and others: autonomy's the whole point of living, and everything should be subservient to it:

> The point of autonomy, the point of choosing and having the freedom to choose between competing conceptions of how, and indeed why, to live, is simply that it is only thus that our lives become in any real sense our own. The value of our lives is the value we give to our lives. And we do this, so far as this is possible at all, by shaping our lives for ourselves. Our own choices, decisions and preferences help to make us what we are, for each helps us to confirm and modify our own character and enables us to develop and to understand ourselves. So autonomy, as the ability and the freedom to make the choices that shape our lives, is quite crucial in giving to each life its own special and peculiar value.
>
> Concern for welfare, and the paternalist control it is so often used to justify, ceases to be legitimate at the point at which, so far from being productive of autonomy, so far from enabling the individual to create her own life, it operates to frustrate the individual's own attempts to create her own life for herself. And of course this also applies in the limiting case of suicide or of course to voluntary euthanasia, where the individual's attempts to create her own life involve creating its ending also.
>
> Welfare thus conceived has a point, as does concern for the welfare of others; it is not simply a good in itself. We need welfare, broadly conceived in terms of health, freedom from pain, mobility, shelter, nourishment and so on, precisely because welfare is liberating. It is what we need to be able to pursue our lives to best advantage. So that where concern for welfare and respect for wishes are incompatible one with another, concern for welfare must give way to respect for autonomy.[14]

Thus, for Harris, withholding from someone the right to die when, where and how they like is:

> simply a form of tyranny; an attempt to control the life of a person who has her own autonomous view about how that life should go. The evil of tyranny does not require explication in terms of the nature of sanctity of life, but rather in terms of respect for persons and of their autonomy. Euthanasia should be permitted, not because everyone should accept that it is right, nor because to fail to do so violates a defensible conception of the sanctity of life, but simply because to deny a person control of what, on any analysis, must be one of the most important decisions of life, is a form of tyranny, which like all acts of tyranny is an ultimate denial of respect for persons.[15]

And then there is Ronald Dworkin's gloss on this, which in a lawyerly way seeks to take the war into his opponents' camp by asking: 'What do you mean by "sanctity of life"?', and quickly putting into their mouths the answer: "Well, I suppose

---

[14] Harris J (1995) 'Euthanasia and the Value of Life' in Keown (ed) *Euthanasia Examined* (Cambridge, CUP) 11.
[15] *Ibid* 19–20.

we mean autonomy, actually." It is a wholescale misrepresentation of the anti-euthanasists' position: they are simply and demonstrably not guilty of the confla-tion of which Dworkin himself is guilty. Here he is in full rhetorical flow:

> Anyone who believes in the sanctity of human life believes that once a human life has begun it matters, intrinsically, that that life goes well, that the investment it represents be realized rather than frustrated. Someone's convictions about his own critical interests are opinions about what it means for his own human life to go well, and these convictions can therefore best be understood as a special application of his general commitment to the sanctity of life.[16]

So you might have thought that you were actually a campaigning, pro-life Catholic, but actually, if you think about it properly, you will realise that you are one of us. If you are not one of us, you are wholly beyond the pale:

> Making someone die in a way that others approve, but he believes is a horrifying contra-diction of his life, is a devastating, odious form of tyranny.[17]

Euthanasia—the deliberate killing of a patient—is straightforward murder in English law. There have of course been vocal calls to make such killing lawful in certain circumstances,[18] and the practice is lawful in several places.[19] Why is the practice unlawful? Because murder is unlawful. And why is murder is unlawful? Ultimately because of the principle of the sanctity of life, which can be framed in various ways. Here is one, from the House of Lords in *R v Brown* [1994] 1 AC 212:

> With the exception of a few exotic specimens which have never come before the courts, euthanasia is in practice the only situation where the recipient expressly consents to being killed. As the law stands today, consensual killing is murder. Why is this so? Professor Glanville Williams suggests (*Textbook of Criminal Law*, 2nd ed pp 579–580) that the arguments in support are transcendental, and I agree. Believer or atheist, the observer grants to the maintenance of human life an overriding imperative, so strong as to outweigh any consent to its termination. Some believers and some atheists now dis-sent from this view.[20]

Autonomy has been the principal spokesman for euthanasia. If one accepts on grounds of autonomy that Miss B should have a right to insist that her invasive life-sustaining treatment be stopped, they say, how can one say that a patient with a miserably painful terminal cancer does not have a right to have her misery stopped by a merciful injection of potassium chloride or a supra-therapeutic dose of morphine? From what we have seen so far, we perhaps ought not to be surprised that autonomy and human rights are hand in glove on the question of euthanasia, but in fact it is rather odd. As we noted in the context of abortion, Article 2 (the

---

[16] Dworkin R (1993) *Life's Dominion* (London, Harper Collins) 215. For the distinction between critical and experiential interests, see ch 1.
[17] *Ibid* 217.
[18] In the UK the most recent such attempt was by Lord Joffe, who tried and failed to put onto the statute book a law permitting physician-assisted suicide (The Assisted Dying for the Terminally Ill Bill).
[19] Eg Switzerland, Belgium, the Netherlands and Oregon.
[20] [1994] 1 AC 212, 261 (Lord Mustill).

right to life) normally leads the pack, leaving Article 8 trailing humbly in its wake. This is a logical hierarchy: unless one has life, one has nothing to which any Article 8 right can attach. But the hierarchy is reversed in the cases of abortion (where maternal Article 8 rights trump any Article 2 right that the foetus might have), and potentially, too, in the case of euthanasia.

The European Court of Human Rights has relied very heavily on the 'margin of appreciation' in avoiding saying anything very useful on the subject.[21] In *Pretty v United Kingdom*[22] (which concerned an attempt by Dianne Pretty to obtain immunity from prosecution for her husband were he to help her to commit suicide) the court carefully said: (a) that if a state recognised a 'right to die' this would necessarily be contrary to Article 2; and (b) that if State X were found not to be in breach of Article 2 by allowing assisted suicide, that it would follow that State Y would be in breach of its obligations under Article 2 by refusing to allow the practice.[23] Personal autonomy was 'an important principle underlying the interpretation of [Article 8's] guarantees.[24] In a masterpiece of equivocation the Court said that it was 'not prepared to exclude' the possibility that the applicant's to 'exercise[e] her choice to avoid what she considers will be an undignified and distressing end to her life' was encompassed by the notion of personal autonomy, and accordingly it was possible that the existing UK law making criminal the action of her husband in helping her commit suicide infringed Article 8(1).[25] But that was not the end of the matter. Could Article 8(2) save the UK law? Indeed it could—via the device of the margin of appreciation. The UK law was not arbitrary or disproportionate, and accordingly the wider societal considerations inherent in Article 8(2) meant that there was no breach.[26]

What this comes to is that Article 8 likes euthanasia and assisted suicide, but cannot bring itself to say so clearly.

In the case of *Burke* at first instance, Munby J was not so coy:

> The personal autonomy which is protected by Article 8 embraces such matters as how one chooses to pass the closing days and moments of one's life and how one manages one's death. . . . The dignity interests protected by the Convention include, under Article 8, the preservation of mental stability and, under Article 3, the right to die with dignity and the right to be protected from treatment, or from a lack of treatment, which will result in one dying in avoidably distressing circumstances. . . . Important as the sanctity of life is, it has to take second place to personal autonomy; and it may have to take second place to human dignity.[27]

21 See Korff D (2006) 'The Right to Life: A Guide to the Implementation of Article 2 of the European Convention on Human Rights' *Council of Europe Human Rights Handbooks No 8* (Strasbourg, Council of Europe) 15–22.
22 (2002) 35 EHRR 1.
23 *Ibid* [41].
24 *Ibid* [61].
25 *Ibid* [67].
26 *Ibid* [76]–[78].
27 *R (Burke) v General Medical Council* [2005] QB 424.

The passage duly appeared in lights on the website of the Voluntary Euthanasia Society.[28] It was the biggest forensic coup in their history.[29]

The rhetorical appeal of the comparison between a 'normal' end-of-life case and the Miss B case is as false as it is compelling. There is a distinction of colossal importance between the withdrawal of life-sustaining treatment and the performance of an act whose intention is to bring about death.[30] This is a distinction recognised in the professional ethical codes of most civilised countries: it survives all the criticism that can be thrown at the distinction between acts and omissions themselves.[31] What was responsible for Miss B's death was ultimately her cervical spinal cord lesion. All that she was complaining of was that she was being technologically prevented from being allowed to suffer the natural consequences of that lesion. That is several moral worlds away from the deliberate execution of a patient with an overdose of opiates. While the acts/omissions distinction may well have considerable moral justification, it is not critical. If one had a case where life-sustaining treatment was withdrawn by a procedure which was properly characterised as an act, the procedure should be regarded as in the same ethical class as one which was an omission. In fact most laymen, describing the procedures used to allow a patient to die naturally, would probably use the word 'act': they would see a feeding tube being actively withdrawn: they would see the switch on a ventilator being turned to 'Off'. It is only the law's historical obsession with acts that led the House of Lords in *Bland* not only to perpetuate the acts/omissions distinction, but to make it the whole philosophical basis of the law relating to the withdrawal of treatment. It cannot bear the weight. The distinction has considerable utility in theology, criminal law and other branches of ethics: it has become a nonsense on the ward. *Bland*'s desire for philosophical consistency in the law has ultimately done nothing for the law's reputation in the eyes of philosophers.

All this obfuscates the plain fact that Miss B died from a spinal cord lesion, not as a result of any medical intervention. Autonomy loves the obfuscation: it allows it to pass off as an ally a principle (the permissibility in some circumstances of the withdrawal of life-sustaining treatment), which is no ally at all.

In fact there are many reasons why autonomy, if it were consistent, would oppose euthanasia/physician-assisted suicide.

(a) The usual and logical hierarchy of Article 2 over Article 8, discussed above.
(b) The related and rather trite observation that dead men have no autonomy at all.
(c) The fact that many decisions about euthanasia are prompted by inadequate or non-existent palliative care. Autonomy should be concerned about this

[28] It now calls itself 'Dignity in Dying'.
[29] His judgment was subsequently excoriated by the Court of Appeal, but there are no signs in the Court of Appeal judgment that they disagree with this section.
[30] For a contrary view, see, eg, Shaw D (2007) 'The Body As Unwarranted Life Support: A New Perspective on Euthanasia' 33 *Journal of Medical Ethics* 519–21.
[31] Perhaps the most potent criticisms are those arising from consideration of the so-called 'trolley problem' (discussed in detail in Foster C (2007) *Elements of Medical Law* (London, Claerhout) 109–11).

because it suggests that fatal decisions are being made under the duress imposed by pain, rather than with the freedom that proper palliation can give.

(d) The fact that the assessment of capacity at the best of times is problematic, and in the seriously, let alone the terminally, ill, can be nightmarish. The fallacy of the 'all-or-nothing' view of capacity has already been highlighted[32] and the wrong assumption of capacity in many patients on ordinary medical wards has been noted.[33] *A fortiori* those problems are practically more acute and their consequences more profound in an end-of-life context. Several related points appear below.

(e) The fact that many decisions about euthanasia are prompted by the depression that is a common adjunct to serious illness. Such depression is often treatable, but while it lasts interferes with the capacity to make a properly free decision.

(f) The fact that many decisions about euthanasia are made on the basis of inadequate information about the palliative options and/or prognosis. It is of course a basic principle of the law of consent that the weightier the decision the more complete should be the information provided and the patient's understanding of it. There is no weightier decision to be made as whether or not to die, and yet that decision is often made in circumstances of reduced capacity or sensory duress (see above), and with the benefit of far less information than would be regarded as necessary to make a validly informed decision about a procedure of far less moment.

The classic example relates to the fear of choking to death in motor neurone disease. It is this fear which seems to have forced Dianne Pretty and several other sufferers to the court. In fact the literature indicates that the fear is groundless.[34] Choking can indeed be a symptom (and it is well controlled with proper palliative care), but it is not a cause of death. If Dianne Pretty had got her way, she would have been killed by her husband on the basis of a misunderstanding of the literature. Autonomy should surely be profoundly unhappy about that.

(g) The possibility of patients opting for bad reasons for euthanasia/Physician-assisted suicide, and coercion. Many patients towards the end of their lives are

[32] See ch 8, above.

[33] See ch 8, above.

[34] See Foster C (2005) 'Misrepresentations About Prognosis and Palliative Options in Motor Neurone Disease: Some Legal Considerations' 11(1) *Journal of Evaluation in Clinical Practice* 21–2; Borasio GD and Miller RG (2001) 'Clinical Characteristics and Management of Amyotrophic Lateral Sclerosis' 21(2) *Seminars in Neurology* 155–166; Bradley WG, Anderson F, Bromberg M, Gutmann L, Harati Y, Ross M, Miller RG, and the ALS CARE Study Group (2001) 'Current Management of ALS: Comparison of the ALS CARE Database and the AAN Practice Parameter' 57 *Neurology* 500–04; Hadjikoutis S, Eccles R and Wiles CM (2000) 'Coughing and Choking in Motor Neurone Disease' 68(5) *Journal of Neurology, Neurosurgery and Psychiatry* 601–4; Neudert CN, Oliver D, Wasner M, and Borasio GD (2001) 'The Course of the Terminal Phase in Patients With Amyotrophic Lateral Sclerosis' 248 *Journal of Neurology* 612–16; O'Brien T, Kelly M, and Saunders C (1992) 'Motor Neurone Disease: A Hospice Perspective' 304 *British Medical Journal* 471–73; Silani V and Borasio GD (1999) 'Honesty and Hope: Announcement of Diagnosis in ALS' 53 (8 Supplement 5) *Neurology* S37–9.

concerned about 'being a burden'. They may, particularly if their lives are oth-erwise slightly burdensome, opt for death in order to save their families or carers the trouble of looking after them. Other factors may well come into play too—for instance concerns about the future costs of care.

(h) The related possibility of a 'slippery slope', resulting in the non-consensual killing of patients in vulnerable groups.[35]

(i) The transformation of the doctor-patient relationship: most patients, particu-larly towards the end of their lives, probably want to be treated by doctors who are not killers. Fear and panic are prevalent enough on cancer wards without them being prowled by doctors who have ushered several patients to the mortuary before they start the ward round. To take away the option of being cared for by non-homicidal clinicians is a serious inroad into freedom.[36]

There is a real danger of over-reaction against autonomy's exaggerated bland-ishments. That over-reaction has been sadly exemplified in some recent litigation in the United Kingdom, sponsored by the pro-life lobby.[37] It seems to be impos-sible for some opponents of euthanasia to mention the words 'autonomy' in the same sentence as 'end of life decision-making', without a curse. But of course autonomy, which has had a legitimately prominent place in decision-making throughout life, should not be elbowed out towards the end. Indeed it could be argued that all decisions about medical treatment (in respect of which autonomy rightly has pride of place) are potentially end-of-life decisions. It is important to consent in an appropriately informed way to the administration of paracetamol because one of the side-effects of the drug could be a life-threatening anaphylactic reaction. The decision about whether or not to have a coronary bypass graft for is plainly tantamount to an end-of-life decision: if you have the operation you have a real, if small, chance of dying on the table. If you do not, and the operation was properly indicated, you are implicitly accepting that you are likely to die earlier than you need to do.

[35] It should be noted, however, that a recent survey found 'no evidence to justify the grave and important concern often expressed about the potential for abuse—namely the fear that legalised physi-cian-assisted dying will target the vulnerable or pose the greatest risk to people in vulnerable groups. The evidence available cannot provide conclusive proof about the impact on vulnerable patients. . . . [I]t does show that there is no current factual support for so-called slippery-slope concerns about the risks of legalisation of assisted dying.': Battin MP, van der Heide A, Ganzini L *et al* (2007) 'Legal Physician-Assisted Dying in Oregon and the Netherlands: Evidence Concerning the Impact on Patients in "Vulnerable Groups"' 33 *Journal of Medical Ethics* 591–7.

[36] Thus, eg, it has been asserted that the ramifications of physician-assisted suicide 'are too disturb-ing for the patient-physician relationship and the trust to sustain it': Snyder L, Sulmasy DP (2001) 'Physician-Assisted Suicide' 135 *Annals of Internal Medicine* 209–16; and that the practice would cause patients 'great difficulty believing their doctor intends their best interests': Weithman PJ (1999) 'Of Assisted Suicide and the Philosopher's Brief' 109 *Ethics* 548–78. However, a recent study showed little empirical evidence to support either side of the debate about the effect on patient trust of legalising physician-assisted suicide: Hall M, Trachtenberg F and Dugan E (2005) 'The Impact on Patient Trust of Legalising Physician Aid in Dying' 31 *Journal of Medical Ethics* 693–7.

[37] The best example was the wholly counter-productive challenge by Leslie Burke to the legality of the GMC's guidelines on the withdrawal of life sustaining treatment: see *R (Burke) v General Medical Council* [2005] QB 424; [2006] QB 273.

That said, we should surely be more careful at the end of life than at its middle about letting autonomy have its head. This is for the rather obvious and brutally practical reason that in an end of life setting, autonomy will all too often, in a moment of relievable depression, despair or pain, ablate itself for good. Simon Woods suggests, plausibly, that this might justify requiring terminally ill patients to receive palliative care before any issue of assisted dying can arise. Surely autonomy should be happy with this conclusion. Yes, there will be a moment of compulsion, but only to ensure that autonomy is not being a victim of other forces, and risking annihilation in circumstances in which, if a look back were possible, it would be regretted.[38]

The difficult cases, which test our devotion to the principle of autonomy, involve questions about the extent to which patients should be involved, in ways that are foreseeably distressing, in matters concerning their health and fate over which the patient has no control.[39] Imagine that a clinician has decided that it would not be in the best interests of patient A to be resuscitated in the event of her suffering a cardiac arrest. The clinician, as we have seen, cannot be compelled to resuscitate. The clinician, the other carers, and patient A's family all agree that A would be enormously upset to be told about this decision. What should be done?[40]

For the autonomist, the ability to plan ahead and ensure that the life-plan is fulfilled is everything. It trumps mere agonising distress every time. The law is kinder, and less prescriptive. While there is an obligation to tell a patient about what one proposes to do to her, there is no obligation to say what you propose not to do. This is a distinction that would be shredded by any first year philosophy student, but it does good and compassionate service. It allows a bespoke service (for 'bespoke', the cynic rightly reads 'paternalistic') instead of autonomy's crude off-the-peg cut.

The high value that the courts and the legislature place on autonomy has led to intense interest in 'advance directives'—declarations by persons with capacity about what they would like to have happen to them should they lose capacity and be in specified medical circumstances.[41] The presumption behind advance directives is that the will of capacitate person A should determine the fate of incapacitate person A. There are practical, legal and philosophical difficulties with this view, to which we will come.

In England and Wales the Mental Capacity Act 2005 purports to have codified the law relating to advance directives.

---

[38] See Woods S (2007) *Death's Dominion—Ethics at the End of Life* (Buckingham, Open University Press).

[39] See, eg, Vince T and Petros A (2006) 'Should Children's Autonomy Be Respected by Telling Them of Their Imminent Death?' 32 *Journal of Medical Ethics* 21–3, and Godkin D (2006) 'Should Children's Autonomy Be Respected by Telling Them of Their Imminent Death?' 32 *Journal of Medical Ethics* 24–5.

[40] In the UK, guidance is given in 'Decisions Relating to Cardiopulmonary Resuscitation' (2001) produced jointly by the British Medical Association, the Royal College of Nursing and the UK Resuscitation Council, 27 *Journal of Medical Ethics* 310–16.

[41] For general discussions of the law and ethics of advance directives, see Hornett S (1995) 'Advance directives: a legal and ethical analysis' in Keown (ed) *Euthanasia Examined* (Cambridge, CUP) 297–314; Heckler C, Moseley R and Vawter DE (1989) *Advance Directives in Medicine* (New York, Westport, CT, and London, Praeger).

Section 4(6)(a) provides that a person making a 'best interests' determination must consider, so far as is reasonably ascertainable, (a) the person's past and present wishes and feelings (and, in particular, any relevant written statement made by him when he had capacity).

Sections 24, 25 and 26 deal with advance directives. The Act calls them 'advance decisions.' It is necessary to set them out in full.

24 Advance decisions to refuse treatment: general

(1) 'Advance decision' means a decision made by a person ('P'), after he has reached 18 and when he has capacity to do so, that if—

(a) at a later time and in such circumstances as he may specify, a specified treatment is proposed to be carried out or continued by a person providing health care for him, and

(b) at that time he lacks capacity to consent to the carrying out or continuation of the treatment,

the specified treatment is not to be carried out or continued.

(2) For the purposes of subsection (1)(a), a decision may be regarded as specifying a treatment or circumstances even though expressed in layman's terms.

(3) P may withdraw or alter an advance decision at any time when he has capacity to do so.

(4) A withdrawal (including a partial withdrawal) need not be in writing.

(5) An alteration of an advance decision need not be in writing (unless section 25(5) applies in relation to the decision resulting from the alteration).

25 Validity and applicability of advance decisions

(1) An advance decision does not affect the liability which a person may incur for carrying out or continuing a treatment in relation to P unless the decision is at the material time—

(a) valid, and

(b) applicable to the treatment

(2) An advance decision is not valid if P—

(a) has withdrawn the decision at a time when he had capacity to do so,

(b) has, under a lasting power of attorney created after the advance decision was made, conferred authority on the donee (or, if more than one, any of them) to give or refuse consent to the treatment to which the advance decision relates, or

(c) has done anything else clearly inconsistent with the advance decision remaining his fixed decision.

(3) An advance decision is not applicable to the treatment in question if at the material time P has capacity to give or refuse consent to it.

(4) An advance decision is not applicable to the treatment in question if—

(a) that treatment is not the treatment specified in the advance decision,

(b) any circumstances specified in the advance decision are absent, or

(c) there are reasonable grounds for believing that circumstances exist which P did not anticipate at the time of the advance decision and which would have affected his decision had he anticipated them.

(5) An advance decision is not applicable to life-sustaining treatment unless—

(a) the decision is verified by a statement by P to the effect that it is to apply to that treatment even if life is at risk, and

(b) the decision and statement comply with subsection (6).

(6) A decision or statement complies with this subsection only if—

(a) it is in writing,

(b) it is signed by P or by another person in P's presence and by P's direction,

(c) the signature is made or acknowledged by P in the presence of a witness, and

(d) the witness signs it, or acknowledges his signature, in P's presence.

(7) The existence of any lasting power of attorney other than one of a description mentioned in subsection (2)(b) does not prevent the advance decision from being regarded as valid and applicable.

26 Effect of advance decisions

(1) If P has made an advance decision which is—

(a) valid, and

(b) applicable to a treatment,

the decision has effect as if he had made it, and had had capacity to make it, at the time when the question arises whether the treatment should be carried out or continued.

(2) A person does not incur liability for carrying out or continuing the treatment unless, at the time, he is satisfied that an advance decision exists which is valid and applicable to the treatment.

(3) A person does not incur liability for the consequences of withholding or withdrawing a treatment from P if, at the time, he reasonably believes that an advance decision exists which is valid and applicable to the treatment.

(4) The court may make a declaration as to whether an advance decision—

(a) exists;

(b) is valid;

(c) is applicable to a treatment.

(5) Nothing in an apparent advance decision stops a person—

(a) providing life-sustaining treatment, or

(b) doing any act he reasonably believes to be necessary to prevent a serious deterioration in P's condition,

while a decision as respects any relevant issue is sought from the court.

There is an obvious discordance here. Section 4(1) provides that an advance directive should be 'considered' as part of a 'best interests' determination: section 26(1) appears to make the advance directive binding. How can these sections be reconciled?

The issue arose in *Burke*.[42] Noting the tension between sections 4 and 26, the Court of Appeal said:

The position of a patient in a PVS was addressed at length by the House of Lords in *Bland* and we do not consider it appropriate in this case to add to what was said by their Lordships, other than to make the following observation. While a number of their

---

[42] *R (Burke) v General Medical Council* [2006] QB 273.

Lordships indicated that an advance directive that the patient should not be kept alive in a PVS should be respected, we do not read that decision as requiring such a patient to be kept alive simply because he has made an advance directive to that effect. Such a proposition would not be compatible with the provisions of the Mental Capacity Act 2005, which we consider accords with the position at common law. While section 26 of that Act requires compliance with a valid advance directive to refuse treatment, section 4 does no more than require this to be taken into consideration when considering what is in the best interests of a patient.[43]

Thus section 4 seems to have trumped section 26. If Parliament intended to make advance directives binding, it failed. There is no magic in an advance directive: it is evidence to be taken into account in deciding where someone's best interests lie.

Since autonomy likes advance directives, this might appear to be something of a rout for autonomy. But is it really? If autonomy is really concerned about freedom, it ought to be more sceptical about advance directives than it often is. If the effect of acting on an advance directive is to rob someone of autonomy, anyone interested in autonomy should be slow to act.

The common law, essentially embodied in section 4 of the 2005 Act, expresses appropriate scepticism.

If it can be shown that the directive in question relates exactly to the circumstances obtaining at the time that it comes to be considered, then it may be decisive evidence. But there will often be real, practical problems facing anyone who wants to say that it is decisive: did the person at the time of making the directive know as much about the prognosis and therapeutic and palliative options as she would need to know in order to make her decision an appropriately informed one?; has medicine moved on significantly since the directive was made?; have the convictions of the patient herself changed in a material way?; and so on. Section 4 requires all these plainly relevant questions to be asked and answered. The result will often be that it is unlawful to act in accordance with an advance directive. Clinicians, courts and other decision-makers should bear in mind too the compelling evidence that when patients are in the situation envisaged by their advance directives, they very commonly value their compromised life far more highly than they thought they would when they were healthy.[44] If you don't have much, it

---

[43] *Ibid* [57].

[44] It does not follow from this that people close to death become opposed to euthanasia and assisted suicide per se: see Chapple A, Ziebland S, McPherson A and Herxheimer A (2006) 'What People Close to Death Say About Euthanasia and Assisted Suicide: A Qualitative Study' 32 *Journal of Medical Ethics* 706–10. But in a study of 21 people paralysed from the neck down, and reliant on artificial ventilation, only one patient wished that she had been allowed to die. Two were unsure. 18 were glad to be alive. It is immensely unlikely that had they made advance directives when healthy, anticipating this situation, that the 18 would have expressed in the directive the preference for life which they in fact had. See Gardner BP, Theocleous F, Watt JW and Krishnan KR (1985) 'Ventilation or Dignified Death for Patients With High Tetraplegia?' 291 *British Medical Journal* 1620–22. In a study of 150 competent patients with advance directives, 61% thought that there could be times when their best interests would be best served by their clinicians failing to follow the advance directive: see Sehgal A *et al* (1992) 'How Strictly Do Dialysis Patients Want Their Advance Directives Followed?' 267 *Journal of the American Medical Association* 59–63.

seems that you value more highly the little that you do have. Disease changes your perceptions of the world and your place in it.

Disease can do more than that. It can sometimes change not just outlook and values, but the person himself.[45]

Consider the following (hypothetical) cases:

Case 1

Ben is 94. He was brought up by Benedictine monks in Galway, but repudiated Catholicism in his mid 40s. He married twice, and has two sons from his first marriage and two daughters from his second. He earned a fortune as a bookie and invested it very prudently. All his children are destitute. Both the daughters and the sons believe that the daughters are the sole beneficiaries under his will. The daughters and the sons don't get on.

A year ago Ben was admitted to a local authority care home. Alzheimer's disease was diagnosed. Now he has a severe chest infection. It will require treatment with antibiotics. If he is not treated he will die. The daughters tell the clinicians that Ben had told them five years earlier that 'If I ever go doollaly I want to go: I don't want you to see your old man like that.' His sons say that Ben, shortly before his admission to the care home, embraced again the Catholicism of his youth and became a dogmatic pro-life activist. His solicitors bring out a formally executed advance directive, duly witnessed, which says that: 'Should I ever suffer from Alzheimer's disease I do not want any treatment to keep me alive.'

What should be done? The facts have been related in detail to emphasise that these situations are rarely pure and never simple. The financial interest of the daughters of course means that one should view their representations with suspicion. Perhaps the sons feel that if the father lives he will alter his will in their favour. Their motives should accordingly be doubted too. But assume that the sons' account is credible. The advance directive is legally impeccable. Would autonomy really want to say that section 26 of the 2005 Act applied, and that that was the end of the matter? Do the values that Ben has embraced really not matter at all? Do those values only matter if they were embraced at a time when Ben was capacitate? And capacitate for what? Should one not respect the decision of an Alzheimer's patient to embrace Catholicism and pro-life values? If autonomy is saying that the advance directive is the end of the matter, then it must be saying that it is not necessary to discover who is telling the truth about Ben's changed views. Can that be right?

Whatever the Act says about this situation, it forbids the assertion: 'Ben has Alzheimer's, and accordingly he does not have capacity for any purposes.' On the contrary, there is a statutory presumption of capacity.[46] If he has capacity, of course the Act does not apply. But assume that he does not have capacity in the sense defined by the Act for the purposes of deciding whether or not to have the antibiotics. Section 4 demands a full inquiry into Ben's change of view: Section

---

[45] Hughes JC (2001) 'Views of the Person With Dementia' 27 *Journal of Medical Ethics* 86–91.
[46] Mental Capacity Act 2005 s 1(2).

26 may very well be frustrated in the light of that inquiry. Should autonomy be outraged if Ben is given his antibiotics? It should not be: if it is really consistent it should agitate for the prescription.

Case 2

John is 80 and has advanced Alzheimer's disease. He made an advance directive in terms identical to Ben's. The indications are that he enjoys life very much. Whereas before he had been prone to depression and anxiety, it seems that the Alzheimer's disease, while robbing him of much cognitive function, has also mercifully robbed him of his angst. He appears to be in a childlike Eden.[47] He smiles constantly, loves joking with the nurses and other patients, and has a religious devotion to certain television programmes. He has difficulty feeding, and if he is to be kept alive he will need a PEG. The clinicians discuss the clinical options with his family, but not with him. He overhears, and understands that one option is not to give him the life-saving PEG. 'They want to put me down like a dog', he says to his family.

This paints a picture of a patient transformed by his disease. The person who made the advance directive is no more. The new John is happier than the old, and wants very much to live. Assume that the old John would be (as the advance directive indicates) horrified at the spectacle of the happily demented new John. Assume that he would use words like 'disgusting', 'humiliating' and 'degrading'. Autonomy would be forthright. The *real* John is the old John, and the old John must rule. The real, old John had a clearly articulated life-plan, which included the desire not to be as the new John is. Not only would it be unethical to frustrate the life-plan by giving him the PEG, it would be unlawful. The new John has no capacity to consent to it. 'Best interests' considerations cannot justify the PEG: the only arbiter of the new John's best interests is the old John. The old John took the trouble to prohibit precisely the sort of intervention that is now proposed: it would be tyrannous (to borrow a word from Ronald Dworkin and John Harris) to put the PEG in. There is a plain biological continuity between the old and the new John: it was precisely the knowledge of that continuity that led to the making of the advance directive.

But where is the tyranny here? Surely if there is any tyranny the tyrant is the old John, and his victim is the new John. Does autonomy have nothing to say about that? If the objection is the magnitude of the intervention, imagine that all that is necessary to sustain life is the wholly non-invasive administration of antibiotics. Should the new John be assassinated in his Edenic bliss by the ghost of the old John? Autonomy should be happy: the disease has created a new John, and if autonomy has to be humoured we can seriously say that the new John has drafted a brand new life-plan which involves watching TV, joking, and staying alive as long as possible to enjoy doing it all.

---

[47] It is interesting, and perhaps significant, that Alzheimer's disease, when it strips away memory, tends to strip away the most recent memories first. The last to go are the memories of childhood. Patients may be left with the memories that they had when they were very young children. That may be a recipe for happiness or horror.

It is not clear what the English law would do in John's case,[48] but on the question of which 'John' should be considered when determining 'best interests', it is submitted that it should plainly be the new John. That is a consequence of something in section 4 of the 2005 Act that is so obvious that it is easily missed: the tense. The opening words of section 4(1) are: 'In determining for the purposes of this Act what *is* in a person's best interests . . .' (emphasis added).

What Parliament commands decision-makers to inquire into is the best interests of the patient *at the time that the decision is made*. If a personality-changing disease has transmuted person A (who made an advance declaration indicating that if he became person B he wanted to die), into person B, it is the patient facing the doctors—patient B—whose best interests fall to be considered. Person A is an irrelevance: he does not exist.[49]

It is easy to dismiss as exotic and fanciful such examples of personhood-transformation. But in fact they will occur very frequently. Perhaps they are the norm. Perhaps most of us will be changed dramatically by the imminence of our death, whether by organic changes to our cerebral cortex wrought by a degenerative disease, by a new appreciation of the preciousness of life, or by the sheer vertigo of teetering on the edge of eternity. Perhaps we only dismiss such examples because we are slaves to the palpably absurd dichotomy of capacity/no capacity. Perhaps a more nuanced view of human choice-making would deprive autonomy of some of the spurious authority with which it speaks at the death-bed. To be fair, the 2005 Act strives hard for that more sophisticated view.

There will always be many situations, however, where it is very difficult to assess where best interests lie. The classically difficult situations are cases involving very young or very disabled children, but there are often profound difficulties in adults too.[50] Until recently, the law has been careful to ensure that fundamental principles guide the assessment of 'best interests'. It has thought that if they do not guide, they are likely to be the victims of the practical difficulties.

As has already been (unnecessarily) observed, in true 'best interests' cases autonomy, by definition, can be no guide. What principles step into the breach?

---

[48] In practice many clinicians would baulk at inserting a PEG, but would think that antibiotics were a different matter.

[49] The explanatory notes to the Act tend to support this construction. They say, at para 28: 'Best interests is not a test of "substituted judgment" (what the person would have wanted), but rather it requires a determination to be made by applying an objective test as to what would be in the person's best interests.' The Code of Practice to the Act is to similar effect. It states, at 5.38: 'In setting out the requirements for working out a person's best interests, section 4 of the Act puts the person who lacks capacity at the centre of the decision to be made. Even if they cannot make the decision, their wishes and feelings, beliefs and values should be taken fully into account—whether expressed in the past or now. But their wishes and feelings, beliefs and values will not necessarily be the deciding factor in working out their best interests. Any such assessment must consider past and present wishes and feelings, beliefs and values alongside all other factors, but the final decision must be based entirely on what is in the person's best interests.'

[50] For surveys of the ethical problems relating to children, see McIntosh N (2002) 'Ethical issues in withdrawing life-sustaining treatment from handicapped neonates' in Dickenson D (ed) *Ethical Issues in Maternal-Fetal Medicine* (Cambridge, CUP) 335–45; Nuffield Council of Bioethics (2006) *Critical Care Decisions in Fetal and Neonatal Medicine: Ethical Issues* (London, Nuffield Council of Bioethics).

As was observed in *Bland*, the sanctity of life is the main benchmark. However important the sanctity of life is, it has to be admitted that (if one repudiates the extreme position of vitalism) it is rather amorphous. Accordingly, if it is to mean anything—if it is to be real—it has to be procedurally entrenched. The lawyers' traditional and most effective way of doing that is by creating a presumption. That is what has been done. The reasoning used to go like this:

(a) Human life is sacred. A corollary of that is that there must be a presumption that it is in the patient's best interests to continue to live.
(b) The presumption can be rebutted.
(c) What is required to rebut it is evidence that continued existence would be intolerable (the so-called 'intolerability test'.)

The test has impeccable forensic lineage.[51] Its clearest statement was by Taylor LJ in *Re J (A Minor) (Wardship: Medical Treatment)*:

> I consider the correct approach is for the court to judge the quality of life the child would have to endure if given the treatment and decide whether in all the circumstances such a life would be so afflicted as to be intolerable to that child. I say 'to that child' because the test should not be whether the life would be intolerable to the decider. The test must be whether the child in question, if capable of exercising sound judgment, would consider the life tolerable.'[52]

This test, despite its august ancestry, appeared to be ignominiously sidelined by the Court of Appeal in *R (on the application of Burke) v General Medical Council*[53]and *Wyatt v Portsmouth Hospitals NHS Trust*.[54] The way in which this sidelining happened was exceedingly odd, but the oddness does not concern us here.[55] The court in *Wyatt* urged a return to an untrammeled 'best interests' test, 'unfettered by any potentially contentious glosses on the best interests test . . ..' Intolerability was not dismissed completely, but was sent to the back of the class: '[I]t should not be seen as a gloss on or a supplementary guide to best interests', but it remained 'a valuable guide in the search for best interests.'[56] Best interests determinations should be made like this:

> The welfare of the child is paramount, and the judge must look at the question of the child's welfare from the assumed point of view of the patient. . . . There is a strong presumption in favour of a course of action which will prolong life, but the presumption is

---

[51] See, eg, *W Healthcare NHS Trust v KH* [2004] EWCA Civ 1324, [26], where Brooke LJ said: '[N]ormally the approach that the law should adopt is to determine whether, in the judgment of the court, the continuation of the life would be intolerable.' In *Re B (A Minor) (Wardship: Medical Treatment)* [1981] 1 WLR 1421, 1424, Templeman LJ said that the issue to be decided was 'whether the life of this child is demonstrably going to be so awful that in effect the child must be condemned to die', and Dunn LJ decided the case on the grounds that there was no evidence that 'this child's short life is likely to be an intolerable one.'

[52] [1991] Fam 33, 55.

[53] See above n 27.

[54] [2005] 1 WLR 3995.

[55] This is commented on in detail in Foster C (2007) *Elements of Medical Law* (London, Claerhout) 120–23.

[56] [2005] 1 WLR 3995, [91].

not irrebuttable. . . . The term 'best interests' encompasses medical, emotional and all other welfare issues. . . . The court must conduct a balancing exercise in which all the relevant factors are weighed . . . and a helpful way of undertaking this exercise is to draw up a balance sheet. . . . We urge caution in the application to children of factors relevant to the treatment of adults, although some general statements of principle plainly apply to both.[57]

This, of course, gives judges considerably less help than the structured approach of intolerability. Although it refers to the presumption in favour of continued life, it does not entrench it evidentially as the intolerability test did. But intolerability is so useful, and such a potent guarantor of the sanctity of life, that it is coming quietly back. Indeed there was a bridge for its return in *Wyatt* itself. It was the reference to the 'balance sheet' in the passage just cited. This was a reference to *In Re A (Male Sterilisation)*,[58] where Thorpe LJ said:

There can be no doubt in my mind that the evaluation of best interests is akin to a welfare appraisal. . . . Pending the enactment of a checklist or other statutory direction it seems to me that the first instance judge with the responsibility to make an evaluation of the best interests of a claimant lacking capacity should draw up a balance sheet. The first entry should be of any factor or factors of actual benefit. . . . Then on the other sheet the judge should write any counterbalancing dis-benefits to the applicant . . . Then the judge should enter on each sheet the potential gains and losses in each instance making some estimate of the extent of the possibility that the gain or loss might accrue. At the end of that exercise the judge should be better placed to strike a balance between the sum of the certain and possible gains against the sum of the certain and possible losses. Obviously, only if the account is in relatively significant credit will the judge conclude that the application is likely to advance the best interests of the claimant.[59]

Note the reference to '*significant* credit'. End-of-life decision-making is not a simple matter of deciding whether the benefits of continued existence outweigh the detriments. Only if it is established that the detriments significantly outweigh the benefits will the presumption in favour of continued life be overturned. This is intolerability by another name.

In *An NHS Trust v MB and Mr and Mrs MB*,[60] Holman J, considering whether life-sustaining ventilation should be withdrawn from a sensate, cognate 18 month old child with Spinal Muscular Atrophy, wondered aloud what the Court of Appeal in *Wyatt* could have meant in commenting as they did on intolerability. Although he thought that use of the word 'intolerable' tended to indicate a conclusion rather than providing a test (an observation not shared by generations of previous judges, who have found it a helpful yardstick), he did go on to say that:

If it is correct to say, or once it has been concluded, that life is literally 'intolerable', then it is hard to see in what circumstances it should be artificially prolonged. If, conversely,

---

[57] [2005] 1 WLR 3995, [87], [90].
[58] [2000] 1 FLR 549.
[59] *Ibid* 560.
[60] [2006] EWHC 507 (Fam).

it is 'tolerable' then it is hard to see in what circumstances it should be permitted, avoidably, to end.[61]

Intolerability is back, and the notion of the sanctity of life is all the safer for it.

What does all this have to do with autonomy? In one way, very little: autonomy is not directly involved in this debate. But in another and more important way, a very great deal. The intolerability test is a stringent one. It is probably a more stringent test than most healthy, fit people, considering what to say in their advance directive, would think of grafting into it. Few would say: 'I want to be kept alive unless it can be demonstrated that my life is intolerable.' Autonomy, looking over the shoulder of that advance directive drafter, would shake its head furiously at such a paragraph. That is because autonomy lacks perspective. It does not take into account how people's views change when faced with the challenges they have always feared most. It lives in a cowardly and blinkered way in the present. The law as it presently stands gives to people in the most vulnerable position—trapped in the dependency created by disease and debility, the benefit of its knowledge of how precious life seems when there is little of it left.

Autonomy, via advance directives, wants to extend its influence even to the very edge of the lives of non-autonomous patients. While giving lip service to autonomy, the law has refused it leave. Instead the sanctity of life, with beneficence and non-maleficence at its shoulder, continues, however tenuously, to rule.

[61] *Ibid* [17].

Part 4

After Death

12

Transplantation

ALTHOUGH THIS SECTION appears in Part 4 of the book, which deals with issues arising after death, many (indeed some would argue all) of the issues relating to autonomy which are pertinent to organ transplantation arise in relation to living donors. One of the most difficult issues is of course that of resource allocation (there are many more would-be recipients than there are organs). That issue is only touched on here. It is dealt with in more detail in chapter 9.

There are broadly three types of organ donation[1]:

(a) Xenotransplantation—in which an organ from species X is transplanted into species Y.
(b) Living donor homotransplantation: from a live donor of species X into a recipient of species X.
(c) Post-mortem homotransplantation: from a dead donor of species X into a recipient of species X.

It is not quite as simple as this, of course. The definition of death is relevant. Although the English courts have adopted the brain stem definition of death,[2] not all relatives will. There will sometimes be a reluctance to allow the removal of organs from a patient who is brain-stem dead, and will only accept death when there is cardio-respiratory failure—which diminishes the chance of a successful transplantation.[3,4]

---

[1] I do not consider here the possibility of artificial organs or genetically created organs. Although progress in both these areas is rapidly being made both are at the experimental stage at the moment. The implantation of artificial organs raises the issues of the sufficiency of information and the adequacy of consent that are raised whenever any experimental procedure is proposed. The implantation of genetically created organs raises similar issues, as well as issues about the autonomy rights of the person from whom any cell line used in the transplant was derived. Those issues are discussed in outline in ch 13.

[2] See *Re A* [1992] 3 *Medical Law Review* 303; *R (Smeaton on behalf of SPUC) v The Secretary of State for Health* [2002] 2 FCR 193.

[3] Some cynics have come close to implying that the criterion of brain stem death is just too convenient for would-be transplanters. The issue is discussed in detail by Lock M (2002) *Twice Dead* (Berkeley, University of California Press).

[4] See generally Parker M and Shemie SD (2002) 'Pro/Con Ethics Debate: Should Mechanical Ventilation Be Continued to Allow for Progression to Brain Death So That Organs Can Be Donated?' 6(5) *Critical Care* 399–402.

Xenotransplantation

If one does not consider that the animal donor has any autonomy rights, xeno-transplantation is relatively uninteresting from our perspective. It has, however, been suggested that the autonomy rights of the wider population might come into play, since there is at least a theoretical possibility of cross-species disease trans-mission—particularly of viruses.[5] This is the same sort of analysis that we saw in examining the tension between Article 8(1) and 8(2) in the context of confiden-tiality and consent. It is rather clumsy: it seeks to deploy autonomy where other language would be neater. The rights of society not to be infected with pig viruses *can* be described in terms of autonomy, but it is better to say simply that it is a bad thing for society to be so infected or, if one insists on being philosophical, that doctors motivated by the principle of non-maleficence will avoid doing xeno-transplantation if it is likely to hurt more people than it helps.

Live Donor Homotransplantation

If a competent adult donor wants altruistically to donate a kidney, is there any reason why she should not? The altruistic motive should surely be applauded, autonomy is happy, and indeed the practice is widespread and encouraged by gov-ernment. It has never been considered in the courts, but if it were, the outcome is certain: the judge would wonder why on earth he was being bothered with the case. And yet it is not absurd to wonder about the legal basis of the donation.

Nephrectomy undoubtedly amounts to serious bodily injury. The general rule is of course that one cannot consent to serious bodily injury.[6] One can consent to some activities (eg boxing), in the course of which there is a *risk* of serious bodily injury, if the activity itself is deemed (rather arbitrarily, in the case of boxing) law-ful. But in the case of nephrectomy there is a certainty of serious injury, and a real, though small, risk of death. There will often, but not always, be a tangible bene-fit—namely the survival or dialysis-free life of a friend or relative. Sometimes— and always in the case of a donation to an unknown recipient—there will be the benefit of knowing that one has done one's best to change the life of another for the better. But although fine metaphysical computation is impossible, these enefits appear to be outweighed by the very real detriments. Altruistic kidney donation is arguably more akin to the nailing of one's scrotum to a board than it does to participation in a boxing match. As we had to do before, we simply have

---

[5] Bach FH, Ivinson AJ and Weeramantry C (2001) 'Ethical and Legal Issues in Technology: Xenotransplantation' 27 *American Journal of Legal Medicine* 283.
[6] *R v Brown* (above): ch 8.

to sigh and acknowledge that the English law is internally inconsistent, but that in this case at least, seems to endorse the right things.

From the point of view of our principles, autonomy here wants to do the decent thing. Non-maleficence and beneficence agree with the final result. The likely result in the case of a live donation of a kidney is of no lasting harm to the donor and a profoundly good life-changing revolution for the recipient.

But there are harder cases. Jonathan Herring discusses the (real) case of a man, Mr P, who had two sons, both of whom had kidney failure. Mr P successfully donated one of his kidneys to one son. The second son, R, had a cadaveric transplant. It failed. The chance of obtaining a matching kidney from the general population was very low. Mr P wanted to donate his remaining kidney to R. He said that it would be much better for him than for R to be on dialysis. Mr P's request was refused by four teams of transplant surgeons. They were concerned, inter alia, about the effect on R of the change to Mr P's life and prognosis, and about the resource implications if the transplant failed and both Mr P and R had to be on dialysis.[7]

Autonomy would be outraged, but beneficence and non-maleficence would tend towards cautious, slightly reluctant agreement with the surgeons' view. Justice would be impressed by the consideration of the wider societal cost.

There are still harder cases. Herring poses another: a parent seeking to donate a heart to save her child.[8] Autonomy must surely pause longer here. Once the parent's heart is removed, the parent will have no autonomy at all. The child, depending on the result of the transplant operation, may have enhanced autonomy, similar autonomy as before or, if it fails completely, no autonomy at all. Herring suggests that the principle of non-maleficence would (or should) preclude the clinicians from agreeing to such a procedure.[9] The argument is brutal but convincing. Society should applaud the parent's desire to make this extraordinary sacrifice, while at the same time protecting her from the desired consequences of her self-immolatory altruism. Society should be strong enough to be able to bear such tensions, and so should the law. It is right that the law should not only refuse to compel the clinicians to carry out such a procedure, but also prohibit them from doing so. A definite prohibition is necessary to ensure that clinicians sleep at night, and it is in the wider interests of us all that they do so.

Should it be unlawful to sell and buy organs?[10] It certainly is unlawful. The Human Tissue Act 2004 creates a series of offences in relation to organ trafficking.[11] The General Medical Council asserts that:

[7] Herring J (2006) *Medical Law and Ethics* (Oxford, OUP) 370–71.

[8] *Ibid* 371.

[9] See too Garwood-Gowers A (1999) *Living Donor Organ Transplantation: Key Legal and Ethical Issues* (Aldershot, Ashgate) 62.

[10] For a detailed discussion, see Council on Ethical and Judicial Affairs of the American Medical Association (1995) 'Financial Incentives for Organ Procurement' 155 *Archives of Internal Medicine* 581–8; Joralemon D and Cox P (2003) 'Body Values: The Case Against Compensating for Transplant Organs' 33 *Hastings Center Report* 27–33; Nelkin D, Andrews L (1998) 'Homo Economicus: Commercialization of Body Tissue in the Age of Biotechnology' 28 *Hastings Center Report* 30–9; Erin CA and Harris J (2003) 'An Ethical Market in Human Organs' 29(3) *Journal of Medical Ethics* 137–8.

[11] Human Tissue Act 2004 s 32.

In no circumstances may doctors participate in or encourage in any way the trade in human organs from live donors. They must not advertise for donors nor make financial medical arrangements for people who wish to sell or buy organs. . . . Doctors must also satisfy themselves that consent to a donation has been given without undue influence of any kind, including the offer of a financial or material benefit. A doctor, or another appropriately qualified professional, independent of the transplantation team, must assess the motivation of each donor.[12]

Autonomy's analysis of this prohibition will always be inadequate. Its knee-jerk response will be: 'Why shouldn't somebody do what they want with their own body?' And later, when it is pointed out that the prohibition is actually an effort to protect the exploitation of the vulnerable by their own greed, or poverty, or by the overbearing influence of others, autonomy will sheepishly acknowledge that there might be something in that point. This highlights the fact that autonomy really cannot cope with anything other than the wholly artificial caricature of a splendidly self-determining person. Any suggestion that autonomy has to be protected will be resisted: if a person's self-determination has to be guarded, that person is by definition not self-determining.

That said, it is not clear that beneficence and non-maleficence (the real builders of all of the obviously necessary legal bulwarks against the exploitation of the vulnerable) will always be opposed to payment for organs. This issue has already been discussed in the context of payment for involvement in research.[13]

This is as good a place as any to mention the unholy alliance (indeed frequent identification) of autonomy and a stern type of utilitarianism.

Imagine that four patients are sitting in a hospital waiting room. A needs a kidney transplant, B needs a heart transplant, C needs a liver transplant and D is perfectly healthy. A simple utilitarianism would say that D should be killed so that A, B and C should live happy and healthy lives. Autonomy, unmitigated by any other principles would agree, and for the same reasons. The total amount of autonomy in the world will be increased by the consequentialist murder of D.[14]

No decent people would agree with this, but it cannot be criticised unless one is prepared to recruit principles other than autonomy.[15] It is a chilling illustration of what happens if one equates autonomy and good, as is so uncritically done in so much of medical ethics.

What about donation by children or incompetent adults?

In *Re Y (Mental Patient: Bone Marrow Donation)*,[16] it was proposed that bone marrow should be taken from a profoundly mentally and physically handicapped

---

[12] General Medical Council (1992) *Guidance for Doctors on Transplantation of Organs from Live Donors* (London, GMC).

[13] See ch 10.

[14] This is urged by John Harris: see Harris J (2005) 'Organ Procurement: Dead Interests, Living Needs' 31 *Journal of Medical Ethics* 242.

[15] The most accessible account of and advocacy of the 'four principles' approach to the ethics of transplantation is in Wigmore SJ and Plant WD (2005) 'The Ethics of Transplantation' in Forsythe JLR (ed) *Transplantation* (Amsterdam, Elsevier). To be fair, even the most hard-line of the autonomists acknowledge that in the realm of resource allocation autonomy cannot supply all the answers.

[16] [1997] Fam 110.

adult (X) and transplanted into her sister, Y, who had a pre-leukaemic bone marrow disorder. Y's only realistic prospect of recovery was from such a transplant, and the prospects of an acceptable match were higher if the bone marrow came from X than from a stranger. X could not validly consent to the procedure.[17] A declaration as to the lawfulness of the procedure was sought.

The test was:

> whether the procedures here envisaged will benefit [X] and accordingly benefits which may flow to [Y] are relevant only in so far as they have a positive effect upon the best interests of [X].[18]

The judge found powerfully persuasive *Curran v Bosze*,[19] a decision of the Supreme Court of Illinois. In *Curran* Calvo J said, having reviewed several authorities:

> In each of the foregoing cases where consent to the kidney transplant was authorised, regardless whether the authority to consent was to be exercised by the court, a parent or a guardian, the key inquiry was the presence or absence of a benefit to the potential donor. Notwithstanding the language used by the courts in reaching their determination that a transplant may or may not occur, the standard by which the determination was made was whether the transplant would be in the best interest of the child or incompetent person. The primary benefit to the donor in these cases arises from the relationship existing between the donor and the recipient. In *Strunk* (1969) 445 SW 2d 145 the donor lived in a state institution. The recipient was a brother who served as the donor's only connection with the outside world. In both *Hart v Brown* (1972) 29 Conn Supp 368 and *Little v Little* (1979) 576 SW 2d 493 there was evidence that the sibling relationship between the donor and the recipient was close.[20]

Accordingly:

> [T]here must be an existing, close relationship between the donor and recipient. The evidence clearly shows that there is no physical benefit to a donor child. If there is any benefit to a child who donates bone marrow to a sibling it will be a psychological benefit. According to the evidence, the psychological benefit is not simply one of personal,

---

[17] As to the ability of a child to consent to organ donation, see *Re W (A Minor) (Medical Treatment)* [1992] 4 All ER 627, in which Lord Donaldson MR said, obiter, 'Organ donations are quite different and, as a matter of law, doctors would have to secure the consent of someone with the right to consent on behalf of a donor under the age of 18 or, if they relied on the consent of the minor himself or herself, be satisfied that the minor was "Gillick" competent in the context of so serious a procedure which would not benefit the minor. . . . It is inconceivable that [the doctor] should proceed in reliance solely upon the consent of an underage patient, however "Gillick-competent", in the absence of supporting parental consent and equally inconceivable that he should proceed in the absence of the patient's consent. In any event he will need to seek the opinions of other doctors and may be well advised to apply to the court for guidance. . . . A minor of any age who is "Gillick-competent" in the context of a particular treatment has a right to consent to that treatment which again cannot be overridden by those with parental responsibility, but can be overridden by the court. Unlike the statutory right this common law right extends to the donation of blood or organs.': 635 and 639. The 'statutory right' referred to is Family Law Reform Act 1969 s 8.

[18] [1997] Fam 110, 113.

[19] (1990) 566 NE 2d 1319.

[20] *Ibid* .1331

individual altruism in an abstract theoretical sense, although that may be a factor. The psychological benefit is grounded firmly in the fact that the donor and recipient are known to each other as family. Only where there is an existing relationship between a healthy child and his or her ill sister or brother may a psychological benefit to the child from donating bone marrow to a sibling realistically be found to exist. The evidence establishes that it is the existing sibling relationship as well as the potential for a continuing sibling relationship, which forms the context in which it may be determined that it will be in the best interests of the child to undergo a bone marrow harvesting procedure for a sibling.[21]

The English court accordingly decided that it was in the interests of X for the transplant to be done. The judge noted, however, that

this is a rather unusual case and that the family of [Y] and [X] are a particularly close family. It is doubtful that this case would act as a useful precedent in cases where the surgery involved is more intrusive than in this case, where the evidence shows that the bone marrow harvested is speedily regenerated and that a healthy individual can donate as much as two pints with no long term consequences at all. Thus the bone marrow donated by [X] will cause her no loss and she will suffer no real long term risk.'[22]

There are various autonomistic analyses of this *result*:

(a) A fascistic one: X has no autonomy, and her life is, generally speaking, not worth living. By chance, though, she has the opportunity to make a difference to somebody who is autonomous, and accordingly does have a life worth living. Accordingly not only is the taking of X's bone marrow justifiable, it is the only right thing to do. It can only increase the amount of autonomy on the planet. The same reasoning would apply if X's heart were needed by Y, or indeed if X's heart were needed for any other person with autonomy.

(b) If X's life is worth living, it is not worth as much as Y's. Therefore all that is said in (a) above applies.

(c) X's life is worth living, notwithstanding her absent or truncated autonomy, and in order to make the most of it (and to make the most of any autonomy that she may have), Y should stay alive and well. By the same reasoning, if Y needed a kidney, it should be compulsorily taken from X.

(d) X's life is worth living, notwithstanding her absent or truncated autonomy, and in order to make the most of it (and to make the most of any autonomy that she may have), Y should stay alive and well. If Y needed a kidney, though, the residual autonomy rights that X has would forbid it.

Note that (d) is the only analysis which is remotely consistent with the *reasoning* in this case, and it demands an assumption that X, despite being profoundly mentally disabled and incompetent by all the usual canons, does have autonomy rights. That is a concession which in other comparable cases it is difficult to extract from autonomy. In fact, though, analysis (d) is very strained. It is yet another

[21] (1990) 566 NE 2d 1343–4.
[22] [1997] Fam 110, 116.

example of what happens if one tries to analyse complex situations using just one principle. The judge in *Re Y* would have been surprised to hear a submission that the only reason why there was any debate before him about whether or not to take bone marrow from X was because X had some sort of autonomy interest which should not be violated. Remember that the question was whether it was in X's 'best interests' for the bone marrow to be taken. Were those 'interests' mere autonomy? Of course not: on one view she had no autonomy interests at all. But even if she did, they were not all she had. She had an interest in being happy, in relating to her family, in not being hurt, in not being bereaved, and so on. Translated into legalese, she had relevant Article 3 and Article 8 interests. The better view is that she would continue to have both even if she were unconscious.[23] It strains language far less to say that the action of taking the bone marrow is action that both beneficence and non-maleficence would urge.

Post-Mortem Homotransplantation

As long as the donor is really dead, these raise no issues in relation to autonomy other than those which are inherent in all cases involving the use of post-mortem tissue. That is the subject of the next chapter. The details of the debate about what amounts to death are technical and irrelevant to our discussion.[24]

[23] But see *NHS Trust A v M* [2001] 2 WLR 942. This concerned patients in PVS. The President held there that Art 8 was engaged, but that Art 3 was not. The gist was that one cannot suffer inhuman or degrading treatment if one is not aware that of it. If right, it is a curious conclusion. Can one not degrade an unconscious person? Should an Article designed to protect the vulnerable falter when it comes to the most vulnerable of all patients? The conclusion was robustly criticised by Munby J in *R (Burke) v General Medical Council* [2005] QB 424, [144]–[146]. Although the Court of Appeal in *Burke* themselves criticised Munby J, they seem implicitly to have endorsed his conclusion on Art 3: see [2006] QB 273, [39]. For a detailed discussion of this issue, see Foster C (2007) *Elements of Medical Law* (London, Claerhout) 112–15.
[24] They are well summarised by Potts M and Evans DW (2005) 'Does It Matter That Organ Donors Are Not Dead? Ethical and Policy Implications' 31 *Journal of Medical Ethics* 406–9; Truog RD and Robinson WM (2003) 'Role of Brain Death and the Dead-Donor Rule in the Ethics of Organ Transplantation' 31 *Critical Care Medicine* 2391–6.

13

The Ownership of Body Parts

THE LAW IS a mess. Every lawyer will remember the old adage that there is no property in a corpse.[1] Many law students' first introduction to practical legal cunning was to be told how body snatchers were charged with the theft of the shroud in order to get round the rule. Like most simple rules of English law, however, there is more law in the exceptions than there is in the rule. If a body or a part of a body acquires different attributes because X has put work into it (for example by dissecting or preserving it), it may: (a) have been transmuted into property; and (b) have become the property of X.[2] But the ability to possess a corpse lawfully does not necessarily imply that it has become property.[3] Who owns the (possibly valuable) dandruff that cascades from the scalps of still-living celebrities? If a maid in a pop idol's hotel room takes away and auctions his nail-clippings, is she guilty of theft? Are the flecks of dandruff and the nail clippings capable of constituting 'property' within the meaning of the Theft Act 1968? Have they been abandoned by their original owner? If they are not property, could they ever be owned even by the person whose cells generated them? Should one assume abandonment if a claim is not explicitly asserted? What if the maid, instead of taking nail clippings, uses a buccal cell from the star's toothbrush to establish an immortal cell line which makes her and a pharmaceutical company millions of dollars?[4] Should the star, having abandoned his cells, be able retroactively to assert a right over them once it is clear that there is money to be made from them? And so on. This is the stuff of which fascinating and pointless papers are made.[5]

Not much of the detail need concern us. There has been a recent attempt in the Human Tissue Act 2004 to codify the law in relation to the ownership of body parts from both living and dead people. The key principle in the Act is the autonomist's favourite—consent.

Philosophically the Act is something of a desert. And that is probably no bad thing. The point of Acts is to act, not to discuss. The Act does not opt obviously and exclusively for either of the two main approaches to the question of the ownership

[1] It is easier to assert it than to find high authority for it. See, however, *Doodeward v Spence* (1908) 6 CLR 906.
[2] See *R v Kelly* [1998] 3 All ER 714; *Dobson v Northern Tyneside Health Authority* [1996] 4 All ER 474.
[3] *AB v A Teaching Hospital NHS Trust* [2004] 3 FCR 324.
[4] See *Moore v Regents of the University of California* 793 P 2d 479 1990 for a discussion of the issues involved here.
[5] For a detailed discussion of these and related issues, see Foster C (2003) 'Dandruff, Data Protection and Dead Bodies' April 2003 *Counsel* 12. See also *Yearworth v N Bristol NHS Trust*, (CA) unreported, 4 February 2009.

of body parts—the property approach and the privacy approach. It pragmatically uses the approach to each issue which seems to make the draftsman's job easier. In its approach to the unauthorised analysis of DNA, for instance, its thinking is very much that of Article 8. This is a relief. DNA has always presented a problem for English lawyers, who are unused to moving outside their own mental pigeon-holes. It is a physical substance: accordingly the law of property should apply to it. It conveys information: therefore the law relating to the control of information should apply. The sort of lawyers who do one sort of law don't (and possibly can't) talk to the other sort—hence a dangerous lack of integrity in the law. Only blissful lack of concern about the analytic niceties can free the law relating to DNA from this sort of forensic constipation. The 2004 Act is blissfully unlettered and unconcerned. It simply notes that the real mischief resulting from the misuse of DNA results from its use as a source of information: hence the very practical prohibitions on *using* it, intending to use it, and so on. It is not a perfect solution for all conceivable purposes, but it is a lot better than one that nods with the undue deference of old towards the notion of DNA as property. In relation to body parts in pots of formalin, though, it steadfastly and rightly holds onto the 'property' analysis.

The Act can be summarised simply: consent is necessary for the removal and use of human tissue—unless it isn't. There are several statutory exceptions to the general principle that consent is required. These are summarised below. There is no way to make the catalogue interesting. It is adduced to illustrate that some of the exceptions cause autonomy's eyebrows to rise.

The Act deals with the removal and use of material from the dead, and with the use of material taken from the living. The common law continues to govern the removal of tissue from the living. The Act does not regulate everything that can be extracted from a human body—just 'relevant material'. This is defined as material that has come from a human body and consists of, or contains, human cells. Cell lines are excluded (although therapeutic cell lines have been shoved under the umbrella of the Human Tissue Authority by a very odd legislative dodge); so are hair and nail from living people. Live gametes and embryos are excluded; they are the province of the Human Fertilisation and Embryology Act 1990.

Consent is required in order to use 'relevant material' for specified purposes. Generally, consent is required, whether the tissue is from the living or the dead, for anatomical examination, determination of the cause of death, establishing after a person's death the efficacy of any drug or other treatment administered to him, obtaining scientific or medical information about a living or deceased person which may be relevant to any other person, public display, research in connection with disorders or the functioning of the human body, and transplantation. In relation to anatomical examination and public display, witnessed consent in writing before death is required. In relation to determining the cause of death, there is an unsurprising exception where a post mortem is ordered by a coroner.

Where the tissue is from a dead person, consent is required for use in clinical audit, education or training relating to human health, performance assessment, public health monitoring and quality assurance.

Tissue From the Living

Lots of tissue is left over from diagnostic or surgical procedures. Consent is not needed for the use of that tissue for clinical audit, education or training relating to human health, performance assessment, public health monitoring or quality assurance. It can be used without consent for research, provided that the researcher cannot identify the donor and is unlikely to be able to do so in the future. The data gleaned from such research can lawfully be linked with patient records, provided that patient-identifying information is not obtained.

Where it proves impossible to get 'appropriate consent' for the use of residual tissue for the purpose of obtaining medical information that may be relevant to another person, the Human Tissue Authority can, in two sets of exceptional circumstances, deem consent to have been given for that use. These circumstances are:

(a) where the donor cannot be traced and there is no reason to believe that he/she has died, has refused consent or lacks capacity;
(b) where the donor has not responded to repeated attempts to obtain consent, and there is no reason to believe that he/she has died, has refused consent, or lacks capacity.

Tissue From the Living and the Dead

The Act gives power to the Secretary of State to make regulations allowing tissue to be used without consent for research. No such regulations have been made.

Tissues that have been imported, and tissues that come from someone who has died at least 100 years previously, can be used without consent. There is no statutory need for the researchers sequencing Tutankhamun's DNA to reach for their ouija boards.

Existing Holdings

Tissue, whether from the living or the dead, which was already in storage in April 2006 can be used for all the 'scheduled purposes' (those set out above under 'What uses require consent?' in relation both to the living and to the deceased).

Who Can Give Consent?

The answers are unsurprising. The Department of Health's explanatory notes[6] set it out well in tabular form:

Living competent adult, or competent child willing to make a decision	His/her consent
Living child (incompetent, or competent but unwilling to make a decision)	Consent of a person with parental responsibility
Deceased adult	i His/her consent before death ii If no prior consent, consent of a nominated representative iii If no representative, the consent of a qualifying relative.

'Qualifying relatives' are spouse/partner/civil partner under the Civil Partnerships Act 2004, parent or child, brother or sister, grandparent or grandchild, child of a brother or sister, stepfather or stepmother, half brother or half sister and a friend of longstanding. The order in which these are cited is important. It represents a statutory hierarchy. Where there is more than one person in the same rank (eg brother or sister), the consent of any one of them will make it lawful (although not obligatory) to store or to use tissue for a statutory purpose. The hierarchy does not apply to consent to analyse the DNA in the tissue of a deceased person: the consent of any qualifying relative will suffice. The reason for this is obvious: any relative might themselves have a particular medical or other interest in that analysis: Other relatives should not be allowed to prevent the analysis that one relative thinks is a good idea.

The central principle, as we have said, is consent. It is perhaps curious that the Act does not define it. It leaves the definition, wholly unsatisfactorily, in the joint hands of the newly created Human Tissue Authority (which has published guidance as to what 'consent' might mean),[7] and the common law. It will presumably require a good deal of expensive litigation to work out the details.[8] Some of the

---

[6] Department of Health (2005) *The Human Tissue Act 2004: New Legislation on Human Organs and Tissue.*

[7] See Human Tissue Authority (July 2006) *Consent: Code of Practice* (HTA, London).

[8] See Liddell K and Hall A (2002) 'Beyond Bristol and Alder Hey: The Future Regulation of Human Tissue' 2005, 13 *Medical Law Review* 171; Brazier M (2002) 'Organ Retention and Return: Problems of Consent' 2002, 29 *Journal of Medical Ethics* 30.

details might matter very much indeed. Jonathan Herring poses the question of whether 'conditional consent' is permitted:

> A Roman Catholic might, for example, be happy for her or his human material to be used for research as long as the research does not involve embryos or concern contraception. Could he or she consent with such a proviso?"[9]

The basic structure is clear, though. For live humans, the common law principles outlined in chapter 8 will apply. The same comments apply as applied there as to whether or not autonomy should be happy with the result. In relation to competent adults the answer, broadly, is that autonomy will indeed be happy—provided that conditional consent is part of the deal; but autonomy does not have a monopoly on the happiness. With a caveat inserted in relation to the issue of conditional consent, the smiles of beneficence and non-maleficence are almost as broad. Justice might prefer tissue to be more readily available than autonomy might allow it to be (so that the lessons from a particular patient's story can be more thoroughly learned), but will not quibble too much. In relation to children and incompetent adults, autonomy may not have anything at all to say, but if it has, it is likely to be between clenched teeth. These are very much the provinces of beneficence and non-maleficence.

The caveat in relation to conditional consent is an important one. We return to it in the context of the use of the tissues from dead people.

But what about dead patients? Should one be able to rule from the grave what is done with parts of your body? Once the seat of your autonomy is destroyed, should you be able to exercise autonomy? Some of the most vocal proponents of autonomy for the living are vocal denouncers of autonomy for the dead.[10]

The history of the Human Tissue Act 2004 is the history of the Alder Hey and Bristol Royal Infirmary debacles.[11] Parents discovered that parts of their dead children were held in vast collections. Often no consent had been obtained for any retention at all. When some retention was authorised, it was often not retention on anything like the scale that actually occurred. The parents felt that their children had been violated and that they themselves had been duped. The resulting inquiries[12]

---

[9] Herring J (2006) *Medical Law and Ethics* (Oxford, OUP) 360–61.

[10] Probably the best example is John Harris. See Harris J (2002) 'Law And Regulation of Retained Organs: The Ethical Issues' 22(4) *Legal Studies* 527–49. His view is not that there should be no right to determine what is done with one's own organs and those of one's children, but that these rights are flimsy compared to the right that society should have to use the organs for research. The most comprehensive discussion of the issues relating to the ownership of body parts is in Gold GA (1996) *Body Parts, Property Rights and the Ownership of Human and Biological Materials* (Washington DC, Georgetown University Press). There is an accessible overview of the issues in Calabresi G (1991) 'Do We Own Our Bodies?' 1 *Health Matrix* 5–18. For a good survey of the issues in the light of Honoré's theory of ownership, see Quigley M (2007) 'Property and the Body: Applying Honoré' 33 *Journal of Medical Ethics* 631–4.

[11] See too The Chief Medical Officer (2001) *The Removal, Retention and Use of Human Organs and Tissue from Post Mortem Examination* (DoH, london), and Department of Health (2002) *Human Bodies, Human Choices*.

[12] The Kennedy Inquiry: see 'Learning from Bristol: The Report of the Public Inquiry into Children's Heart Surgery at the Bristol Royal Infirmary 1984–1995' (Cm 5207, 2002)

found that the communication of doctors' intentions was often dismal. The justification for poor communication was often that the doctors felt that the parents would be distressed if the subject were broached, and that no harm was done by retaining some tissue. Although there were undoubtedly medical justifications for at least some retention, there were no justifications for the paternalism that characterised the hospitals' attitude to retention.

So it was the outrage about the abnegation of an autonomy right that drove the 2004 Act onto the statute book. The autonomy right concerned was basically the rights of the parents to be informed about their children's organs.[13] Accordingly it is rather strange for John Harris to complain so loudly about it. Presumably he would think it outrageous medical paternalism for a doctor, without consulting the parents, to conduct a surgical procedure on a child. Does he really not think that the parents, as custodians of the child's autonomy interests and as holders of engaged autonomy interests themselves, should not have a say about how and where their children's remains are kept? This is quintessential Article 8(1) territory. In almost all other contexts Harris is a fiercely vigilant watchdog of these Article 8(1) rights.

When one comes to decisions by competent adults about their organs, should death really change things so fundamentally? Should the law protect with the extraordinary rigour that it does the integrity of an arm that has blood pumping through it, and the almost unfettered right of the person to whom the arm happens to be attached to do anything with it, and yet be haughtily dismissive of the ability of the former owner to determine what happens to the arm as soon as the heart that has done the pumping stops. Would not (should not?) autonomy go to the wire to insist on the ability of a person to leave Blackacre to whomever he wants? Is an arm not more fundamental than a field? Why should one's decision about what happens to the arm evaporate off as the electrical activity in your brainstem falls off, whereas a decision about the field persists?

Surely here, if anywhere, autonomy ought (with the caveat of conditional consent) to speak consistently and unchallenged.[14] It is rather strange that it does not

<http://www.bristol-inquiry.org.uk> accessed 27 December 2007; The Redfern Inquiry: see 'Report of the Royal Liverpool Children's Inquiry' (The Stationery Office, 2001): <http://www.rlcinquiry.org.uk> accessed 27 December 2007.

[13] See Knowles D (2001) 'Parents' Consent to the Post-Mortem Removal and Retention of Organs' 18(3) *Journal of Applied Philosophy* 225.

[14] Many disagree, for reasons with which, in other contexts and other chapters, I would have agreed wholeheartedly. Thus Jonathan Zimmern (2007) says: 'New medical technologies and research projects are continually being developed which highlight the web of family bonds, genetic dependency and social obligation that underlie human society. However we constitute or choose to live our lives, we do so in a community. The [Human Tissue] Act anchors many of its provisions on informed consent requirements. Over reliance on consent fails to acknowledge the point that wider familial dependencies and relationships are also engaged by genetic data. Consent has an important role to play in the concerns surrounding the analysis of DNA, but it cannot provide the answer on its own. Our emphasis on the centrality of individual autonomy has obscured other equally important values. We would do well to acknowledge the inherent weaknesses within this position and accept that consent procedures cannot provide every answer to the dilemmas faced by modern medicine.': 'Consent and Autonomy in the Human Tissue Act 2004' 18 *King's Law Journal* 313, 328.

appear to. Yes, one can imagine situations where other principles might want a voice—for example if there were a clear indication that retention and examination of tissue would produce a real and immediate public health benefit, but retention was being objected to. But whatever Harris says, such situations will be few and far between.[15] Most would be prepared to cede most of this ground, most of the time, to autonomy.

The fact that the autonomists say what they do (or some of them do) about body parts is extraordinarily interesting and significant. It does not indicate muddled thinking: far from it. It indicates an icy consistency. We have seen repeatedly that autonomy is the creed of the selfish brat; we have seen its sinister alliance with some of the more disreputable elements of utilitarianism; we have seen how its defining egocentricity means that it does not have the perspective to comment safely, without the help of other principles, on life and death matters. And here, at the end and beyond the end of life, we see it in its true colours. When the self dissipates, it has nothing more to say. It responds to a grieving mother by telling her that information from the heart of her unlawfully plundered child will form part of a potentially useful computer database. It cannot comfort, because it really understands very little.

Autonomy perhaps has a legitimate complaint with the ability of 'nominated representatives' or 'qualifying relatives' to give consent under the 2004 Act when the person him or herself has failed to do so.[16] It means that we do not have a strict opt-in system of organ donation in the UK. We have an 'opt-in, or if you don't, your representative or relative might opt-in for you' system. But it is plain why this is the case. It is because of the manifest failure of the UK opt-in system. A straightforward opt-in system would leave the organ transplant system floundering: there just would not be enough organs.

This is best viewed as a failure of autonomy itself. The reason that people don't carry donor cards is not because they are reluctant to donate their organs. We know this very well. Where 'mandated choice' systems operate (requiring people to indicate—for example when voting or applying for a driving licence—whether or not they are prepared to donate organs), a hugely greater number of people agree to donate than actually carry donor cards in an opt-in system. The reason that the opt-in system fails is because, contrary to autonomy's assumption of a well-examined life and a carefully scripted life-plan, people are simply, benignly thoughtless. Unless they are forced to choose (itself something that autonomy squirms about), they will not. It is easy to force choice in the name of beneficence: it is harder to do it coherently in the name of autonomy.

We return finally to the question of conditional consent. It is best illustrated by taking the case of organ donation. What if X states that he is happy to donate his

[15] Harris's justification for his position is that the research benefit from retained tissue is so obvious and usual that the public interest in the research should trump any private concerns about the retention of tissue.
[16] For a discussion of this double veto, see Wilkinson TM (2005) 'Individual and Family Consent to Organ and Tissue Donation: Is the Current Position Coherent?' 31 *Journal of Medical Ethics* 587–90.

kidneys after his death, provided that the kidneys are not given to a Jew? Should his kidneys be accepted? Autonomy, and its bedfellow, utilitarianism, would have no hesitation. Of course they should be accepted, and the condition honoured. The lives (and the autonomy) of potentially two people waiting for a kidney could be revolutionised. One should not deny them this chance on the basis of a politically correct scruple: the potential recipients should not be sacrificed on the altar of a liberal principle. Beneficence is not so sure. It has a holistic view of 'good'. Although the kidneys of a rabid anti-semite might do physiological good to two recipients, accepting them might well do harm overall to society. Non-maleficence has similar reservations. Justice is quite clear: this sort of condition is entirely unacceptable. On balance, then, autonomy is outvoted in the case of the kidney donation. Does this mean a ban on all conditional donations? What about the Catholic who does not want her tissue to be used in research involving embryos or contraception? Although in some circumstances the practical difficulties of restricting use to particular purposes can be profound, there can be no coherent objection of principle to such a condition. It is not akin to the Catholic saying: 'I will donate my kidney to anyone, provided that they have not had an abortion.' That would be offensive for precisely the same reason as in the anti-semite example. It is offensive because it implies distaste for a person as opposed to a practice. Distaste for a practice is fine; it is recognised in all civilised societies that expression of distaste is legitimate and important. It is the personalising of the distaste that is rightly unacceptable.

14

Epilogue

I N MANY WAYS this book is utterly trite. It states something that is obvious—that medical law and ethics, dealing with the whole of the immensely variegated human condition, need to listen to other principles as well as autonomy. It is only necessary to do this because the academic world roars out deafeningly exaggerated praise of the Emperor's non-existent clothes. It points out that the law very often does indeed listen, and where the law does not do it adequately, suggests how the law might benefit by pricking up its philosophical ears.

Any society that does not have an immense respect for human autonomy is misguided. Any society that does not have laws robustly protecting autonomy is an unsafe and unhappy one. But any society whose sole principle is autonomy is unreflective, shallow and dangerous. Indeed it is hardly a society at all. Its national boundaries will simply be the walls of a box containing selfish atomistic units.

Medical law is good philosophical litmus. The law is forced to be obviously principled when dealing with the stuff of life and death. This book has examined what medical law says about its own actuating principles. It has noted that the judges in medical cases pay eloquent lip service to autonomy. Often they talk as if they regard it as the only principle in play. Yet very rarely is this really the case. Even in the heartlands of autonomy—the law relating to medical consent—the courts are very ready to find that an obviously autonomous person is not legally autonomous in order to achieve the result that is plainly right. The caesarean section cases illustrate the point best. There are other anomalies. A competent patient can sue her doctors for failing to comply with her request to turn off her life-sustaining ventilation, but the relatives of a competent prisoner who succeeds entirely voluntarily in hanging himself from his cell door can sue the police for failing to stop the suicide. If you nail your competent friend's scrotum to a board because he has asked you to, or sell a kidney to pay off your mortgage, you will be prosecuted.

In the law of confidentiality the nature of the right to confidence is generally (although perhaps unsatisfactorily) explained in terms of autonomy, but the right gives way constantly and rightly to wider societal considerations. You have an absolute autonomistic right to determine what happens to your body parts after your death—unless you don't. This last sentence stands well as a general summary of the English law's relationship with autonomy.

If one looked simply at the facts of English medical law cases, and then at the results of the judicial determinations, one would almost never be compelled to conclude that autonomy was the main reason for the decision. Beneficence and non-maleficence, yes. The sanctity of life, certainly. Professional probity (insofar as it adds anything to beneficence and non-maleficence), plainly. Justice; of course. But autonomy, very rarely. One would only necessarily deduce its influence in some of the more extreme consent cases (like that of Miss B), and in the bizarrely anomalous case of abortion (when you would also be forced to conclude that *any* autonomistic maternal whim trumped all foetal rights).

Although autonomy's stranglehold on the academic world of medical ethics has loosened slightly over recent years, it is still very hard for alternative theses to breathe. The main opponents of self-determination's hegemony have been the proponents of 'relational autonomy'. Their hearts are in the right place, and so are their conclusions, but it is illuminating and significant that they feel the need to wrap up their contentions in the language of autonomy. It is like a convinced free-marketeer in 1980s Russia urging the adoption of capitalist practice on the grounds that it would mean that more money flowed into the coffers of the Communist Party.

What are we to make of this discordanice between the judges' words and their decisions, and between the law as a whole (shown in the courts' decisions, rather than their reasoning) and the academic world? These two related questions can be answered together. The elements of the answer were outlined in chapter 1. By and large academic ethicists never have to decide anything at all. Indeed it is better for them if they don't, because if something is finally decided there is less to discuss in a subsequent paper. But judges don't have the luxury of discussion for discussion's sake. They are paid to decide. The discussion is a means to an end. The discussion, at least in appellate cases, is infused, if not informed, by academic writing, and that necessarily means that autonomy, the sole language of academic discourse, will be prominent in the judgments. As discussed earlier, the judges probably have a temperamental and cultural tendency towards that sort of language anyway. But beneficence, non-maleficence, probity, justice and downright decency are so much part of the intellectual wallpaper of western judges that they tend to be deployed entirely unconsciously. The judges would no more think of saying that they are deciding a case on the ground of medical beneficence than they would think of saying: 'In this case I am going to assume that it is a good thing to be just.' Hence principles of decisive importance tend to go unmentioned. This makes it possible for the academics to make the claim, based on the stated judicial reasoning, that autonomy is the only driving force.

I suggested in the first chapter that we see a new form of Kantism in medical ethics, but with a sort of dogmatic, hectoring liberalism replacing Christian morality as the Universal Law. One is only regarded as truly free insofar as one's opinions and one's choices are in line with that Law. For the reasons we have already noted, the law is less enslaved to that Law than are the academics, but legal enslavement appears complete in the case of abortion. If one takes out of the equation the given, unargued liberal axiom that abortion is a Good Thing, and drafted abortion legislation from first principles (amongst which autonomy must of course be prominent), one would never begin to have an abortion law that looked like ours.

If we are to have the robust, coherent sort of liberalism that we all surely want, it is no good for liberalism to be irrationally tyrannical. We need a new fundamentalism. We need to go back to philosophical basics. Judges need to be more explicit in spelling out just why they hold what they hold. This will require some self-examination. They need to remember that what might be blindingly obvious to them may not be so obvious to someone sitting in a law library, and that it is not patronising to say that beneficence is important. They need to be less reverential towards academics. The academics are, ironically, tremendously and often inappropriately deferential to the judges: the cycle of deference can be paralysing, and not just paralysingly funny. Academics need to (but won't) remember that their abstraction is not only dull but can also, when read out in a courtroom, be life-threatening. There should be a sort of academic Hippocratic Oath, administered to anyone doing tertiary-level studies in medical ethics. It should make it an offence to judge any problem using only one principle unless it has been conclusively demonstrated that no other principle has anything to contribute. This is really a very modest demand. It is a demand for intellectual democracy, which is actually a demand for intellectual integrity.

INDEX

Introductory Note

References such as '178–9' indicate (not necessarily continuous) discussion of a topic across a range of pages. Wherever possible, topics with many references have either been divided into sub-topics or the most significant discussions of the topic highlighted in bold type. Because the entire volume is about 'autonomy' and 'medical ethics', the use of these terms (and certain others occurring throughout the work) as index entry points has been minimised. Information will be found under the corresponding detailed topics.

Index

of expression, 71, 79
language of, 141
of others, 32, 35, 112, 124, 136
from pain, 146, 150
religious, 25
of thought, 25, 27, 124
fundamental human rights, 38, 44
see also Strasbourg Court

gay couples, adoption, 35–6
General Medical Council (GMC), 26–7, 65–7,
   75–6, 98–9, 103, 129, 138–9
   guidelines, 68–9, 75, 99, 101–3
genes, 37, 56, 61, 74
genetic counselling, 73–6
genetic engineering, 48, 61
genetic testing, 38–9, 60, 74
Gillick competency, 36, 77–81, 92, 121–2, 124–5,
   169
Gillon, R, 3, 17, 65
GMC *see* General Medical Council
government, 25, 47–8, 166
guidance, 25, 27, 41, 77–8, 80–1, 99, 168–9

harm, 17–18, 45, 50, 53, 74–6, 86, 117
   avoiding, 59–60
   bodily, 90, 106, 140
Harris J, 31, 41, 51, 60–2, 146, 167–8, 177–8
Helsinki Declaration, 133–4, 136–41
Herring, J, 14
HFEA (Human Fertilisation and Embryology
   Authority), 31, 34, 55–61
HIV, 75, 106–7, 140
holistic care, 23
homotransplantation *see* transplants
human embryos *see* embryos
Human Fertilisation and Embryology Authority
   see HFEA
humility, xii, 11, 121

immunities, blanket, 127
impairment, 92–3, 137
implied consent, 110–11
imprisonment, 37–8, 87–8, 94
incapacitated patients, 27, 52, 118, 120, 152
incapacity, 42, 93, 114–15, 118
   see also capacity
incompetent adults, 55, 85, 133, 137–9, 168–9
   see also capacity
   and best interests, 115–21
incompetent patients, 96, 114, 119–21
   see also capacity
individual autonomy, 11, 84, 104, 178
individuality, 43, 56, 143
information, 26–7, 65–8, 71–3, 78–9, 97–9,
   101–5, 114–16
   disclosure *see* disclosure

relevant *see* relevant information
informed consent, 18, 84, 89, 97, 99–104,
   106–7, 110
inhuman or degrading treatment, 112,
   171
injury, 88, 90, 140
   serious, 46, 107, 140, 166
inquiries, 81, 104, 127, 156–7, 177
integrity, bodily, 44–5, 51, 144
intention, 52, 59, 66, 149, 178
interests:
   best *see* best interests
   competing, 46, 50
   foetal, 42, 48
   societal, 38, 84, 111, 128
interference, 32, 35, 38, 80, 90, 108, 111
international instruments, 133–4
intolerability test, 159–61
invasive research, 137, 139
invasive treatment, 123, 141, 145, 147, 157

Johnston, C, 114, 123–4
justice, principle of in medical ethics, 18

Kant, E, 4, 7–8, 11, 125, 140
Keown, J, 10, 144, 146, 152
kidneys, 166–70, 180–1
Knoppers, BA, 110

language, xii–xiii, 8, 28, 36, 70–1, 73, 182
   autonomistic, 62, 98, 131, 182
lasting powers of attorney, 116–18, 153–4
law of confidentiality, 65–82, 111, 181
law of consent, 83–125
   best interests and incompetent adults,
      115–21
   and biobanks, 109–13
   Caesarean sections, 91–5
   and capacity, 114–25
   and children, 121–5
   incidental findings on operation, 108–9
   limits of consent, 105–8
   and patient responsibility, 104
   Reeves case, 85–9
   relevant information, 98–104
   sexual autonomy, 90–1
   suicide prevention, 85–9
law of medical consent *see* law of consent
legal personality, 48, 59, 75–6
liability, 43, 45, 66, 91, 100, 153–4
   financial, 33
life-plans, 3, 5, 8–9, 97, 102, 104, 157
   autonomy, 67, 84
life-sustaining treatment, 103, 116, 145, 149,
   154, 158
   continuation of, 117–18
   invasive *see* invasive treatment
   withdrawal of, 149

187

Index

Index

religion, 25, 27, 37, 124
reproductive autonomy, 7, 31–9, 60–1, 74, 118
  adoption, 34–7
  entitlement to have a child, 34
  prisoners, 37–9
  requirement to reproduce, 31–4
reproductive technology, 34, 55–62, 75
research, 48, 110–11, 174–5, 177, 179–80
  invasive, 137, 139
  medical, 117, 121, 133–42
  non-therapeutic, 133, 138–9
resources, 129, 131–2
respect, 41, 55, 66–7, 71, 79, 138, 145–6
responsibility:
  parental, xiii, 3, 14, 49, 88, 122, 138–9
  patients *see* patient responsibility
  social, 131
responsible body of professional opinion, 5, 66,
  99, 118–19
rights:
  and duties, 19, 127–32
  foetal, 42, 182
  to life, 49, 148
  moral, 6, 51–2
  parental, 56, 78–80, 176
risks, 22, 53, 98–102, 104–8, 121–2, 134–5,
  139–42
  of death, 75–6, 166
Rothstein, MA, 110
rule of law, 6

sanctity of life, 9, 84, 89, 142, 144–8, 159–61, 182
Savulescu, J, 3, 21–3, 60, 62, 96, 129
self-determination, 32, 50, 83–4, 89, 99, 101, 145
semen, 31–3, 56
sensual world, 7–8
serious bodily injury *see* serious injury
serious harm, 75–6, 101, 103, 108–9, 135
serious injury, 46, 107, 140, 166
sexual autonomy, 50, 83, 90–1
sexual intercourse, 7, 77–8, 80–1, 90, 105–8, 121
siblings, 57, 169–70
  see also brothers; sisters
Silber guidelines, 81
Singer, P, 3, 38, 45, 65, 133
sisters, 74, 143, 169, 176
  see also siblings
social responsibility, 131
societal interests, 38, 84, 111, 128
sons, 14, 31, 52–3, 156, 167
sound mind, 83–5, 87, 100, 144–5

  see also capacity
sperm *see* semen
Spriggs, M, 7, 31, 58
statutory checklist (in ascertaining best
  interests), 35–6
sterilisation, 118–19
Strasbourg Court, 32, 35, 46–7, 49–50, 66,
  111–13, 148
suicide, 7, 146, 148, 151, 155, 181
  prevention, 85–9
surgeons, 28, 83, 91, 95, 99, 108–9, 143
surgical separation, 143–4

termination of pregnancy *see* abortion
testing *see* genetic testing
therapeutic necessity, 112–13
thoroughgoing autonomists, 50, 94, 107, 110
tissue:
  existing holdings, 175
  from the living, 175
  from the living and the dead, 175
tort, 12, 28, 45, 70, 127–9
traditional autonomy, 14, 82, 109
transplants, 165–7, 174
  live donor homotransplantation, 166–71
  post-mortem homotransplantation, 171
  xenotransplantation, 166
treatment, 24–8, 77–81, 84–5, 91–3, **98–104**,
  112–25, 153–6
  compulsory, 43, 93, 111
  invasive, 86, 123, 137, 139, 141, 145, 147
  life-sustaining, 103, 116, 145, 149, 154, 158
  non-consensual, 10, 92–3
  withdrawal of, 120–1, 149
truncated autonomy, 53, 121, 170
trust, 13–14, 65, 70, 77, **95–7**, 103–4, 138

unborn children, 11, 21, 42–9, 51
utilitarianism, 18, 168, 179–80

ventilation, 83, 130, 155
volunteers, 138–9
vulnerable patients, 12, 18, 151

Weait, M, 91, 107
welfare, 57, 116, 119, 134, 146
  children, 35–6, 57, 78–9, 81, 112, 123, 159
withdrawal of treatment, 120–1, 149
women, 27–8, 31–2, 44, 50–1, 53, 92–3, 105–6

xenotransplantation, 165–6

189